ENGLISH/
CHINESE
(Simplified)

英汉图画词典

PEARSON
Longman

Steven J. Molinsky • Bill Bliss

Hellen Hu and Peter V. S. Smith, Translators

Illustrated by
Richard E. Hill

Word by Word Picture Dictionary,
English/Simplified Chinese, second edition

Pearson Education, 10 Bank Street, White Plains, NY 10606

Editorial director: Pam Fishman
Vice president, director of design and production: Rhea Banker
Director of electronic production: Aliza Greenblatt
Director of manufacturing: Patrice Fraccio
Senior manufacturing manager: Edith Pullman
Marketing manager: Oliva Fernandez
Associate development editor: Mary Perrotta Rich
Assistant editor: Katherine Keyes
Senior digital layout specialist: Wendy Wolf
Text design: Wendy Wolf
Cover design: Tracey Munz Cataldo
Realia creation: Warren Fischbach, Paula Williams
Illustrations: Richard E. Hill
Contributing artists: Steven Young, Charles Cawley, Willard Gage, Marlon Violette
Reviewers: James C. Bao, Ph.D., Susan Y. Rui; Yun Xiao, Bryant University
Project management by TransPac Education Services, Victoria, BC, Canada with assistance from Robert Zacharias

ISBN-10 0-13-815484-8 ISBN-13 978-0-13-815484-4
Longman on the Web
Longman.com offers online resources for teachers and students. Access our Companion Websites, our online catalog, and our local offices around the world.

Visit us at www.pearsonlongman.com.

Printed in the United States of America
17

CONTENTS

目录

COMMUNICATION

Principles for a Lifetime

Unit / Theme	Communication Skills	Writing & Discussion
1 Personal Information and Family	• Asking for & giving personal information • Identifying information on a form • Spelling name aloud • Identifying family members • Introducing others	• Telling about yourself • Telling about family members • Drawing a family tree
2 Common Everyday Activities and Language	• Identifying classroom objects & locations • Identifying classroom actions • Giving & following simple classroom commands • Identifying everyday & leisure activities • Inquiring by phone about a person's activities • Asking about a person's plan for future activities • Social communication: Greeting people, Leave taking, Introducing yourself & others, Getting someone's attention, Expressing gratitude, Saying you don't understand, Calling someone on the telephone • Describing the weather • Interpreting temperatures on a thermometer (Fahrenheit & Centigrade) • Describing the weather forecast for tomorrow	• Describing a classroom • Making a list of daily activities • Describing daily routine • Making a list of planned activities • Describing favorite leisure activities • Describing the weather
3 Numbers/ Time/ Money/ Calendar	• Using cardinal & ordinal numbers • Giving information about age, number of family members, residence • Telling time • Indicating time of events • Asking for information about arrival & departure times • Identifying coins & currency – names & values • Making & asking for change • Identifying days of the week • Identifying months of the year • Asking about the year, month, day, date • Asking about the date of a birthday, anniversary, appointment • Giving date of birth	• Describing numbers of students in a class • Identifying a country's population • Describing daily schedule with times • Telling about time management • Telling about the use of time in different cultures or countries • Describing the cost of purchases • Describing coins & currency of other countries • Describing weekday & weekend activities • Telling about favorite day of the week & month of the year
4 Home	• Identifying types of housing & communities • Requesting a taxi • Calling 911 for an ambulance • Identifying rooms of a home • Identifying furniture • Complimenting • Asking for information in a store • Locating items in a store • Asking about items on sale • Asking the location of items at home • Telling about past weekend activities • Identifying locations in an apartment building • Identifying ways to look for housing: classified ads, listings, vacancy signs • Renting an apartment • Describing household problems • Securing home repair services • Making a suggestion • Identifying household cleaning items, home supplies, & tools • Asking to borrow an item • Describing current home activities & plans for future activities	• Describing types of housing where people live • Describing rooms & furniture in a residence • Telling about baby products & early child-rearing practices in different countries • Telling about personal experiences with repairing things • Describing an apartment building • Describing household cleaning chores
5 Community	• Identifying places in the community • Exchanging greetings • Asking & giving the location of places in the community • Identifying government buildings, services, & other places in a city/town center • Identifying modes of transportation in a city/town center	• Describing places in a neighborhood • Making a list of places, people, & actions observed at an intersection

Unit / Theme	Communication Skills	Writing & Discussion
6 Describing	• Describing people by age • Describing people by physical characteristics • Describing a suspect or missing person to a police officer • Describing people & things using adjectives • Describing physical states & emotions • Expressing concern about another person's physical state or emotion	• Describing physical characteristics of yourself & family members • Describing physical characteristics of a favorite actor or actress or other famous person • Describing things at home & in the community • Telling about personal experiences with different emotions
7 Food	• Identifying food items (fruits, vegetables, meat, poultry, seafood, dairy products, juices, beverages, deli, frozen foods, snack foods, groceries) • Identifying non-food items purchased in a supermarket (e.g., household supplies, baby products, pet food) • Determining food needs to make a shopping list • Asking the location of items in a supermarket • Identifying supermarket sections • Requesting items at a service counter in a supermarket • Identifying supermarket checkout area personnel & items • Identifying food containers & quantities • Identifying units of measure • Asking for & giving recipe instructions • Complimenting someone on a recipe • Offering to help with food preparation • Identifying food preparation actions • Identifying kitchen utensils & cookware • Asking to borrow an item • Comprehending product advertising • Ordering fast food items, coffee shop items, & sandwiches • Indicating a shortage of supplies to a co-worker or supervisor • Taking customers' orders at a food service counter • Identifying restaurant objects, personnel, & actions • Making & following requests at work • Identifying & correctly positioning silverware & plates in a table setting • Inquiring in person about restaurant job openings • Ordering from a restaurant menu • Taking customers' orders as a waiter or waitress in a restaurant	• Describing favorite & least favorite foods • Describing foods in different countries • Making a shopping list • Describing places to shop for food • Telling about differences between supermarkets & food stores in different countries • Making a list of items in kitchen cabinets & the refrigerator • Describing recycling practices • Describing a favorite recipe using units of measure • Telling about use of kitchen utensils & cookware • Telling about experience with different types of restaurants • Describing restaurants and menus in different countries • Describing favorite foods ordered in restaurants
8 Colors and Clothing	• Identifying colors • Complimenting someone on clothing • Identifying clothing items, including outerwear, sleepwear, underwear, exercise clothing, footwear, jewelry, & accessories • Talking about appropriate clothing for different weather conditions • Expressing clothing needs to a store salesperson • Locating clothing items • Inquiring about ownership of found clothing items • Indicating loss of a clothing item • Asking about sale prices in a clothing store • Reporting theft of a clothing item to the police • Stating preferences during clothing shopping • Expressing problems with clothing & the need for alterations • Identifying laundry objects & activities • Locating laundry products in a store	• Describing the flags of different countries • Telling about emotions associated with different colors • Telling about clothing & colors you like to wear • Describing clothing worn at different occasions (e.g., going to schools, parties, weddings) • Telling about clothing worn in different weather conditions • Telling about clothing worn during exercise activities • Telling about footwear worn during different activities • Describing the color, material, size, & pattern of favorite clothing items • Comparing clothing fashions now & a long time ago • Telling about who does laundry at home

Unit / Theme	Communication Skills	Writing & Discussion
9 **Shopping**	• Identifying departments & services in a department store • Asking the location of items in a department store • Asking to buy, return, exchange, try on, & pay for department store items • Asking about regular & sales prices, discounts, & sales tax • Interpreting a sales receipt • Offering assistance to customers as a salesperson • Expressing needs to a salesperson in a store • Identifying electronics products, including video & audio equipment, telephones, cameras, & computers • Identifying components of a computer & common computer software • Complimenting someone about an item & inquiring where it was purchased • Asking a salesperson for advice about different brands of a product • Identifying common toys & other items in a toy store • Asking for advice about an appropriate gift for a child	• Describing a department store • Telling about stores that have sales • Telling about an item purchased on sale • Comparing different types & brands of video & audio equipment • Describing telephones & cameras • Describing personal use of a computer • Sharing opinions about how computers have changed the world • Telling about popular toys in different countries • Telling about favorite childhood toys
10 **Community Services**	• Requesting bank services & transactions (e.g., deposit, withdrawal, cashing a check, obtaining traveler's checks, opening an account, applying for a loan, exchanging currency) • Identifying bank personnel • Identifying bank forms • Asking about acceptable forms of payment (cash, check, credit card, money order, traveler's check) • Identifying household bills (rent, utilities, etc.) • Identifying family finance documents & actions • Following instructions to use an ATM machine • Requesting post office services & transactions • Identifying types of mail & mail services • Identifying different ways to buy stamps • Requesting non-mail services available at the post office (money order, selective service registration, passport application) • Identifying & locating library sections, services, & personnel • Asking how to find a book in the library • Identifying community institutions, services, and personnel (police, fire, city government, public works, recreation, sanitation, religious institutions) • Identifying types of emergency vehicles • Reporting a crime • Identifying community mishaps (gas leak, water main break, etc.) • Expressing concern about community problems	• Describing use of bank services • Telling about household bills & amounts paid • Telling about the person responsible for household finances • Describing use of ATM machines • Describing use of postal services • Comparing postal systems in different countries • Telling about experience using a library • Telling about the location of community institutions • Describing experiences using community institutions • Telling about crime in the community • Describing experience with a crime or emergency
11 **Health**	• Identifying parts of the body & key internal organs • Describing ailments, symptoms, & injuries • Asking about the health of another person • Identifying items in a first-aid kit • Describing medical emergencies • Identifying emergency medical procedures (CPR, rescue breathing, Heimlich maneuver) • Calling 911 to report a medical emergency • Identifying major illnesses • Talking with a friend or co-worker about illness in one's family • Following instructions during a medical examination • Identifying medical personnel, equipment, & supplies in medical & dental offices • Understanding medical & dental personnel's description of procedures during treatment • Understanding a doctor's medical advice and instructions • Identifying over-the-counter medications • Understanding dosage instructions on medicine labels • Identifying medical specialists • Indicating the date & time of a medical appointment • Identifying hospital departments & personnel • Identifying equipment in a hospital room • Identifying actions & items related to personal hygiene • Locating personal care products in a store • Identifying actions & items related to baby care	• Describing self • Telling about a personal experience with an illness or injury • Describing remedies or treatments for common problems (cold, stomachache, insect bite, hiccups) • Describing experience with a medical emergency • Describing a medical examination • Describing experience with a medical or dental procedure • Telling about medical advice received • Telling about over-the-counter medications used • Comparing use of medications in different countries • Describing experience with a medical specialist • Describing a hospital stay • Making a list of personal care items needed for a trip • Comparing baby products in different countries

Unit / Theme	Communication Skills	Writing & Discussion

12 School, Subjects, and Activities	• Identifying types of educational institutions
	• Giving information about previous education during a job interview
	• Identifying school locations & personnel
	• Identifying school subjects
	• Identifying extracurricular activities
	• Sharing after-school plans
	• MATH:
	  • Asking & answering basic questions during a math class
	  • Using fractions to indicate sale prices
	  • Using percents to indicate test scores & probability in weather forecasts
	  • Identifying high school math subjects
	  • Using measurement terms to indicate height, width, depth, length, distance
	  • Interpreting metric measurements
	  • Identifying types of lines, geometric shapes, & solid figures
	• ENGLISH LANGUAGE ARTS:
	  • Identifying types of sentences
	  • Identifying parts of speech
	  • Identifying punctuation marks
	  • Providing feedback during peer-editing
	  • Identifying steps of the writing process
	  • Identifying types of literature
	  • Identifying forms of writing
	• GEOGRAPHY:
	  • Identifying geographical features & bodies of water
	  • Identifying natural environments (desert, jungle, rainforest, etc.)
	• SCIENCE:
	  • Identifying science classroom/laboratory equipment
	  • Asking about equipment needed to do a science procedure
	  • Identifying steps of the scientific method
	  • Identifying key terms to describe the universe, solar system, & space exploration
		• Telling about different types of schools in the community
		• Telling about schools attended, where, when, & subjects studied
		• Describing a school
		• Comparing schools in different countries
		• Telling about favorite school subject
		• Telling about extracurricular activities
		• Comparing extracurricular activities in different countries
		• Describing math education
		• Telling about something bought on sale
		• Researching & sharing information about population statistics using percents
		• Describing favorite books & authors
		• Describing newspapers & magazines read
		• Telling about use of different types of written communication
		• Describing the geography of your country
		• Describing geographical features experienced
		• Describing experience with scientific equipment
		• Describing science education
		• Brainstorming a science experiment & describing each step of the scientific method
		• Drawing & naming a constellation
		• Expressing an opinion about the importance of space exploration

13 Work	• Identifying occupations • Stating work experience (including length of time in an occupation) during a job interview • Talking about occupation during social conversation • Expressing job aspirations • Identifying job skills & work activities • Indicating job skills during an interview (including length of time) • Identifying types of job advertisements (help wanted signs, job notices, classified ads) • Interpreting abbreviations in job advertisements • Identifying each step in a job-search process • Identifying workplace locations, furniture, equipment, & personnel • Identifying common office tasks • Asking the location of a co-worker • Engaging in small-talk with co-workers • Identifying common office supplies • Making requests at work • Repeating to confirm understanding of a request or instruction • Identifying factory locations, equipment, & personnel • Asking the location of workplace departments & personnel to orient oneself as a new employee • Asking about the location & activities of a co-worker • Identifying construction site machinery, equipment, and building materials • Asking a co-worker for a workplace item • Warning a co-worker of a safety hazard • Asking whether there is a sufficient supply of workplace materials • Identifying job safety equipment • Interpreting warning signs at work • Reminding someone to use safety equipment • Asking the location of emergency equipment at work	• Career exploration: sharing ideas about occupations that are interesting, difficult • Describing occupation & occupations of family members • Describing job skills • Describing a familiar job (skill requirements, qualifications, hours, salary) • Telling about how people found their jobs • Telling about experience with a job search or job interview • Describing a familiar workplace • Telling about office & school supplies used • Describing a nearby factory & working conditions there • Comparing products produced by factories in different countries • Describing building materials used in ones dwelling • Describing a nearby construction site • Telling about experience with safety equipment • Describing the use of safety equipment in the community

Unit / Theme	Communication Skills	Writing & Discussion
14 Transportation and Travel	• Identifying modes of local & inter-city public transportation • Expressing intended mode of travel • Asking about a location to obtain transportation (bus stop, bus station, train station, subway station) • Locating ticket counters, information booths, fare card machines, & information signage in transportation stations • Identifying types of vehicles • Indicating to a car salesperson need for a type of vehicle • Describing a car accident • Identifying parts of a car & maintenance items • Indicating a problem with a car • Requesting service or assistance at a service station • Identifying types of highway lanes & markings, road structures (tunnels, bridges, etc.), traffic signage, & local intersection road markings • Reporting the location of an accident • Giving & following driving directions (using prepositions of motion) • Interpreting traffic signs • Warning a driver about an upcoming sign • Interpreting compass directions • Asking for driving directions • Following instructions during a driver's test • Repeating to confirm instructions • Identifying airport locations & personnel (check-in, security, gate, baggage claim, Customs & Immigration) • Asking for location of places & personnel at an airport • Indicating loss of travel documents or other items • Identifying airplane sections, seating areas, emergency equipment, & flight personnel • Identifying steps in the process of airplane travel (actions in the security area, at the gate, boarding, & being seated) • Following instructions of airport security personnel, gate attendants, & flight crew • Identifying sections of a hotel & personnel • Asking for location of places & personnel in a hotel	• Describing mode of travel to different places in the community • Describing local public transportation • Comparing transportation in different countries • Telling about common types of vehicles in different countries • Expressing opinion about favorite type of vehicle & manufacturer • Expressing opinion about most important features to look for when making a car purchase • Describing experience with car repairs • Describing a local highway • Describing a local intersection • Telling about dangerous traffic areas where many accidents occur • Describing your route from home to school • Describing how to get to different places from home and school • Describing local traffic signs • Comparing traffic signs in different countries • Describing a familiar airport • Telling about an experience with Customs & Immigration • Describing an air travel experience • Using imagination: being an airport security officer giving passengers instructions; being a flight attendant giving passengers instructions before take-off • Describing a familiar hotel • Expressing opinion about hotel jobs that are most interesting, most difficult
15 Recreation and Entertainment	• Identifying common hobbies, crafts, & games & related materials/equipment • Describing favorite leisure activities • Purchasing craft supplies, equipment, & other products in a store • Asking for & offering a suggestion for a leisure activity • Identifying places to go for outdoor recreation, entertainment, culture, etc. • Describing past weekend activities • Describing activities planned for a future day off or weekend • Identifying features & equipment in a park & playground • Asking the location of a park feature or equipment • Warning a child to be careful on playground equipment • Identifying features of a beach, common beach items, & personnel • Identifying indoor & outdoor recreation activities & sports, & related equipment & supplies • Asking if someone remembered an item when preparing for an activity • Identifying team sports & terms for players, playing fields, & equipment • Commenting on a player's performance during a game • Indicating that you can't find an item • Asking the location of sports equipment in a store • Reminding someone of items needed for a sports activity • Identifying types of winter/water sports, recreation, & equipment • Engaging in small talk about favorite sports & recreation activities • Using the telephone to inquire whether a store sells a product • Making & responding to an invitation • Following a teacher or coach's instructions during sports practice, P.E. class, & an exercise class • Identifying types of entertainment & cultural events, & the performers • Commenting on a performance • Identifying genres of music, plays, movies, & TV programs • Expressing likes about types of entertainment • Identifying musical instruments • Complimenting someone on musical ability	• Describing a favorite hobby, craft, or game • Comparing popular games in different countries, and how to play them • Describing favorite places to go & activities there • Describing a local park & playground • Describing a favorite beach & items used there • Describing an outdoor recreation experience • Describing favorite individual sports & recreation activities • Describing favorite team sports & famous players • Comparing popular sports in different countries • Describing experience with winter or water sports & recreation • Expressing opinions about Winter Olympics sports (most exciting, most dangerous) • Describing exercise habits & routines • Using imagination: being an exercise instructor leading a class • Telling about favorite types of entertainment • Comparing types of entertainment popular in different countries • Telling about favorite performers • Telling about favorite types of music, movies, & TV programs • Describing experience with a musical instrument • Comparing typical musical instruments in different countries

Unit / Theme	Communication Skills	Writing & Discussion
16 **Nature**	• Identifying places & people on a farm • Identifying farm animals & crops • Identifying animals & pets • Identifying birds & insects • Identifying fish, sea animals, amphibians, & reptiles • Asking about the presence of wildlife in an area • Identifying trees, plants, & flowers • Identifying key parts of a tree and flower • Asking for information about trees & flowers • Warning someone about poisonous vegetation in an area • Identifying sources of energy • Describing the kind of energy used to heat homes & for cooking • Expressing an opinion about good future sources of energy • Identifying behaviors that promote conservation (recycling, conserving energy, conserving water, carpooling) • Expressing concern about environmental problems • Identifying different kinds of natural disasters	• Comparing farms in different countries • Telling about local animals, animals in a zoo, & common local birds & insects • Comparing common pets in different countries • Using imagination: what animal you would like to be, & why • Telling a popular folk tale or children's story about animals, birds, or insects • Describing fish, sea animals, & reptiles in different countries • Identifying endangered species • Expressing opinions about wildlife – most interesting, beautiful, dangerous • Describing local trees & flowers, & favorites • Comparing different cultures' use of flowers at weddings, funerals, holidays, & hospitals • Expressing an opinion about an environmental problem • Telling about how people prepare for natural disasters
17 **U.S. Civics**	• Producing correct form of identification when requested (driver's license, social security card, student I.D. card, employee I.D. badge, permanent resident card, passport, visa, work permit, birth certificate, proof of residence) • Identifying the three branches of U.S. government (legislative, executive, judicial) & their functions • Identifying senators, representatives, the president, vice-president, cabinet, Supreme Court justices, & the chief justice, & the branches of government in which they work • Identifying the key buildings in each branch of government (Capitol Building, White House, Supreme Court Building) • Identifying the Constitution as "the supreme law of the land" • Identifying the Bill of Rights • Naming freedoms guaranteed by the 1st Amendment • Identifying key amendments to the Constitution • Identifying key events in United States history • Answering history questions about events and the dates they occurred • Identifying key holidays & dates they occur • Identifying legal system & court procedures (arrest, booking, obtaining legal representation, appearing in court, standing trial, acquittal, conviction, sentencing, prison, release) • Identifying people in the criminal justice system • Engaging in small talk about a TV crime show's characters & plot • Identifying rights & responsibilities of U.S. citizens • Identifying steps in applying for citizenship	• Telling about forms of identification & when needed • Describing how people in a community "exercise their 1st Amendment rights" • Brainstorming ideas for a new amendment to the Constitution • Expressing an opinion about the most important event in United States history • Telling about important events in the history of different countries • Describing U.S. holidays you celebrate • Describing holidays celebrated in different countries • Describing the legal system in different countries • Telling about an episode of a TV crime show • Expressing an opinion about the most important rights & responsibilities of people in their communities • Expressing an opinion about the rights of citizens vs. non-citizens

Welcome to the second edition of the WORD BY WORD Picture Dictionary! This text presents more than 4,000 vocabulary words through vibrant illustrations and simple accessible lesson pages that are designed for clarity and ease-of-use with learners at all levels. Our goal is to prepare students for success using English in everyday life, in the community, in school, and at work.

WORD BY WORD organizes the vocabulary into 17 thematic units, providing a careful research-based sequence of lessons that integrates students' development of grammar and vocabulary skills through topics that begin with the immediate world of the student and progress to the world at large. Early lessons on the family, the home, and daily activities lead to lessons on the community, school, workplace, shopping, recreation, and other topics. The text offers extensive coverage of important lifeskill competencies and the vocabulary of school subjects and extracurricular activities, and it is designed to meet the objectives of current national, state, and local standards-based curricula you can find in the Scope & Sequence on the previous pages.

Since each lesson in *Word by Word* is self-contained, it can be used either sequentially or in any desired order. For users' convenience, the lessons are listed in two ways: sequentially in the Table of Contents, and alphabetically in the Thematic Index. These resources, combined with the Glossary in the appendix, allow students and teachers to quickly and easily locate all words and topics in the Picture Dictionary.

The *Word by Word* Picture Dictionary is the centerpiece of the complete *Word by Word* Vocabulary Development Program, which offers a wide selection of print and media support materials for instruction at all levels.

A unique choice of workbooks at Beginning and Intermediate levels offers flexible options to meet students' needs. Vocabulary Workbooks feature motivating vocabulary, grammar, and listening practice, and standards-based Lifeskills Workbooks provide competency-based activities and reading tied to national, state, and local curriculum frameworks. A Literacy Workbook is also available.

The Teacher's Guide and Lesson Planner with CD-ROM includes lesson-planning suggestions, community tasks, Internet weblinks, and reproducible masters to save teachers hours of lesson preparation time. An Activity Handbook with step-by-step teaching strategies for key vocabulary development activities is included in the Teacher's Guide.

The Audio Program includes all words and conversations for interactive practice and —as bonus material—an expanded selection of WordSongs for entertaining musical practice with the vocabulary.

Additional ancillary materials include Color Transparencies, Vocabulary Game Cards, and a Testing Program. Bilingual Editions are also available.

Teaching Strategies

Word by Word presents vocabulary words in context. Model conversations depict situations in which people use the words in meaningful communication. These models become the basis for students to engage in dynamic, interactive practice. In addition, writing and discussion questions in each lesson encourage students to relate the vocabulary and themes to their own lives as they share experiences, thoughts, opinions, and information about themselves, their cultures, and their countries. In this way, students get to know each other "word by word."

In using *Word by Word*, we encourage you to develop approaches and strategies that are compatible with your own teaching style and the needs and abilities of your students. You may find it helpful to incorporate some of the following techniques for presenting and practicing the vocabulary in each lesson.

1. **Preview the Vocabulary:** Activate students' prior knowledge of the vocabulary by brainstorming with students the words in the lesson they already know and writing them on the board, or by having students look at the transparency or the illustration in *Word by Word* and identify the words they are familiar with.

2. **Present the Vocabulary:** Using the transparency or the illustration in the Picture Dictionary, point to the picture of each word, say the word, and have the class repeat it chorally and individually. (You can also play the word list on the Audio Program.) Check students' understanding and pronunciation of the vocabulary.

3. **Vocabulary Practice:** Have students practice the vocabulary as a class, in pairs, or in small groups. Say or write a word, and have students point to the item or tell the number. Or, point to an item or give the number, and have students say the word.

4. **Model Conversation Practice:** Some lessons have model conversations that use the first word in the vocabulary list. Other models are in the form of skeletal dialogs, in which vocabulary words can be inserted. (In many skeletal dialogs, bracketed numbers indicate which words can be used for practicing the conversation. If no bracketed numbers appear, all the words in the lesson can be used.)

   The following steps are recommended for Model Conversation Practice:

   a. Preview: Have students look at the model illustration and discuss who they think the speakers are and where the conversation takes place.
   b. The teacher presents the model or plays the audio one or more times and checks students' understanding of the situation and the vocabulary.
   c. Students repeat each line of the conversation chorally and individually.
   d. Students practice the model in pairs.
   e. A pair of students presents a conversation based on the model, but using a different word from the vocabulary list.
   f. In pairs, students practice several conversations based on the model, using different words on the page.
   g. Pairs present their conversations to the class.

5. **Additional Conversation Practice:** Many lessons provide two additional skeletal dialogs for further conversation practice with the vocabulary. (These can be found in the yellow-shaded area at the bottom of the page.) Have students practice and present these conversations using any words they wish. Before they practice the additional conversations, you may want to have students listen to the sample additional conversations on the Audio Program.

6. **Spelling Practice:** Have students practice spelling the words as a class, in pairs, or in small groups. Say a word, and have students spell it aloud or write it. Or, using the transparency, point to an item and have students write the word.

7. **Themes for Discussion, Composition, Journals, and Portfolios:** Each lesson of *Word by Word* provides one or more questions for discussion and composition. (These can be found in a blue-shaded area at the bottom of the page.) Have students respond to the questions as a class, in pairs, or in small groups. Or, have students write their responses at home, share their written work with other students, and discuss as a class, in pairs, or in small groups.

   Students may enjoy keeping a journal of their written work. If time permits, you may want to write a response in each student's journal, sharing your own opinions and experiences as well as reacting to what the student has written. If you are keeping portfolios of students' work, these compositions serve as excellent examples of students' progress in learning English.

8. **Communication Activities:** The *Word by Word* Teacher's Guide and Lesson Planner with CD-ROM provides a wealth of games, tasks, brainstorming, discussion, movement, drawing, miming, role-playing, and other activities designed to take advantage of students' different learning styles and particular abilities and strengths. For each lesson, choose one or more of these activities to reinforce students' vocabulary learning in a way that is stimulating, creative, and enjoyable.

WORD BY WORD aims to offer students a communicative, meaningful, and lively way of practicing English vocabulary. In conveying to you the substance of our program, we hope that we have also conveyed the spirit: that learning vocabulary can be genuinely interactive . . . relevant to our students' lives . . . responsive to students' differing strengths and learning styles . . . and fun!

Steven J. Molinsky
Bill Bliss

个人资料

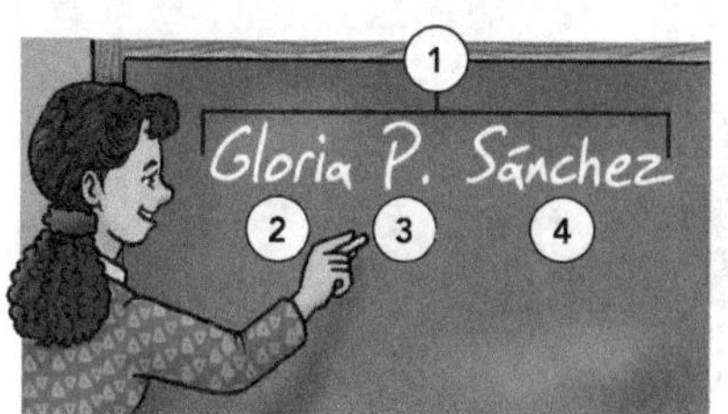

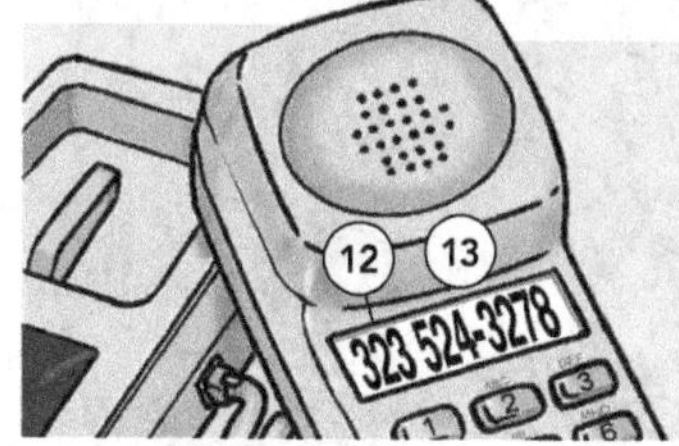

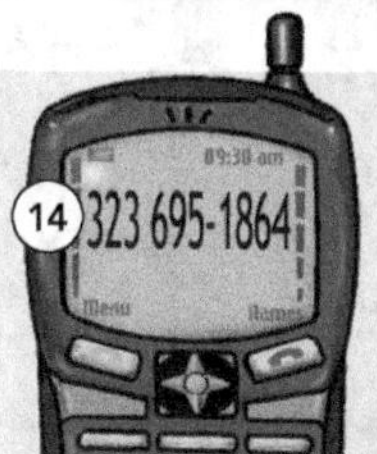

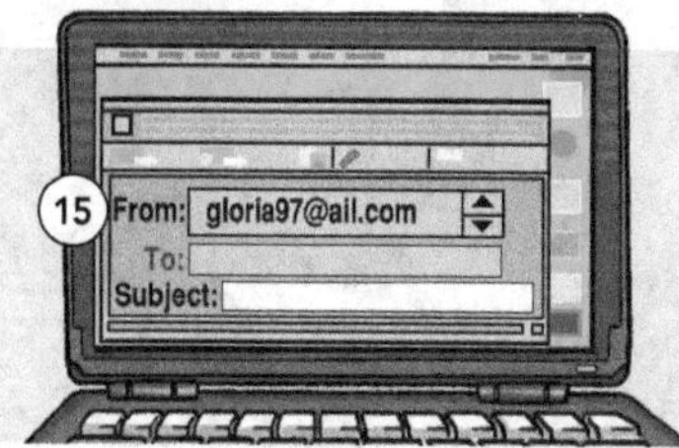

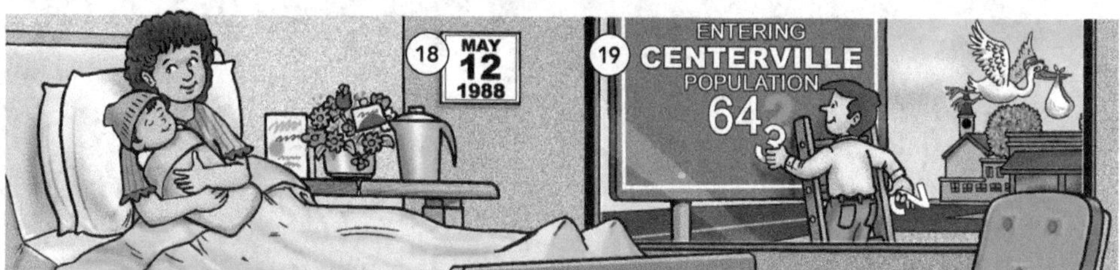

Registration Form

Name: Gloria (First) P. (Middle Initial) Sánchez (Last)

Address: 95 (Number) Garden Street (Street) 3G (Apartment Number)

Los Angeles (City) CA (State) 90036 (Zip Code)

Telephone: 323-524-3278 Cell Phone: 323-695-1864

E-Mail Address: gloria97@ail.com SSN: 227-93-6185 Sex: M__ F X

Date of Birth: 5/12/88 Place of Birth: Centerville, Texas

- 姓名 **1** name
- 名字(不含姓) **2** first name
- 中间名的首字母 **3** middle initial
- 姓 **4** last name/family name/surname
- 地址 **5** address
- 门牌号码 **6** street number
- 街道 **7** street
- 公寓号码 **8** apartment number
- 城市 **9** city
- 州 **10** state
- 邮政编码 **11** zip code
- 电话区号 **12** area code
- 电话号码 **13** telephone number/phone number
- 手机号码 **14** cell phone number
- 电子邮件地址 **15** e-mail address
- 社会保险号码 **16** social security number
- 性别 **17** sex
- 出生日期 **18** date of birth
- 出生地 **19** place of birth

A. What's your **name**?
B. Gloria P. Sánchez.

A. What's your ________?
B. ....
A. Did you say ....?
B. Yes. That's right.

A. What's your last name?
B. ....
A. How do you spell that?
B. ....

Tell about yourself:
My name is ....
My address is ....
My telephone number is ....
Now interview a friend.

FAMILY MEMBERS I

家庭成员 1

丈夫 **1** husband
妻子 **2** wife

父母（双亲） **parents**
父亲 **3** father
母亲 **4** mother

孩子们 **children**
女儿 **5** daughter
儿子 **6** son
婴儿 **7** baby

兄弟姐妹 **siblings**
姐姐/妹妹 **8** sister
哥哥/弟弟 **9** brother

(外)祖父母 **grandparents**
(外)祖母 **10** grandmother
(外)祖父 **11** grandfather

(外)孙儿孙女们 **grandchildren**
(外)孙女 **12** granddaughter
(外)孙子 **13** grandson

A. Who is he?
B. He's my **husband**.
A. What's his name?
B. His name is *Jack*.

A. Who is she?
B. She's my **wife**.
A. What's her name?
B. Her name is *Nancy*.

A. I'd like to introduce my ________.
B. Nice to meet you.
C. Nice to meet you, too.

A. What's your ________'s name?
B. His/Her name is ....

Who are the people in your family?
What are their names?

Tell about photos of family members.

FAMILY MEMBERS II

家庭成员 2

Helen 6
Walter 7
Jack 1 8
Nancy 2
Frank 10
Linda 9 11
Jennifer 3
Timmy 4
Alan 5

伯父/叔父/舅父/姑丈/姨丈等	1	uncle
姑母/姨母/婶母/伯母/舅母等	2	aunt
侄女/外甥女	3	niece
侄儿/外甥	4	nephew
(堂)表兄弟姊妹	5	cousin
婆婆/岳母	6	mother-in-law
公公/岳父	7	father-in-law
女婿	8	son-in-law
媳妇	9	daughter-in-law
内兄/内弟/大伯/小叔/姊夫/妹夫/连襟(配偶之姊妹的丈夫)	10	brother-in-law
大姑/小姑/小姨/大姨/嫂嫂/弟媳/妯娌/丈夫的嫂子/弟媳	11	sister-in-law

① Jack is Alan's ____.
② Nancy is Alan's ____.
③ Jennifer is Frank and Linda's ____.
④ Timmy is Frank and Linda's ____.
⑤ Alan is Jennifer and Timmy's ____.
⑥ Helen is Jack's ____.
⑦ Walter is Jack's ____.
⑧ Jack is Helen and Walter's ____.
⑨ Linda is Helen and Walter's ____.
⑩ Frank is Jack's ____.
⑪ Linda is Jack's ____.

A. Who is he/she?
B. He's/She's my ________.
A. What's his/her name?
B. His/Her name is ________.

A. Let me introduce my ________.
B. I'm glad to meet you.
C. Nice meeting you, too.

Tell about your relatives:
What are their names?
Where do they live?

Draw your family tree and tell about it.

THE CLASSROOM

教室

老师	1	teacher
助教	2	teacher's aide
学生	3	student
书桌	4	desk
座位/椅子	5	seat/chair
桌子	6	table
电脑	7	computer
投影机	8	overhead projector
银幕	9	screen
黑板	10	chalkboard/board
时钟	11	clock
地图	12	map
布告栏	13	bulletin board
公共广播系统/扩音器	14	P.A. system/loudspeaker
白板	15	whiteboard/board
地球仪	16	globe
书柜/书架	17	bookcase/bookshelf
老师书桌	18	teacher's desk
废纸篓	19	wastebasket

笔 **20** pen
铅笔 **21** pencil
橡皮擦 **22** eraser
削铅笔机 **23** pencil sharpener
书/课本 **24** book/textbook
练习本 **25** workbook
线圈笔记本 **26** spiral notebook

活页夹/笔记本 **27** binder/notebook
活页纸 **28** notebook paper
方格绘图纸 **29** graph paper
尺 **30** ruler
计算器 **31** calculator
粉笔 **32** chalk
黑（白）板擦 **33** eraser

白板笔 **34** marker
图钉 **35** thumbtack
键盘 **36** keyboard
电脑显示器 **37** monitor
鼠标 **38** mouse
打印机 **39** printer

A. Where's the **teacher**?
B. The **teacher** is *next to* the **board**.

A. Where's the **globe**?
B. The **globe** is *on* the **bookcase**.

A. Is there a/an _____ in your classroom?*
B. Yes. There's a/an _____ next to/on the _____.

A. Is there a/an _____ in your classroom?*
B. No, there isn't.

Describe your classroom.
(There's a/an ....)

* *With 28, 29, 32, use:* Is there _____ in your classroom?

CLASSROOM ACTIONS

教室动作

说出你的名字。	1	Say your name.
重复你的名字。	2	Repeat your name.
拼出你的名字。	3	Spell your name.
写出你的名字。	4	Print your name.
请你签名。	5	Sign your name.
站起来。	6	Stand up.
走到黑板/走到白板前。	7	Go to the board.
写在黑板上/写在白板上。	8	Write on the board.
擦黑板/擦白板。	9	Erase the board.
坐下。	10	Sit down./Take your seat.
打开书本。	11	Open your book.
读第10页。	12	Read page ten.
学习第10页。	13	Study page ten.
合起书本。	14	Close your book.
把书收起来。	15	Put away your book.
请举手。	16	Raise your hand.
问问题。	17	Ask a question.
听问题。	18	Listen to the question.
回答问题。	19	Answer the question.
听答案。	20	Listen to the answer.
做家庭作业。	21	Do your homework.
带家庭作业。	22	Bring in your homework.
对答案。	23	Go over the answers.
订正错误。	24	Correct your mistakes.
交家庭作业。	25	Hand in your homework.
共用一本书。	26	Share a book.
讨论问题。	27	Discuss the question.
互相帮助。	28	Help each other.
分工合作。	29	Work together.
和同学分享。	30	Share with the class.

查词典。 **31** Look in the dictionary.
查一个单词。 **32** Look up a word.
发出单词的音。 **33** Pronounce the word.
念出定义。 **34** Read the definition.
抄写单词。 **35** Copy the word.
自己做功课。/做自己的功课。 **36** Work alone./ Do your own work.
和搭挡合作。 **37** Work with a partner.
分成小组。 **38** Break up into small groups.
做小组活动。 **39** Work in a group.
做全班活动。 **40** Work as a class.
拉下窗帘。 **41** Lower the shades.
关灯。 **42** Turn off the lights.
看银幕。 **43** Look at the screen.
做笔记。 **44** Take notes.
开灯。 **45** Turn on the lights.
拿出一张纸。 **46** Take out a piece of paper.
发考卷。 **47** Pass out the tests.
回答问题 。 **48** Answer the questions.
检查答案。 **49** Check your answers.
收考卷。 **50** Collect the tests.
选出正确答案。 **51** Choose the correct answer.
圈选正确答案。 **52** Circle the correct answer.
填写空格。 **53** Fill in the blank.
在答案卷(纸/卡)上作答。/将答案涂黑。 **54** Mark the answer sheet./ Bubble the answer.
单词配对。 **55** Match the words.
在单词下画线。 **56** Underline the word.
在单词上打叉。 **57** Cross out the word.
字母重组，完成单词。 **58** Unscramble the word.
重组单词，完成正确的句子。 **59** Put the words in order.
写在另一张纸上。 **60** Write on a separate sheet of paper.

You're the teacher! Give instructions to your students!

PREPOSITIONS

介词

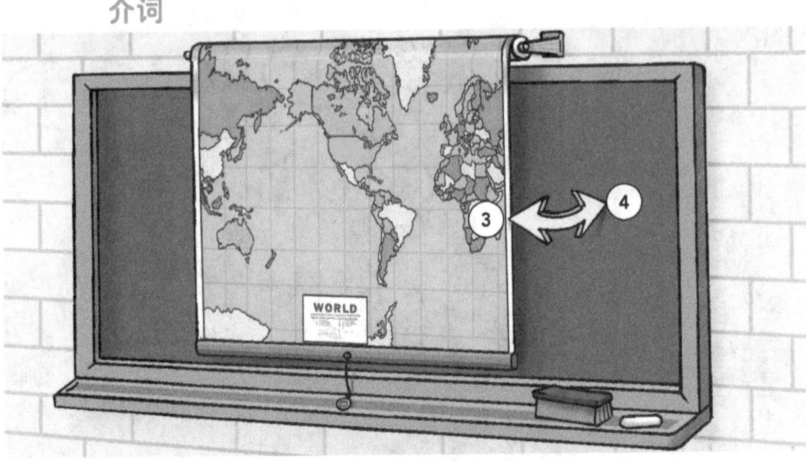

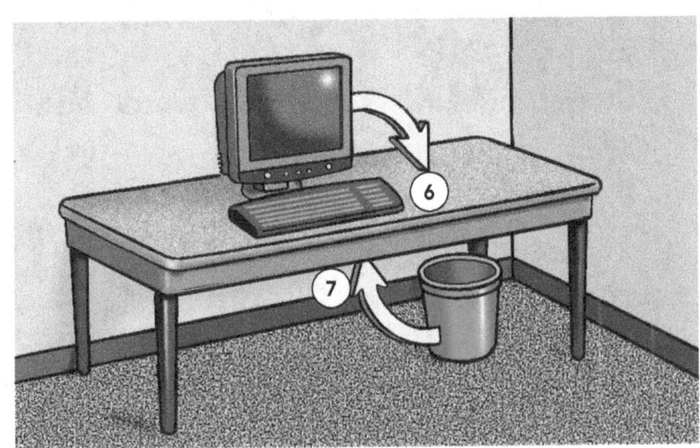

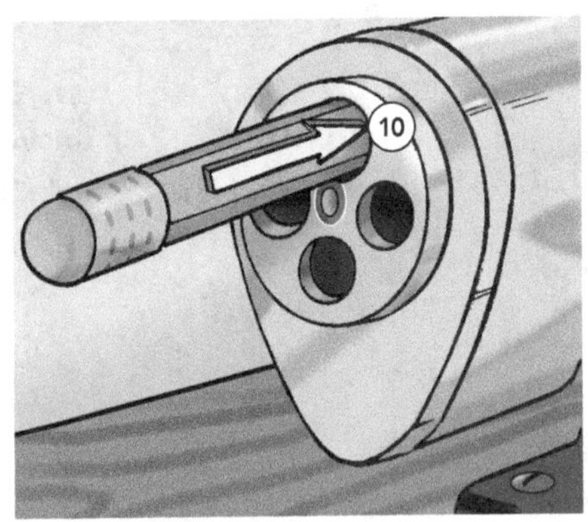

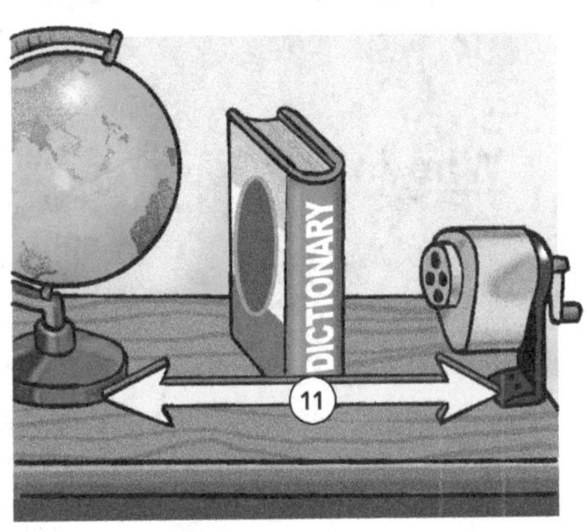

在……之上 **1** above
在……之下 **2** below

在……之前 **3** in front of
在……后面 **4** behind

在……旁边 **5** next to

在……上面 **6** on
在……下面 **7** under

在……左边 **8** to the left of
在……右边 **9** to the right of

在……里面 **10** in

在……和……之间 **11** between

[1–10]
A. Where's the *clock*?
B. The *clock* is **above** the *bulletin board*.

[11]
A. Where's the *dictionary*?
B. The *dictionary* is **between** the *globe* and the *pencil sharpener*.

Tell about the classroom on page 4. Use the prepositions in this lesson.

Tell about your classroom.

日常活动 1

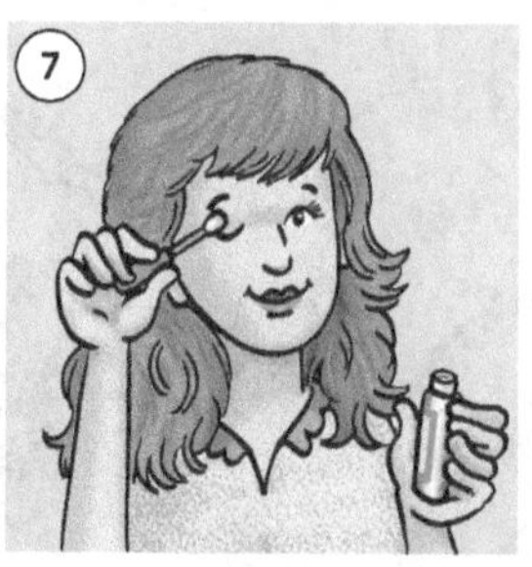

起床 1 get up
洗淋浴 2 take a shower
刷我的牙齿 3 brush *my** teeth
刮胡子 4 shave
穿衣服 5 get dressed
洗我的脸 6 wash *my** face
化妆 7 put on makeup
梳我的头发 8 brush *my** hair
梳理我的头发 9 comb *my** hair
整理床铺 10 make the bed

* my, his, her, our, your, their

脱衣服 11 get undressed
洗澡 12 take a bath
去睡觉 13 go to bed
睡觉 14 sleep
做早餐 15 make breakfast
做午餐 16 make lunch
做晚餐 17 cook/make dinner
吃早餐 18 eat/have breakfast
吃午餐 19 eat/have lunch
吃晚餐 20 eat/have dinner

A. What do you do every day?
B. I **get up**, I **take a shower**, and I **brush my teeth**.

A. What does he do every day?
B. He ________s, he ________s, and he ________s.

A. What does she do every day?
B. She ________s, she ________s, and she________s.

What do you do every day? Make a list.

Interview some friends and tell about their everyday activities.

EVERYDAY ACTIVITIES II

日常活动 2

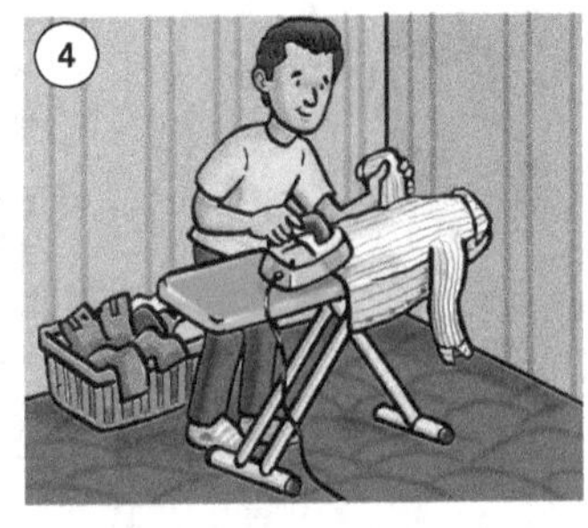
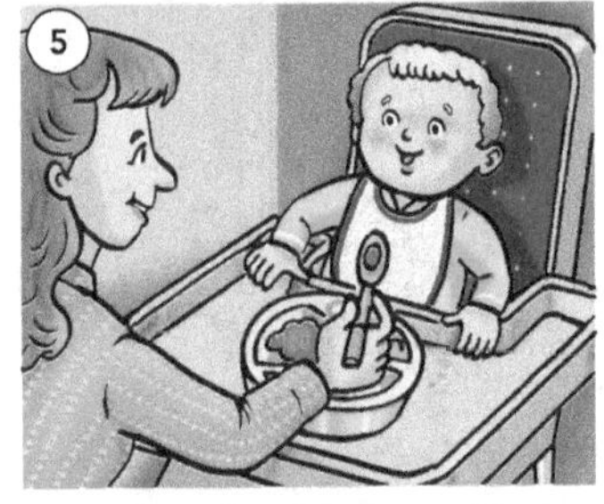

打扫公寓/打扫房子 **1** clean the apartment/ clean the house
洗餐具 **2** wash the dishes
洗衣服 **3** do the laundry
烫衣服 **4** iron
喂婴儿 **5** feed the baby
喂猫 **6** feed the cat
溜狗 **7** walk the dog
学习 **8** study

上班 **9** go to work
上学 **10** go to school
开车上班 **11** drive to work
搭乘公车上学 **12** take the bus to school
工作 **13** work
下班 **14** leave work
去商店 **15** go to the store
回家/回到家 **16** come home/get home

A. Hello. What are you doing?
B. I'm **clean**ing the **apartment**.

A. Hello, ... This is ....
What are you doing?
B. I'm ________ing. How about you?
A. I'm ________ing.

A. Are you going to ________ soon?
B. Yes. I'm going to ________ in a little while.

What are you going to do tomorrow? Make a list of everything you are going to do.

休闲活动

看电视 **1** watch TV
听收音机 **2** listen to the radio
听音乐 **3** listen to music
看书 **4** read a book
看报纸 **5** read the newspaper
玩耍 **6** play
玩牌 **7** play cards
打篮球 **8** play basketball
弹吉他 **9** play the guitar
练习弹钢琴 **10** practice the piano
运动 **11** exercise
游泳 **12** swim
种花 **13** plant flowers
用电脑 **14** use the computer
写信 **15** write a letter
放松/休息一下 **16** relax

A. Hi. What are you doing?
B. I'm **watch**ing **TV**.

A. Hi, ... Are you ________ing?
B. No, I'm not. I'm ________ing.

A. What's your (husband/wife/son/daughter/. . .) doing?
B. He's/She's ________ing.

What leisure activities do you like to do?

What do your family members and friends like to do?

日常会话

Greeting People 问候他人

Leave Taking 告别

哈啰。/你好。/嗨。 **1** Hello./Hi.

早安。 **2** Good morning.

午安。 **3** Good afternoon.

晚上好(傍晚见面时用语)。 **4** Good evening.

你好吗？ **5** How are you?/ How are you doing?

很好。/很好，谢谢。/还好。 **6** Fine./Fine, thanks./Okay.

近来怎样？/你近来怎样？ **7** What's new?/ What's new with you?

没什么。 **8** Not much./Not too much.

再见。 **9** Good-bye./Bye.

晚安(晚上道别时用语)。 **10** Good night.

待会见。 **11** See you later./ See you soon.

Introducing Yourself and Others 介绍自己及他人

Getting Someone's Attention
引起他人注意

Expressing Gratitude
表示感谢

Saying You Don't Understand
表示不明白

Calling Someone on the Telephone
打电话给某人

你好，我的名字叫……。/ 嗨，我是……。 **12** Hello. My name is ..../ Hi. I'm ....

很高兴认识你。 **13** Nice to meet you.

我也很高兴认识你。 **14** Nice to meet you, too.

让我向你介绍……。/ 这位是……。 **15** I'd like to introduce ..../ This is ....

对不起。 **16** Excuse me.

我可以问一个问题吗？ **17** May I ask a question?

谢谢你。/谢谢。 **18** Thank you./Thanks.

不用客气。 **19** You're welcome.

我不懂。/ 对不起，我不懂。 **20** I don't understand./ Sorry. I don't understand.

你可以重复一遍吗？ **21** Can you please repeat that?/ Can you please say that again?

你好，我是……。我可以和…说话吗？ **22** Hello. This is .... May I please speak to ....?

可以，等一下。 **23** Yes. Hold on a moment.

对不起…现在不在这里。 **24** I'm sorry. .... isn't here right now.

Practice conversations with other students. Use all the expressions on pages 12 and 13.

天气

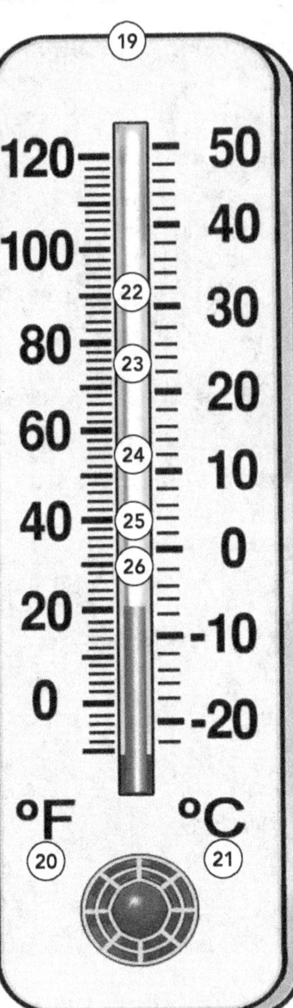

天气	**Weather**
晴天	**1** sunny
多云	**2** cloudy
晴朗	**3** clear
有薄雾	**4** hazy
多雾	**5** foggy
烟雾弥漫	**6** smoggy
大风	**7** windy
潮湿/闷热	**8** humid/muggy
下雨	**9** raining
下毛毛雨	**10** drizzling
下雪	**11** snowing
下冰雹	**12** hailing
下冻雨	**13** sleeting
闪电	**14** lightning
大雷雨	**15** thunderstorm
暴风雪	**16** snowstorm
尘暴	**17** dust storm
热浪	**18** heat wave
气温/温度	**Temperature**
温度计	**19** thermometer
华氏	**20** Fahrenheit
摄氏	**21** Centigrade/Celsius
热	**22** hot
暖和	**23** warm
凉	**24** cool
寒冷	**25** cold
严寒	**26** freezing

[1–13]
A. What's the weather like?
B. It's ________.

[14–18]
A. What's the weather forecast?
B. There's going to be ___[14]___/ a ___[15–18]___.

[20–26]
A. How's the weather?
B. It's ___[22–26]___.
A. What's the temperature?
B. It's . . . degrees ___[20–21]___.

What's the weather like today? What's the temperature?

What's the weather forecast for tomorrow?

NUMBERS

数字

Cardinal Numbers 基数

0 zero
1 one
2 two
3 three
4 four
5 five
6 six
7 seven
8 eight
9 nine
10 ten

11 eleven
12 twelve
13 thirteen
14 fourteen
15 fifteen
16 sixteen
17 seventeen
18 eighteen
19 nineteen
20 twenty

21 twenty-one
22 twenty-two
30 thirty
40 forty
50 fifty
60 sixty
70 seventy
80 eighty
90 ninety
100 one hundred

101 one hundred (and) one
102 one hundred (and) two
1,000 one thousand
10,000 ten thousand
100,000 one hundred thousand
1,000,000 one million
1,000,000,000 one billion

A. How old are you?

B. I'm ________ years old.

A. How many people are there in your family?
B. ________.

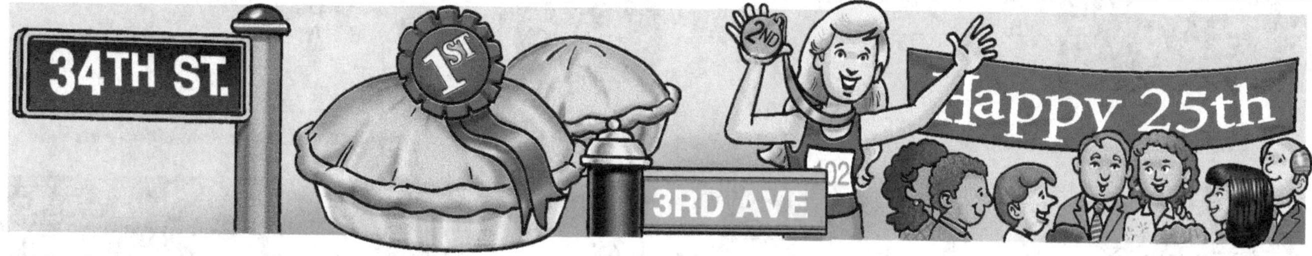

Ordinal Numbers 序数

1st first
2nd second
3rd third
4th fourth
5th fifth
6th sixth
7th seventh
8th eighth
9th ninth
10th tenth

11th eleventh
12th twelfth
13th thirteenth
14th fourteenth
15th fifteenth
16th sixteenth
17th seventeenth
18th eighteenth
19th nineteenth
20th twentieth

21st twenty-first
22nd twenty-second
30th thirtieth
40th fortieth
50th fiftieth
60th sixtieth
70th seventieth
80th eightieth
90th ninetieth
100th one hundredth

101st one hundred (and) first
102nd one hundred (and) second
1,000th one thousandth
10,000th ten thousandth
100,000th one hundred thousandth
1,000,000th one millionth
1,000,000,000th one billionth

A. What floor do you live on?
B. I live on the ________ floor.

A. Is this your first trip to our country?
B. No. It's my ________ trip.

How many students are there in your class?

How many people are there in your country?

What were the names of your teachers in elementary school?
(My *first*-grade teacher was Ms./Mrs./Mr. . . .)

TIME

时间

two o'clock

two fifteen/
a quarter after *two*

two thirty/
half past *two*

two forty-five/
a quarter to *three*

two oh five

two twenty/
twenty after *two*

two forty/
twenty to *three*

two fifty-five/
five to *three*

A. What time is it?
B. It's .

A. What time does the movie begin?
B. At ________.

two A.M.

two P.M.

noon/
twelve noon

midnight/
twelve midnight

A. When does the train leave?
B. At ________.

A. What time will we arrive?
B. At ________.

Tell about your daily schedule:
What do you do? When?
(I get up at ________. I.............)

Do you usually have enough time to do things, or do you "run out of time"? Tell about it.

Tell about the use of time in different cultures or countries you know:
Do people arrive on time for work? appointments? parties?
Do trains and buses operate exactly on schedule?
Do movies and sports events begin on time?
Do workplaces use time clocks or timesheets to record employees' work hours?

Coins 钱币

	Name	Value	Written as:	
1	penny	one cent	1¢	$ .01
2	nickel	five cents	5¢	$ .05
3	dime	ten cents	10¢	$ .10
4	quarter	twenty-five cents	25¢	$ .25
5	half dollar	fifty cents	50¢	$ .50
6	silver dollar	one dollar		$1.00

A. How much is a **penny** worth?
B. A **penny** is worth **one cent.**

A. *Soda* costs *ninety-five cents.* Do you have enough change?
B. Yes. I have a/two/three _____(s) and . . . .

Currency 货币

	Name	We sometimes say:	Value	Written as:
7	(one-) dollar bill	a one	one dollar	$ 1.00
8	five-dollar bill	a five	five dollars	$ 5.00
9	ten-dollar bill	a ten	ten dollars	$ 10.00
10	twenty-dollar bill	a twenty	twenty dollars	$ 20.00
11	fifty-dollar bill	a fifty	fifty dollars	$ 50.00
12	(one-) hundred dollar bill	a hundred	one hundred dollars	$100.00

A. I'm going to the supermarket. Do you have any cash?
B. I have a **twenty-dollar bill**.
A. **Twenty dollars** is enough. Thanks.

A. Can you change a **five-dollar bill/a five**?
B. Yes. I have ***five* one-dollar bills/ *five* ones.**

Written as:	We say:
$1.30	a dollar and thirty cents a dollar thirty
$2.50	two dollars and fifty cents two fifty
$56.49	fifty-six dollars and forty-nine cents fifty-six forty-nine

Tell about some things you usually buy. What do they cost?

Name and describe the coins and currency in your country. What are they worth in U.S. dollars?

THE CALENDAR

日历

年 **1** year
月 **2** month
星期 **3** week
日 **4** day
周末 **5** weekend

一周的日子 **Days of the Week**
星期日 **6** Sunday
星期一 **7** Monday
星期二 **8** Tuesday
星期三 **9** Wednesday
星期四 **10** Thursday
星期五 **11** Friday
星期六 **12** Saturday

月份 **Months of the Year**
一月 **13** January
二月 **14** February
三月 **15** March
四月 **16** April
五月 **17** May
六月 **18** June
七月 **19** July
八月 **20** August
九月 **21** September
十月 **22** October
十一月 **23** November
十二月 **24** December

2012年1月3日 **25** January 3, 2012
January third, two thousand twelve
生日 **26** birthday
周年纪念 **27** anniversary
约定时间 **28** appointment

A. What year is it?
B. It's ________.

[13–24]
A. What month is it?
B. It's ________.

[6–12]
A. What day is it?
B. It's ________.

A. What's today's date?
B. It's ________.

[26–28]
A. When is your ________?
B. It's on ________.

Which days of the week do you go to work/school?
(I go to work/school on ________.)

What do you do on the weekend?

What is your date of birth?
(I was born on ....*month day, year*.......)

What's your favorite day of the week? Why?

What's your favorite month of the year? Why?

时间表达及季节

昨天 1 yesterday
今天 2 today
明天 3 tomorrow
早上 4 morning
下午 5 afternoon
傍晚 6 evening
夜晚 7 night
昨天早上 8 yesterday morning
昨天下午 9 yesterday afternoon
昨天傍晚 10 yesterday evening
昨晚 11 last night

今天早上 12 this morning
今天下午 13 this afternoon
今天傍晚 14 this evening
今晚 15 tonight
明天早上 16 tomorrow morning
明天下午 17 tomorrow afternoon
明天傍晚 18 tomorrow evening
明晚 19 tomorrow night
上周 20 last week
本周 21 this week
下周 22 next week

每周一次 23 once a week
每周两次 24 twice a week
每周三次 25 three times a week
每天 26 every day

季节 **Seasons**
春天 27 spring
夏天 28 summer
秋天 29 fall/autumn
冬天 30 winter

What did you do yesterday morning/afternoon/evening? What did you do last night?

What are you going to do tomorrow morning/afternoon/evening/night?

What did you do last week?

What are your plans for next week?

How many times a week do you have English class?/go to the supermarket?/exercise?

What's your favorite season? Why?

TYPES OF HOUSING AND COMMUNITIES

房屋及社区种类

公寓大楼 **1** apartment building
房子 **2** house
双联式房屋/双门联式房屋（两家合居，但各自分开） **3** duplex/two-family house
二层或三层楼多栋联建住宅 **4** townhouse/townhome
各户有独立产权的公寓(大楼) **5** condominium/condo
宿舍 **6** dormitory/dorm
移动式房屋 **7** mobile home
养老院 **8** nursing home

庇护所 **9** shelter
农场 **10** farm
牧场 **11** ranch
船屋 **12** houseboat
城市 **13** the city
郊区 **14** the suburbs
乡村 **15** the country
小镇/村庄 **16** a town/village

A. Where do you live?

B. I live
- in a/an ___[1–9]___.
- on a ___[10–12]___.
- in ___[13–16]___.

[1–12]

A. Town Taxi Company.

B. Hello. Please send a taxi to ....*(address)*.....

A. Is that a house or an apartment building?

B. It's a/an ________.

A. All right. We'll be there right away.

[1–12]

A. This is the Emergency Operator.

B. Please send an ambulance to ....*(address)*.....

A. Is that a private home?

B. It's a/an ________.

A. What's your name and telephone number?

B. ....

Tell about people you know and where they live.

Discuss:
- Who lives in dormitories?
- Who lives in nursing homes?
- Who lives in shelters?
- Why?

客厅

书柜 **1** bookcase
照片 **2** picture/photograph
画 **3** painting
壁炉台 **4** mantel
壁炉 **5** fireplace
壁炉屏风 **6** fireplace screen
DVD播放机 **7** DVD player
电视 **8** television/TV
卡式影像录放机 **9** VCR/video cassette recorder

墙壁 **10** wall
天花板 **11** ceiling
窗帘 **12** drapes
窗户 **13** window
双人沙发 **14** loveseat
墙柜 **15** wall unit
喇叭 **16** speaker
立体声音响系统 **17** stereo system
杂志架 **18** magazine holder
抱枕 **19** (throw) pillow

沙发 **20** sofa/couch
植物 **21** plant
茶几 **22** coffee table
小地毯 **23** rug
灯 **24** lamp
灯罩 **25** lampshade
小茶几 **26** end table
地板 **27** floor
落地灯 **28** floor lamp
单人沙发椅 **29** armchair

A. Where are you?
B. I'm in the living room.
A. What are you doing?
B. I'm dusting* the **bookcase**.

* dusting/cleaning

A. You have a very nice living room!
B. Thank you.
A. Your ________ is/are beautiful!
B. Thank you for saying so.

A. Uh-oh! I just spilled coffee on your ________!
B. That's okay. Don't worry about it.

Tell about your living room.
(In my living room there's ....)

THE DINING ROOM

饭厅

餐桌	1	(dining room) table
餐椅	2	(dining room) chair
餐具柜	3	buffet
托盘	4	tray
茶壶	5	teapot
咖啡壶	6	coffee pot
糖罐	7	sugar bowl
鲜奶壶	8	creamer
水壶	9	pitcher
吊灯	10	chandelier
瓷器柜	11	china cabinet
瓷器	12	china*
沙拉碗	13	salad bowl
盛菜碗	14	serving bowl
盛菜盘	15	serving dish
花瓶	16	vase
蜡烛	17	candle
烛台	18	candlestick
大浅盘	19	platter
奶油盘	20	butter dish
盐瓶	21	salt shaker
胡椒瓶	22	pepper shaker
桌巾/桌布	23	tablecloth
餐巾	24	napkin
叉子	25	fork
盘子	26	plate
餐刀	27	knife
汤匙	28	spoon
碗	29	bowl
马克杯	30	mug
玻璃杯	31	glass
茶杯	32	cup
浅盘	33	saucer

* 也可叫做 *chinaware*。在 China 当作瓷器时，字首 c 必须小写。在 China 当作国名中国时，字首 C 必须大写。

A. This **dining room table** is very nice.
B. Thank you. It was a gift from my *grandmother.**

*grandmother/grandfather/aunt/uncle/. . .

[In a store]

A. May I help you?
B. Yes, please. Do you have ________s?*
A. Yes. ________s* are right over there.
B. Thank you.

**With 12, use the singular.*

[At home]

A. Look at this old ________ I just bought!
B. Where did you buy it?
A. At a yard sale. How do you like it?
B. It's VERY unusual!

Tell about your dining room.
(In my dining room there's ....)

THE BEDROOM

卧室

- 床 **1** bed
- 床头板 **2** headboard
- 枕头 **3** pillow
- 枕头套 **4** pillowcase
- 床垫套 **5** fitted sheet
- 床单 **6** (flat) sheet
- 毯子 **7** blanket
- 电热毯 **8** electric blanket
- 床裙 **9** dust ruffle
- 床罩 **10** bedspread
- 被子/拼凑图案的被褥 **11** comforter/quilt
- 地毯 **12** carpet
- 五斗柜/衣柜 **13** chest (of drawers)
- 百叶窗 **14** blinds
- 窗帘 **15** curtains
- 灯 **16** lamp
- 闹钟 **17** alarm clock
- 闹钟收音机 **18** clock radio
- 床头柜 **19** night table/nightstand
- 镜子 **20** mirror
- 首饰盒 **21** jewelry box
- 五斗柜/梳妆台 **22** dresser/bureau
- 床垫 **23** mattress
- 弹簧座 **24** box spring
- 床架 **25** bed frame

A. Ooh! Look at that big bug!
B. Where?
A. It's on the **bed**!
B. I'LL get it.

[In a store]

A. Excuse me. I'm looking for a/an ________.*
B. We have some very nice ________s, and they're all on sale this week!
A. Oh, good!

* *With 14 & 15, use:* Excuse me. I'm looking for ______.

[In a bedroom]

A. Oh, no! I just lost my contact lens!
B. Where?
A. I think it's on the ________.
B. I'll help you look.

Tell about your bedroom.
(In my bedroom there's ....)

THE KITCHEN

厨房

电冰箱 **1** refrigerator
冷冻柜 **2** freezer
垃圾桶 **3** garbage pail
电动搅拌器 **4** (electric) mixer
厨柜 **5** cabinet
纸巾架 **6** paper towel holder
罐子 **7** canister
厨房工作台面 **8** (kitchen) counter
洗碗机专用洗洁剂 **9** dishwasher detergent
洗碗液 **10** dishwashing liquid
水龙头 **11** faucet
厨房水槽 **12** (kitchen) sink
洗碗机 **13** dishwasher

垃圾清除器 **14** (garbage) disposal
擦碗巾 **15** dish towel
碗碟沥水架/碗碟架 **16** dish rack/ dish drainer
调味品架 **17** spice rack
电动开罐器 **18** (electric) can opener
搅拌机 **19** blender
小烤箱 **20** toaster oven
微波炉 **21** microwave (oven)
隔热垫 **22** potholder
烧水壶 **23** tea kettle
炉台 **24** stove/range

炉头 **25** burner
烤箱 **26** oven
烤面包机 **27** toaster
咖啡机 **28** coffeemaker
垃圾压缩机 **29** trash compactor
切菜板/砧板 **30** cutting board
食谱 **31** cookbook
食物加工机 **32** food processor
厨房椅子 **33** kitchen chair
厨房桌子 **34** kitchen table
餐桌垫 **35** placemat

A. I think we need a new **refrigerator**.
B. I think you're right.

[In a store]

A. Excuse me. Are your ________s still on sale?
B. Yes, they are. They're twenty percent off.

[In a kitchen]

A. When did you get this/these new ________(s)?
B. I got it/them last week.

Tell about your kitchen.
(In my kitchen there's ....)

THE BABY'S ROOM

婴儿房

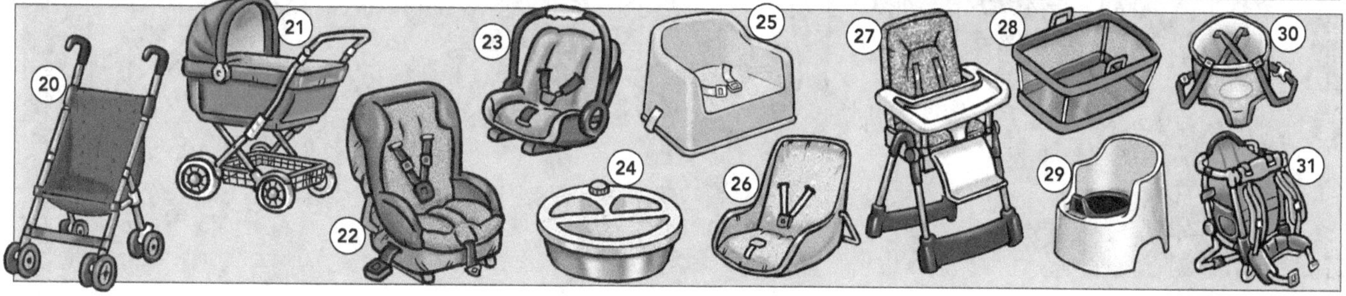

泰迪熊	1	teddy bear
婴儿监听器/对讲机	2	baby monitor/ intercom
抽屉柜	3	chest (of drawers)
婴儿床	4	crib
床围	5	crib bumper/ bumper pad
婴儿床吊饰玩具	6	mobile
换尿布台	7	changing table
连身衣	8	stretch suit
换尿布护垫	9	changing pad
尿布垃圾桶	10	diaper pail
小夜灯	11	night light
玩具箱	12	toy chest
填充动物玩具	13	stuffed animal
洋娃娃	14	doll
婴儿秋千	15	swing
婴儿围栏	16	playpen
手摇铃	17	rattle
学步车	18	walker
摇篮	19	cradle
婴儿推车	20	stroller
婴儿车	21	baby carriage
儿童安全座椅	22	car seat/ safety seat
婴儿提篮	23	baby carrier
食物加热盒	24	food warmer
幼儿加高座椅	25	booster seat
婴儿座椅	26	baby seat
高脚椅	27	high chair
便携式婴儿床	28	portable crib
婴儿便盆	29	potty
胸前婴儿背袋	30	baby frontpack
婴儿背架	31	baby backpack

A. Thank you for the **teddy bear**. It's a very nice gift.
B. You're welcome. Tell me, when are you due?
A. In a few more weeks.

A. That's a very nice ________.
Where did you get it?
B. It was a gift from ....

A. Do you have everything you need before the baby comes?
B. Almost everything. We're still looking for a/an ________ and a/an ________.

Tell about your country:
What things do people buy for a new baby?
Does a new baby sleep in a separate room, as in the United States?

THE BATHROOM

浴室

废纸篓 **1** wastebasket
梳妆台/洗手台 **2** vanity
肥皂 **3** soap
肥皂盒 **4** soap dish
皂液器 **5** soap dispenser
洗脸槽 **6** (bathroom) sink
水龙头 **7** faucet
药柜 **8** medicine cabinet
镜子 **9** mirror
茶杯 **10** cup
牙刷 **11** toothbrush
牙刷架 **12** toothbrush holder
电动牙刷 **13** electric toothbrush

吹风机 **14** hair dryer
架子 **15** shelf
脏衣篮 **16** hamper
风扇 **17** fan
浴巾 **18** bath towel
手巾 **19** hand towel
洗脸毛巾 **20** washcloth/facecloth
毛巾架 **21** towel rack
橡胶吸盘 **22** plunger
马桶刷 **23** toilet brush
卫生纸 **24** toilet paper
空气清香剂 **25** air freshener

马桶 **26** toilet
马桶座 **27** toilet seat
淋浴 **28** shower
莲蓬头/淋浴头 **29** shower head
浴帘 **30** shower curtain
浴缸 **31** bathtub/tub
橡胶垫 **32** rubber mat
排水孔 **33** drain
海绵 **34** sponge
浴垫 **35** bath mat
体重计 **36** scale

A. Where's the **hair dryer**?
B. It's *on* the **vanity**.

A. Where's the **soap**?
B. It's *in* the **soap dish**.

A. Where's the **plunger**?
B. It's *next to* the **toilet brush**.

A. [Knock. Knock.] Did I leave my glasses in there?
B. Yes. They're on/in/next to the ________.

A. *Bobby*? You didn't clean up the bathroom! There's toothpaste on the ________, and there's powder all over the ________!
B. Sorry. I'll clean it up right away.

Tell about your bathroom. (In my bathroom there's ....)

OUTSIDE THE HOME

家的外围

前院 **Front Yard**

路灯 **1** lamppost
信箱 **2** mailbox
前门小路 **3** front walk
前门阶梯 **4** front steps
前门门廊 **5** (front) porch
防风门/外重门 **6** storm door
前门 **7** front door
门铃 **8** doorbell
前门灯 **9** (front) light
窗户 **10** window
纱窗 **11** (window) screen
窗板 **12** shutter
屋顶 **13** roof
车库 **14** garage
车库门 **15** garage door
车道 **16** driveway

后院 **Backyard**

躺椅 **17** lawn chair
割草机 **18** lawnmower
工具房 **19** tool shed
纱门 **20** screen door
后门 **21** back door
门把 **22** door knob
屋外的平台 **23** deck
烧烤架/户外烤架 **24** barbecue/(outdoor) grill
露台 **25** patio
排水沟 **26** gutter
排水管 **27** drainpipe
卫星接收器 **28** satellite dish
电视天线 **29** TV antenna
烟囱 **30** chimney
侧门 **31** side door
篱笆 **32** fence

A. When are you going to repair the **lamppost**?
B. I'm going to repair it next Saturday.

[On the telephone]
A. Harry's Home Repairs.
B. Hello. Do you fix ________s?
A. No, we don't.
B. Oh, okay. Thank you.

[At work on Monday morning]
A. What did you do this weekend?
B. Nothing much. I repaired my ________ and my ________.

Do you like to repair things?
What things can you repair yourself?
What things can't you repair? Who repairs them?

THE APARTMENT BUILDING

公寓大楼

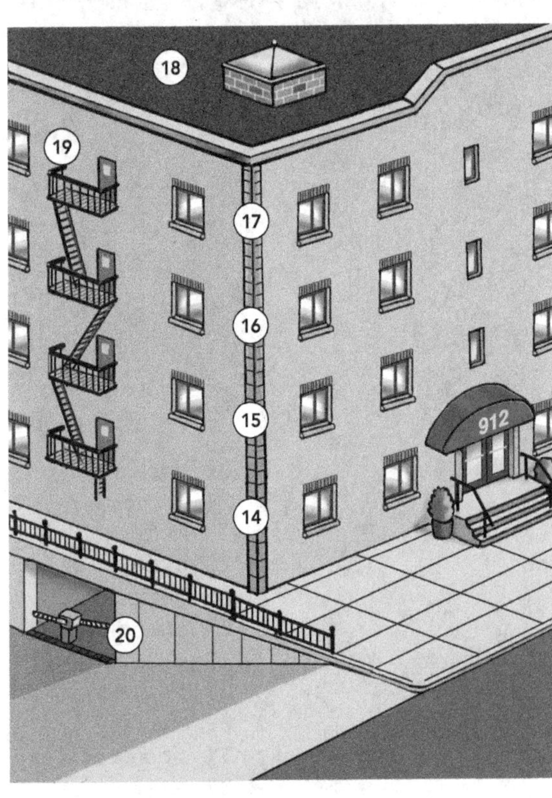

找公寓 **Looking for an Apartment**

租房广告/分类广告 **1** apartment ads/ classified ads

公寓出租广告 **2** apartment listings

空屋出租广告 **3** vacancy sign

签租约 **Signing a Lease**

房客 **4** tenant

房东 **5** landlord

租约 **6** lease

押金 **7** security deposit

搬入 **Moving In**

搬家卡车/搬家货车 **8** moving truck/ moving van

邻居 **9** neighbor

大楼管理员 **10** building manager

看门人 **11** doorman

钥匙 **12** key

锁 **13** lock

一楼 **14** first floor

二楼 **15** second floor

三楼 **16** third floor

四楼 **17** fourth floor

屋顶 **18** roof

室外逃生梯 **19** fire escape

室内停车场 **20** parking garage

阳台 **21** balcony

庭院 **22** courtyard

停车场 **23** parking lot

停车位 **24** parking space

游泳池 **25** swimming pool

水力按摩池 **26** whirlpool

垃圾桶 **27** trash bin

空调设备 **28** air conditioner

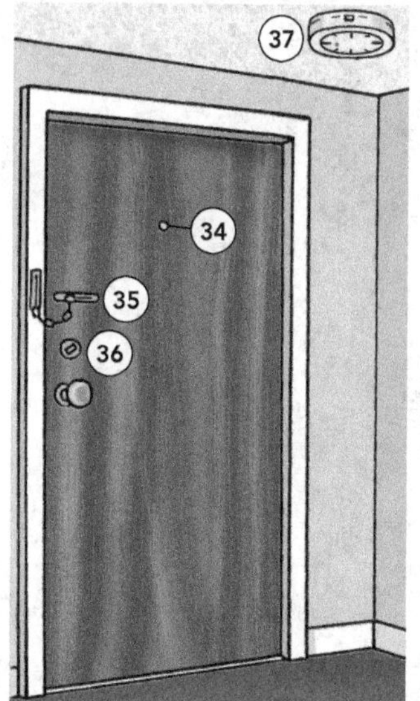

一楼大厅 **Lobby**

- 对讲电话装置/对讲机 **29** intercom/speaker
- 门铃 **30** buzzer
- 信箱 **31** mailbox
- 电梯 **32** elevator
- 楼梯 **33** stairway

门口 **Doorway**

- 门镜/窥视孔 **34** peephole
- 门链 **35** (door) chain
- 弹子门锁 **36** dead-bolt lock
- 烟雾探测器 **37** smoke detector

走廊 **Hallway**

- 紧急出口/安全出口 室内逃生梯 **38** fire exit/emergency stairway
- 火警警报 **39** fire alarm
- 喷水灭火系统 **40** sprinkler system
- 管房人 **41** superintendent
- 垃圾滑槽 **42** garbage chute/trash chute

地下室 **Basement**

- 储藏室 **43** storage room
- 储藏柜 **44** storage locker
- 自助洗衣房 **45** laundry room
- 安检门 **46** security gate

[19–46]

A. Is there a **fire escape**?

B. Yes, there is. Do you want to see the apartment?

A. Yes, I do.

[19–46]

[Renting an apartment]

A. Let me show you around.

B. Okay.

A. This is the ________, and here's the ________.

B. I see.

[19–46]

[On the telephone]

A. Mom and Dad? I found an apartment.

B. Good. Tell us about it.

A. It has a/an ________ and a/an ________.

B. That's nice. Does it have a/an ________?

A. Yes, it does.

Do you or someone you know live in an apartment building? Tell about it.

HOUSEHOLD PROBLEMS AND REPAIRS

房屋问题及修理

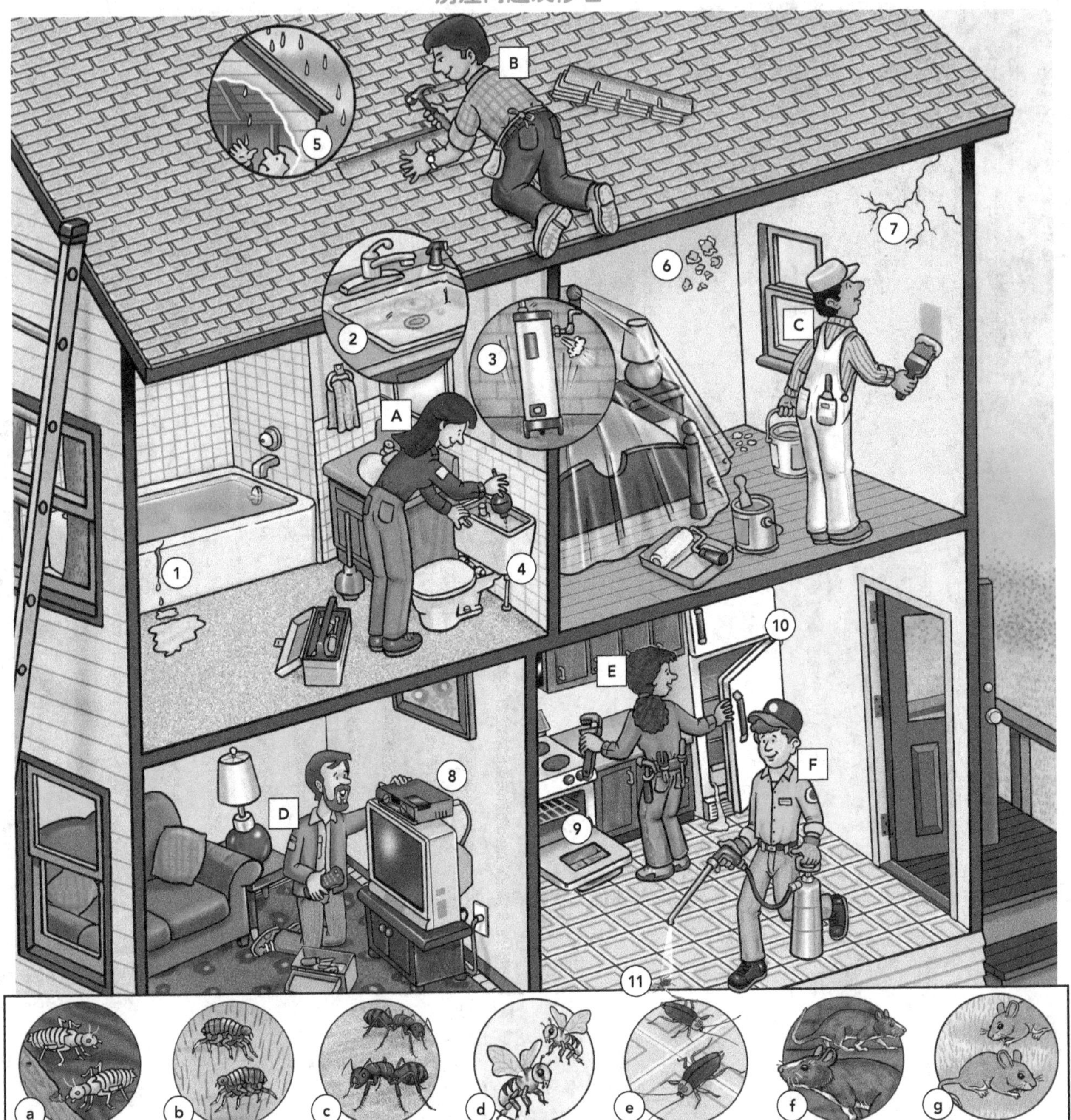

水管工人 **A plumber**
浴缸漏水。 **1** The bathtub is leaking.
洗脸槽堵塞了。 **2** The sink is clogged.
热水器故障。 **3** The hot water heater isn't working.
马桶坏了。 **4** The toilet is broken.

屋顶修理工 **B roofer**
屋顶漏水。 **5** The roof is leaking.

油漆工人 **C (house) painter**
油漆剥落。 **6** The paint is peeling.
墙壁有裂缝。 **7** The wall is cracked.

有线电视公司 **D cable TV company**
有线电视故障。 **8** The cable TV isn't working.

家电修理人员 **E appliance repairperson**
炉具故障。 **9** The stove isn't working.
电冰箱坏了。 **10** The refrigerator is broken.

灭虫人员 **F exterminator/ pest control specialist**
厨房里有……。 **11** There are ____ in the kitchen.
白蚁 **a** termites
跳蚤 **b** fleas
蚂蚁 **c** ants
蜜蜂 **d** bees
蟑螂 **e** cockroaches
老鼠 **f** rats
小老鼠 **g** mice

锁匠 **G locksmith**
锁坏了。**12** The lock is broken.

电工 **H electrician**
前门灯不亮。**13** The front light doesn't go on.
门铃不响。**14** The doorbell doesn't ring.
客厅没电。**15** The power is out in the living room.

烟囱清洁工 **I chimneysweep**
烟囱脏了。**16** The chimney is dirty.

杂活工/修理工 **J home repairperson/"handyman"**
浴室的瓷砖松动了。**17** The tiles in the bathroom are loose.

木工/木匠 **K carpenter**
台阶坏了。**18** The steps are broken.
门打不开。**19** The door doesn't open.

暖气及空调服务 **L heating and air conditioning service**
供暖系统坏了。**20** The heating system is broken.
空调故障。**21** The air conditioning isn't working.

A. What's the matter?
B. ___[1–21]___.
A. I think we should call a/an ___[A–L]___.

[1–21]
A. I'm having a problem in my apartment/house.
B. What's the problem?
A. ________.

[A–L]
A. Can you recommend a good ________?
B. Yes. You should call ....

What do you do when there are problems in your home? Do you fix things yourself, or do you call someone?

打扫房屋

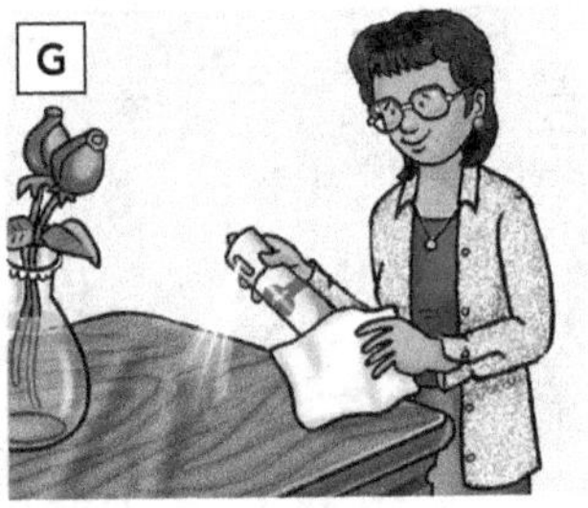

扫地	A	sweep the floor
吸尘器	B	vacuum
拖地板	C	mop the floor
洗窗户	D	wash the windows
除灰尘	E	dust
地板打蜡	F	wax the floor
擦亮家具	G	polish the furniture
清理浴室	H	clean the bathroom
丢垃圾	I	take out the garbage
扫把	1	broom
簸箕	2	dustpan
小扫帚	3	whisk broom
扫毯器	4	carpet sweeper
吸尘器	5	vacuum (cleaner)
吸尘器附件	6	vacuum cleaner attachments
吸尘器袋	7	vacuum cleaner bag
手提吸尘器	8	hand vacuum
抹尘拖把/干拖把	9	(dust) mop/(dry) mop
海绵拖把	10	(sponge) mop
湿拖把	11	(wet) mop
纸巾	12	paper towels
玻璃清洁剂	13	window cleaner
氨水	14	ammonia
擦尘布	15	dust cloth
羽毛掸子	16	feather duster
地板打蜡剂	17	floor wax
木制家具亮光蜡	18	furniture polish
清洁剂	19	cleanser
刷子	20	scrub brush
海绵	21	sponge
水桶/桶子	22	bucket/pail
垃圾桶	23	trash can/ garbage can
回收桶	24	recycling bin

[A–I]
A. What are you doing?
B. I'm **sweeping the floor**.

[1–24]
A. I can't find the **broom**.
B. Look over there!

[1–12, 15, 16, 20–24]
A. Excuse me. Do you sell ________(s)?
B. Yes. They're at the back of the store.
A. Thanks.

[13, 14, 17–19]
A. Excuse me. Do you sell ________?
B. Yes. It's at the back of the store.
A. Thanks.

What household cleaning chores do people do in your home? What things do they use?

HOME SUPPLIES
家用器具

码尺 **1** yardstick
苍蝇拍 **2** fly swatter
橡胶吸盘 **3** plunger
手电筒 **4** flashlight
延长线 **5** extension cord
测量卷尺 **6** tape measure
踏板梯子 **7** step ladder
捕鼠器 **8** mousetrap
遮蔽胶带 **9** masking tape
电工胶带/绝缘带 **10** electrical tape
管道胶带 **11** duct tape
电池 **12** batteries
电灯泡 **13** lightbulbs/bulbs
保险丝 **14** fuses
机油 **15** oil
胶水 **16** glue
工作手套 **17** work gloves
杀虫剂 **18** bug spray/insect spray
杀蟑螂剂 **19** roach killer
沙纸 **20** sandpaper
油漆 **21** paint
油漆稀释剂 **22** paint thinner
油漆刷子 **23** paintbrush/brush
油漆盘 **24** paint pan
滚漆筒 **25** paint roller
喷漆枪 **26** spray gun

A. I can't find the **yardstick**!
B. Look in the utility cabinet.
A. I did.
B. Oh! Wait a minute! I lent the **yardstick** to the neighbors.

[1–8, 23–26]
A. I'm going to the hardware store. Can you think of anything we need?
B. Yes. We need a/an ______.
A. Oh, that's right.

[9–22]
A. I'm going to the hardware store. Can you think of anything we need?
B. Yes. We need ______.
A. Oh, that's right.

What home supplies do you have? How and when do you use each one?

TOOLS AND HARDWARE

工具及五金器具

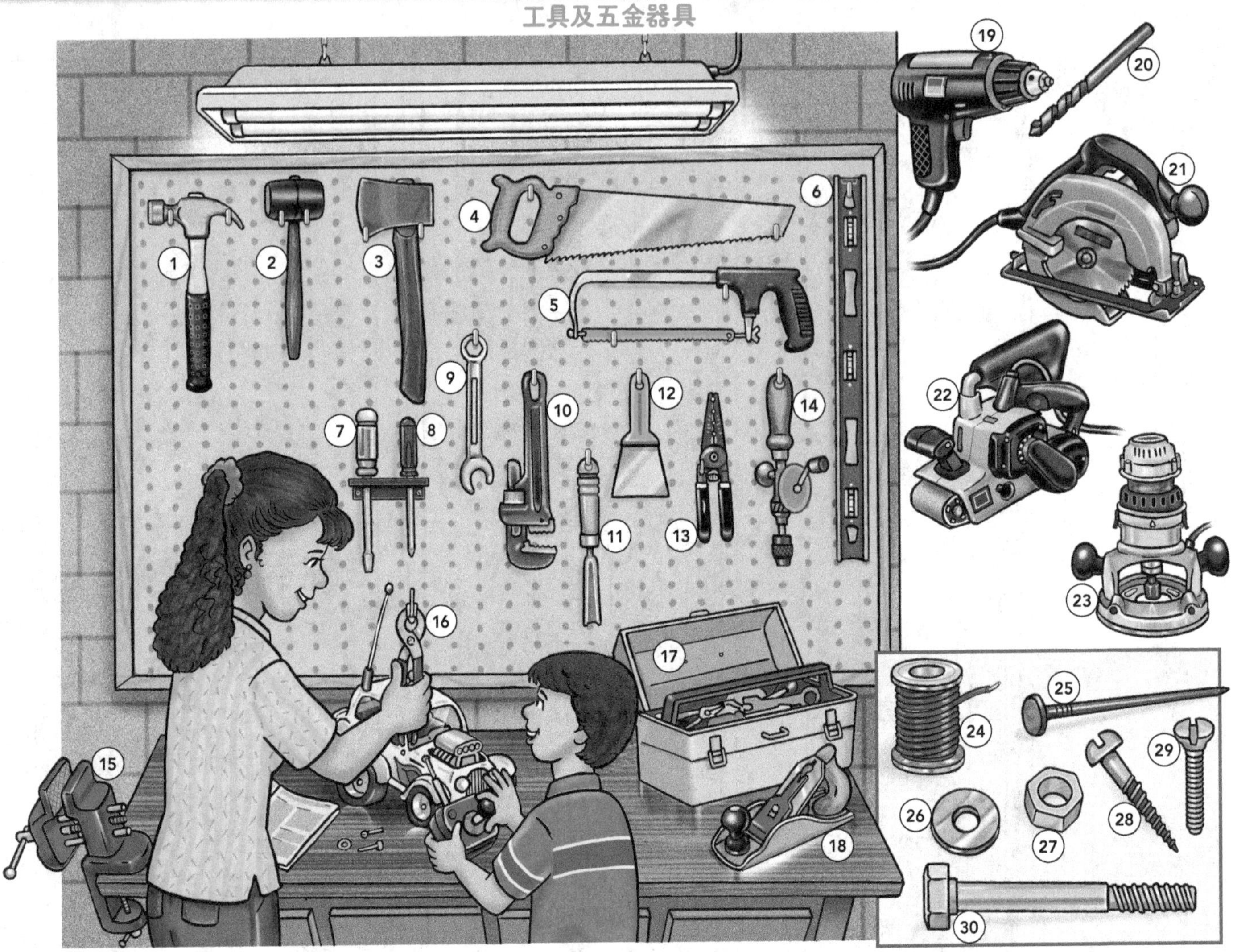

锤子	1	hammer
大头锤	2	mallet
斧头	3	ax
锯子/手锯	4	saw/handsaw
钢锯	5	hacksaw
水平仪	6	level
螺丝刀	7	screwdriver
十字型螺丝刀	8	Phillips screwdriver
扳钳	9	wrench
活动扳手/管钳	10	monkey wrench/pipe wrench
凿子	11	chisel
刮刀	12	scraper
剥皮钳	13	wire stripper
手钻	14	hand drill
台虎钳	15	vise
钳子	16	pliers
工具箱	17	toolbox
刨子	18	plane
电钻	19	electric drill
钻头	20	(drill) bit
圆锯/电锯	21	circular saw/power saw
电动砂磨机	22	power sander
手动木工钻	23	router
电线	24	wire
钉子	25	nail
垫圈	26	washer
螺帽	27	nut
木用螺丝钉	28	wood screw
机械螺丝	29	machine screw
螺栓	30	bolt

A. Can I borrow your **hammer**?
B. Sure.
A. Thanks.

* *With 25–30, use:* Could I borrow some ________s?

[1–15, 17–24]
A. Where's the ________?
B. It's on/next to/near/over/under the ________.

[16, 25–30]
A. Where are the ________s?
B. They're on/next to/near/over/under the ________.

Do you like to work with tools? What tools do you have in your home?

园艺工具及活动

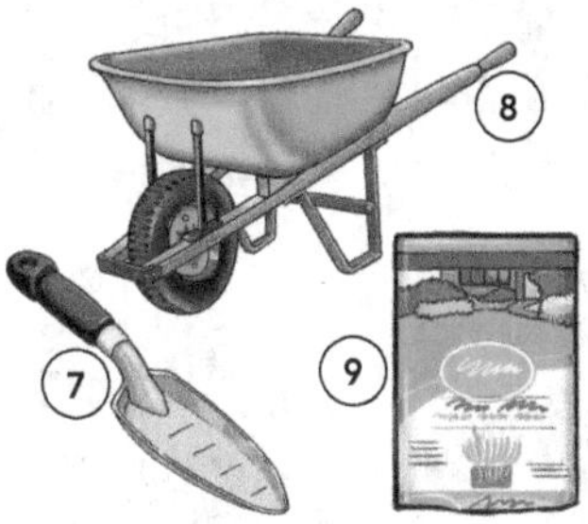

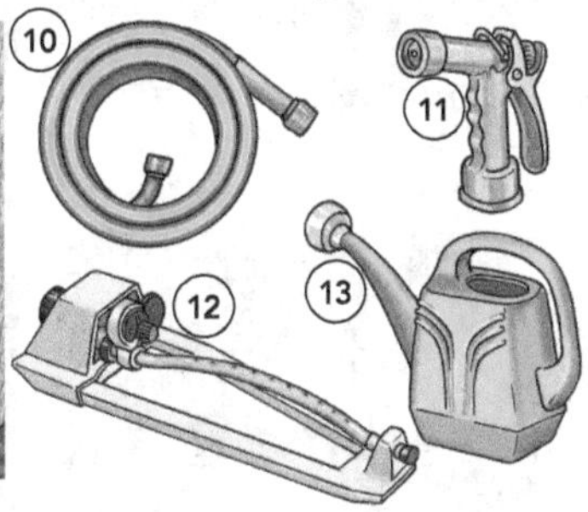

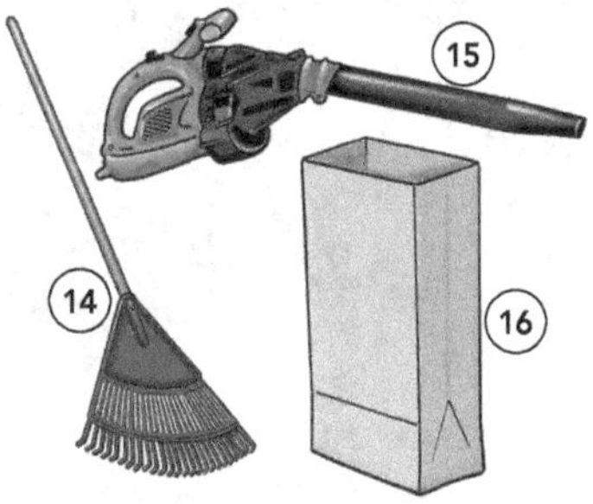

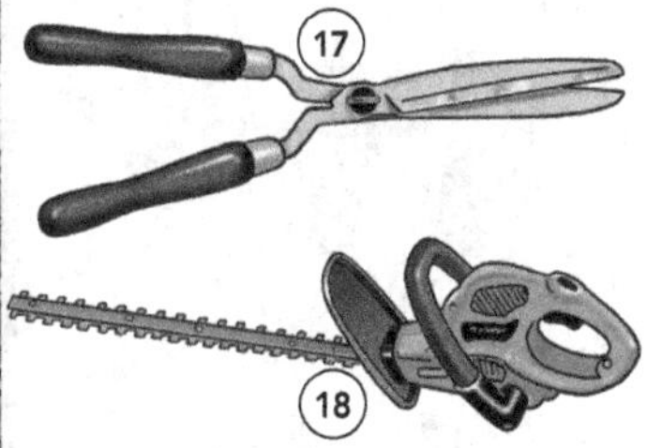

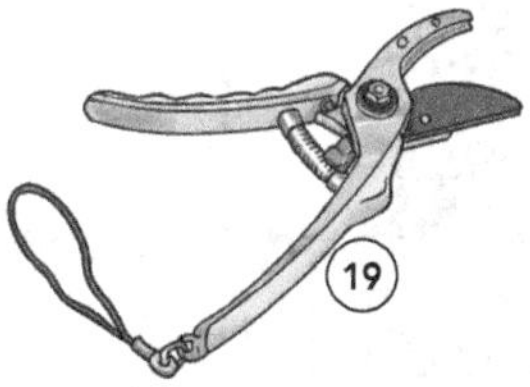

割草坪	A mow the lawn	割草机	1 lawnmower	喷嘴	11 nozzle
种菜	B plant vegetables	汽油桶	2 gas can	洒水器	12 sprinkler
种花	C plant flowers	割灌机	3 line trimmer	浇水壶	13 watering can
浇花	D water the flowers	铲子	4 shovel	草耙	14 rake
耙叶子	E rake leaves	菜种子	5 vegetable seeds	吹叶机	15 leaf blower
修剪树篱	F trim the hedge	锄头	6 hoe	庭院垃圾袋	16 yard waste bag
修剪灌木丛	G prune the bushes	泥刀/小铲子	7 trowel	树篱剪	17 (hedge) clippers
除杂草	H weed	独轮手推车	8 wheelbarrow	树篱修剪器	18 hedge trimmer
		肥料	9 fertilizer	修枝剪	19 pruning shears
		橡胶水管/花园水管	10 (garden) hose	除草器	20 weeder

[A–H]
A. Hi! Are you busy?
B. Yes. I'm **mowing the lawn**.

[1–20]
A. What are you looking for?
B. The **lawnmower**.

[A–H]
A. What are you going to do tomorrow?
B. I'm going to ________.

[1–20]
A. Can I borrow your ________?
B. Sure.

Do you ever work with any of these tools? Which ones? What do you do with them?

PLACES AROUND TOWN I

城镇场所 1

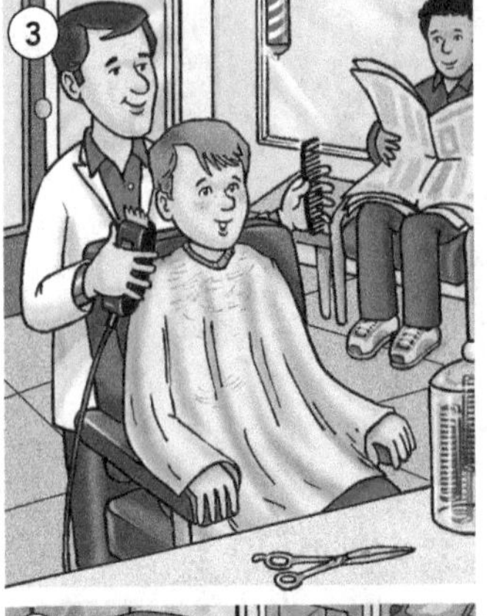

面包店/糕饼店 1 bakery
银行 2 bank
理发店 3 barber shop
书店 4 book store
公共汽车站 5 bus station
糖果店 6 candy store

卖车行 7 car dealership
贺卡店 8 card store
托儿所 9 child-care center/ day-care center
洗衣店/干洗店 10 cleaners / dry cleaners

诊所 11 clinic
服饰店 12 clothing store
咖啡店 13 coffee shop
电脑商店 14 computer store
便利店 15 convenience store
复印店 16 copy center

熟食店 **17** delicatessen/deli
百货公司 **18** department store
廉价商店/折扣商店 **19** discount store
甜甜圈商店 **20** donut shop
药房 **21** drug store/pharmacy
电子商店 **22** electronics store
眼科中心/眼镜店 **23** eye-care center/optician
快餐店 **24** fast-food restaurant
花店 **25** flower shop/florist
家具店 **26** furniture store
加油站 **27** gas station/service station
杂货店 **28** grocery store

A. Where are you going?
B. I'm going to the **bakery**.

A. Hi! How are you today?
B. Fine. Where are you going?
A. To the ________. How about you?
B. I'm going to the ________.

A. Oh, no! I can't find my wallet/purse!
B. Did you leave it at the ________?
A. Maybe I did.

Which of these places are in your neighborhood?
(In my neighborhood there's a/an ....)

PLACES AROUND TOWN II

城镇场所 2

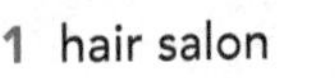

发廊	1	hair salon
五金行	2	hardware store
健康俱乐部/健身中心	3	health club
医院	4	hospital
旅馆	5	hotel
冰淇淋店	6	ice cream shop
珠宝店	7	jewelry store
自助洗衣店	8	laundromat
图书馆	9	library
孕妇商店	10	maternity shop
汽车旅馆	11	motel
电影院	12	movie theater
音乐商店	13	music store
美甲沙龙	14	nail salon
公园	15	park
宠物店	16	pet shop/ pet store

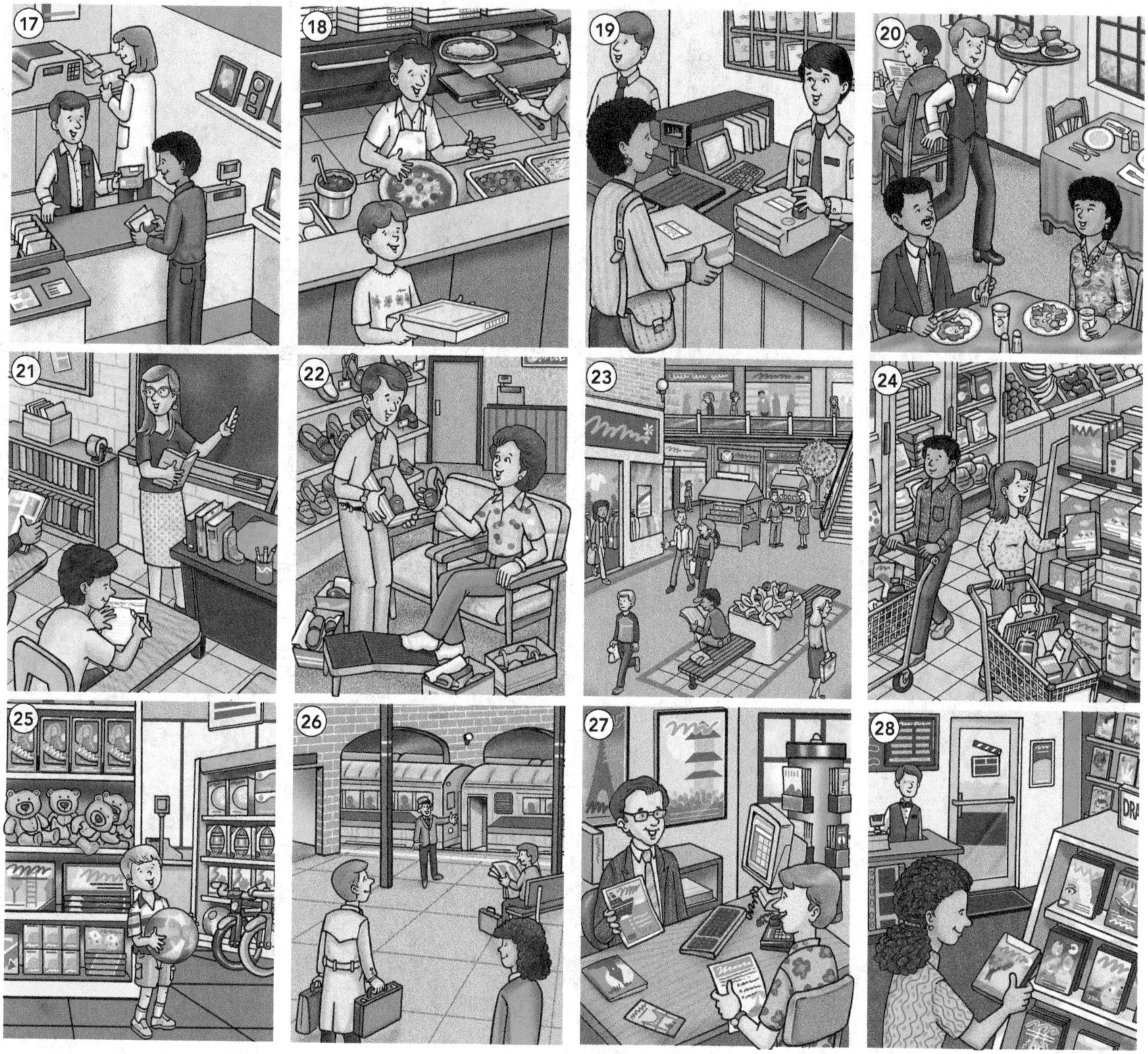

照片冲洗店 **17** photo shop
比萨饼店 **18** pizza shop
邮局 **19** post office
餐厅 **20** restaurant

学校 **21** school
鞋店 **22** shoe store
购物中心 **23** (shopping) mall
超级市场 **24** supermarket

玩具店 **25** toy store
火车站 **26** train station
旅行社 **27** travel agency
音像商店 **28** video store

A. Where's the **hair salon**?
B. It's right over there.

A. Is there a/an ________ nearby?
B. Yes. There's a/an ________ around the corner.
A. Thanks.

A. Excuse me. Where's the ________?
B. It's down the street, next to the ________.
A. Thank you.

Which of these places are in your neighborhood?
(In my neighborhood there's a/an ....)

THE CITY

城市

法院大楼	1	courthouse
出租车	2	taxi/cab/ taxicab
出租车等候站	3	taxi stand
出租车司机	4	taxi driver/ cab driver
消防栓	5	fire hydrant
垃圾桶	6	trash container
市政厅	7	city hall
火警箱	8	fire alarm box
邮筒	9	mailbox
下水道	10	sewer
警察局	11	police station
监狱	12	jail
人行道	13	sidewalk
街道	14	street
街灯	15	street light
停车场	16	parking lot
开停车罚单女警	17	meter maid
停车收费器	18	parking meter
垃圾车	19	garbage truck
地铁	20	subway
地铁站	21	subway station

报摊 22 newsstand
红绿灯 23 traffic light/traffic signal
十字路口 24 intersection
警察 25 police officer
行人穿越道 26 crosswalk
行人 27 pedestrian

冰淇淋贩卖车 28 ice cream truck
路缘/路边 29 curb
室内停车场 30 parking garage
消防队 31 fire station
公车站 32 bus stop
公车 33 bus
公车司机 34 bus driver

办公大楼 35 office building
公用电话 36 public telephone
路牌 37 street sign
下水道出入孔 38 manhole
摩托车 39 motorcycle
街头小贩 40 street vendor
免下车服务窗口 41 drive-through window

A. Where's the ______?
B. On/In/Next to/Between/Across from/In front of/Behind/Under/Over the ______.

[An Election Speech]

If I am elected mayor, I'll take care of all the problems in our city. We need to do something about our ______s. We also need to do something about our ______s. And look at our ______s! We REALLY need to do something about THEM! We need a new mayor who can solve these problems. If I am elected mayor, we'll be proud of our ______s, ______s, and ______s again! Vote for me!

Go to an intersection in your city or town. What do you see? Make a list. Then tell about it.

人物及身体特征

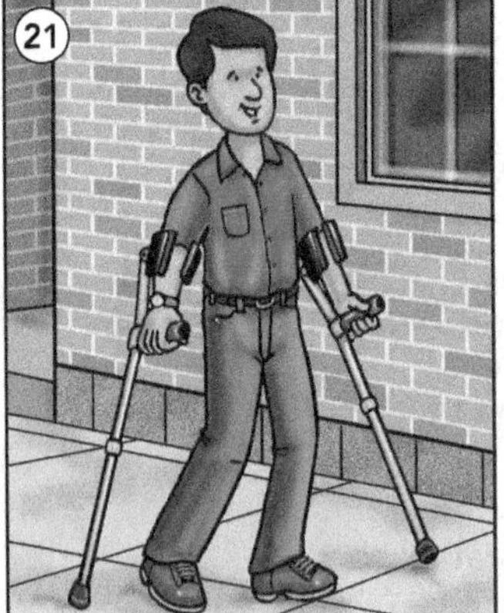

孩子(单数)－孩子(复数) **1 child–children**
婴儿 2 baby/infant
幼童 3 toddler
男孩 4 boy
女孩 5 girl
青少年 6 teenager

成人 **7 adult**
男人(单数)－男人(复数) 8 man–men
女人(单数)－女人(复数) 9 woman–women
年长者 10 senior citizen/elderly person

年纪 **age**
年轻 11 young
中年 12 middle-aged
年老/年长 13 old/elderly

身高 **height**
高 14 tall
中等高度 15 average height
矮 16 short

体重 **weight**
重 17 heavy
中等体重 18 average weight
苗条 19 thin/slim
怀孕 20 pregnant

身体残疾 21 physically challenged
视障 22 vision impaired
听障 23 hearing impaired

描述头发 **Describing Hair**

长 **24** long
齐肩长 **25** shoulder length
短 **26** short

直 **27** straight
波浪 **28** wavy
卷 **29** curly

黑色 **30** black
褐色 **31** brown
金色 **32** blond
红色 **33** red
灰色 **34** gray

秃 **35** bald
下颚、两颊的胡子 **36** beard
嘴唇之上的胡子 **37** mustache

A. Tell me about *your brother*.
B. *He's a tall heavy boy* with *short curly brown* hair.

A. What does *your new boss* look like?
B. *She's average height*, and *she* has *long straight black* hair.

A. Can you describe *the person*?
B. *He's a tall thin middle-aged man*.
A. Anything else?
B. Yes. *He's bald*, and *he* has *a mustache*.

A. Can you describe *your grandmother*?
B. *She's a short thin elderly person* with *long wavy gray* hair.
A. Anything else?
B. Yes. *She's hearing impaired*.

Tell about yourself.

Tell about people in your family.

Tell about your favorite actor or actress or other famous person.

描述人物和物品

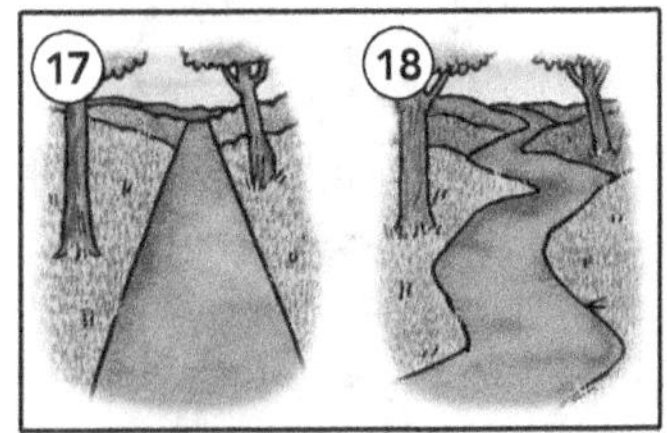

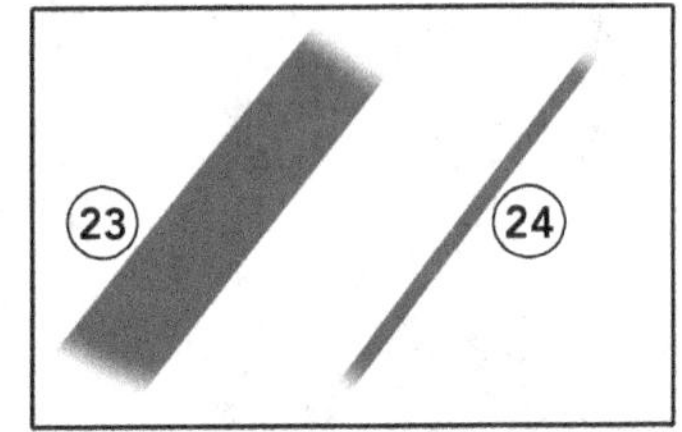

新－旧	**1–2**	new – old
年轻－年老	**3–4**	young – old
高－矮	**5–6**	tall – short
长－短	**7–8**	long – short
大－小	**9–10**	large/big – small/little
快－慢	**11–12**	fast – slow
胖/重－苗条/瘦	**13–14**	heavy/fat – thin/skinny
重－轻	**15–16**	heavy – light
直－弯曲的	**17–18**	straight – crooked
直的－卷的	**19–20**	straight – curly
宽－窄	**21–22**	wide – narrow
厚－薄	**23–24**	thick – thin
暗－亮	**25–26**	dark – light
高－低	**27–28**	high – low
松－紧	**29–30**	loose – tight
好－坏	**31–32**	good – bad
热－冷	**33–34**	hot – cold
整齐－乱七八糟	**35–36**	neat – messy
干净－脏	**37–38**	clean – dirty
软－硬	**39–40**	soft – hard
简单－困难/难	**41–42**	easy – difficult/hard
光滑－粗糙	**43–44**	smooth – rough
大声/吵－安静	**45–46**	noisy/loud – quiet
已婚－单身	**47–48**	married – single

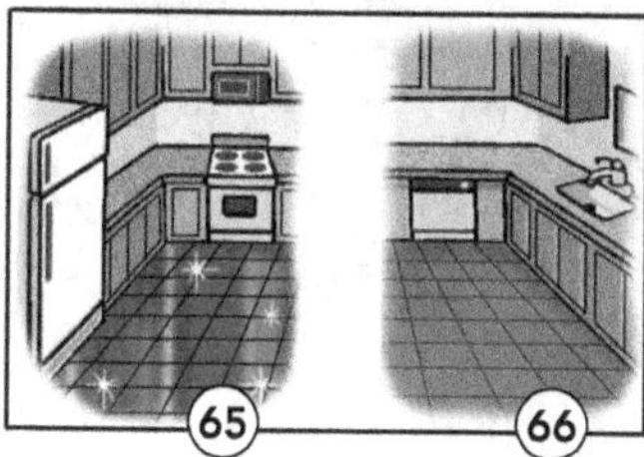

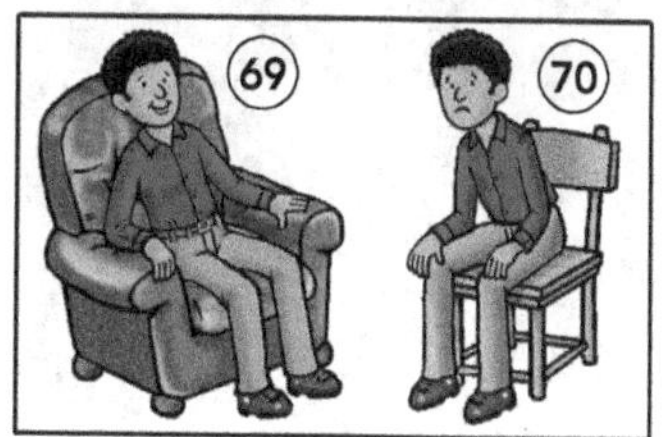

富有/富裕－贫穷 **49–50** rich/wealthy – poor
漂亮/美丽－难看 **51–52** pretty/beautiful – ugly
英俊－丑陋 **53–54** handsome – ugly
湿－干 **55–56** wet – dry
打开－关着 **57–58** open – closed
满的－空的 **59–60** full – empty

昂贵－便宜/不贵 **61–62** expensive – cheap/inexpensive
华丽－朴素 **63–64** fancy – plain
亮丽－无光泽 **65–66** shiny – dull
尖锐－钝的 **67–68** sharp – dull
舒服－不舒服 **69–70** comfortable – uncomfortable
诚实－不诚实 **71–72** honest – dishonest

[1–2]
A. Is your car **new**?
B. No. It's **old**.

1–2 Is your car ______?
3–4 Is he ______?
5–6 Is your sister ______?
7–8 Is his hair ______?
9–10 Is their dog ______?
11–12 Is the train ______?
13–14 Is your friend ______?
15–16 Is the box ______?
17–18 Is the road ______?
19–20 Is her hair ______?
21–22 Is the tie ______?
23–24 Is the line ______?

25–26 Is the room ______?
27–28 Is the bridge ______?
29–30 Are the pants ______?
31–32 Are your neighbor's children ______?
33–34 Is the water ______?
35–36 Is your desk ______?
37–38 Are the windows ______?
39–40 Is the mattress ______?
41–42 Is the homework ______?
43–44 Is your skin ______?
45–46 Is your neighbor ______?
47–48 Is your sister ______?

49–50 Is your uncle ______?
51–52 Is the witch ______?
53–54 Is the pirate ______?
55–56 Are the clothes ______?
57–58 Is the door ______?
59–60 Is the pitcher ______?
61–62 Is that restaurant ______?
63–64 Is the dress ______?
65–66 Is your kitchen floor ______?
67–68 Is the knife ______?
69–70 Is the chair ______?
71–72 Is he ______?

A. Tell me about your ....
B. He's/She's/It's/They're ______.

A. Do you have a/an ______ ....?
B. No. I have a/an ______ ....

Describe yourself.
Describe a person you know.
Describe some things in your home.
Describe some things in your community.

DESCRIBING PHYSICAL STATES AND EMOTIONS

描述身体状况及情绪

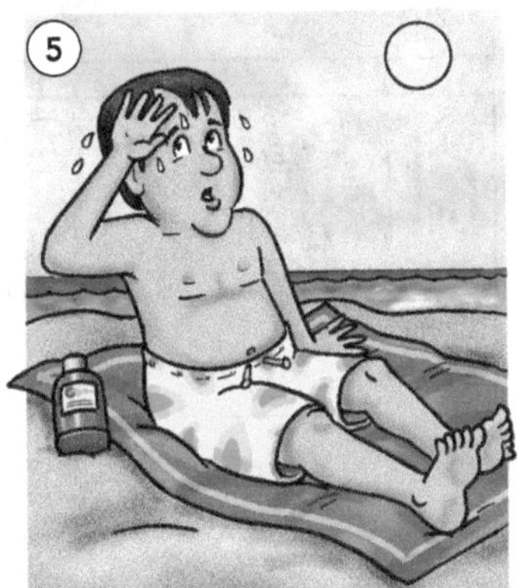

疲累 1 tired
想睡 2 sleepy
精疲力竭 3 exhausted
生病 4 sick/ill
热 5 hot
冷 6 cold
饿 7 hungry
渴 8 thirsty
饱 9 full
高兴 10 happy
难过/悲伤/ 不高兴 11 sad/unhappy
痛苦 12 miserable
兴奋 13 excited
失望 14 disappointed
心烦/不高兴 15 upset
气恼 16 annoyed

生气 **17** angry/mad
大怒 **18** furious
厌恶 **19** disgusted
烦/为……伤脑筋 **20** frustrated
惊喜 **21** surprised
震惊 **22** shocked
孤独 **23** lonely
想家 **24** homesick
紧张 **25** nervous
担心 **26** worried
害怕 **27** scared/afraid
无聊 **28** bored
以……为荣 **29** proud
窘困 **30** embarrassed
忌妒 **31** jealous
困惑 **32** confused

A. You look ______.
B. I am. I'm VERY ______.

A. Are you ______?
B. No. Why do you ask? Do I LOOK ______?
A. Yes. You do.

What makes you happy? sad? mad?

What do you do when you feel nervous? annoyed?

Do you ever feel embarrassed? When?

FRUITS

水果

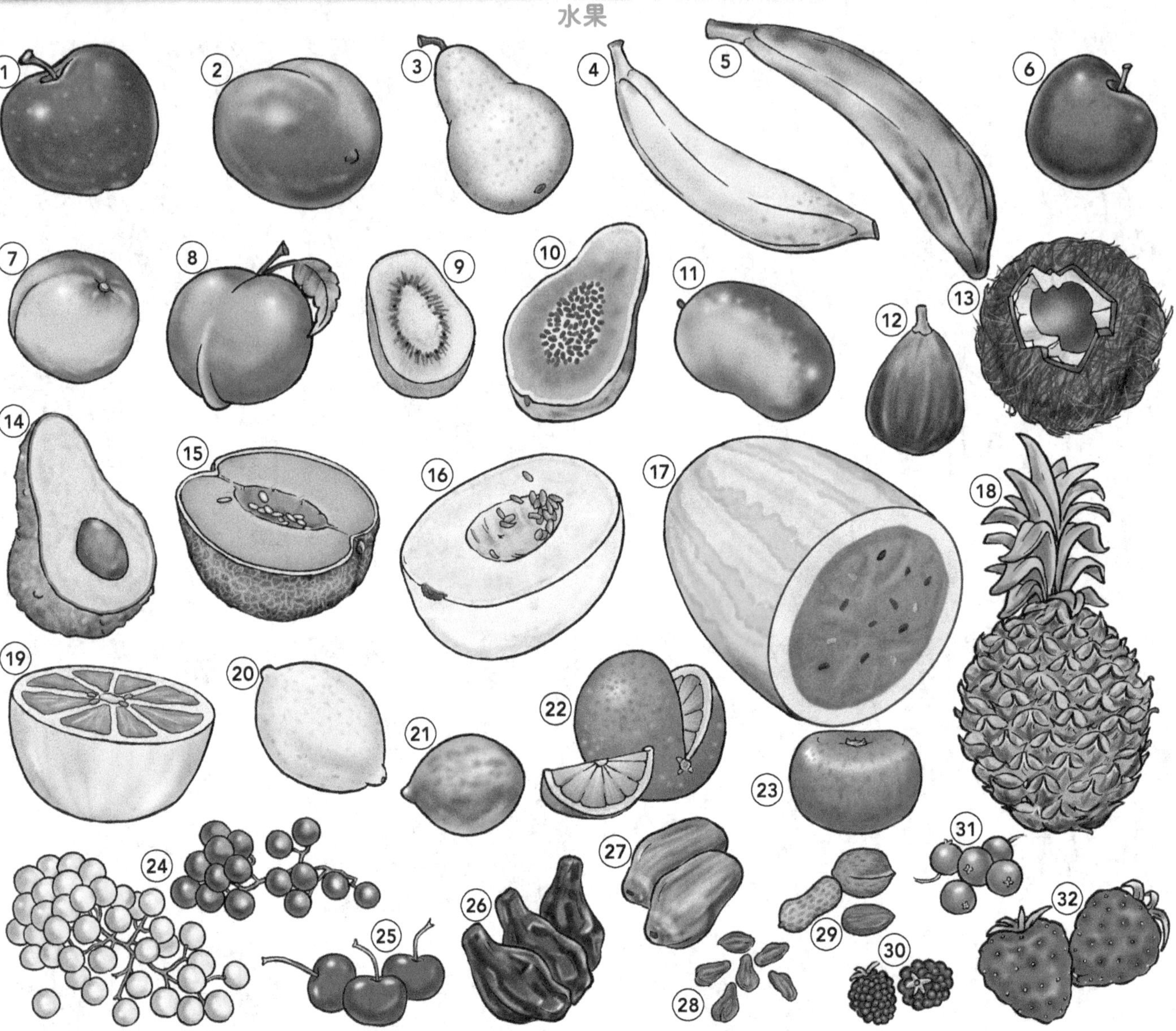

苹果 **1** apple	无花果 **12** fig	橙 **22** orange
桃子 **2** peach	椰子 **13** coconut	橘子 **23** tangerine
梨 **3** pear	鳄梨 **14** avocado	葡萄 **24** grapes
香蕉 **4** banana	哈密瓜 **15** cantaloupe	樱桃 **25** cherries
大蕉 **5** plantain	蜜瓜 **16** honeydew (melon)	梅干 **26** prunes
李子 **6** plum	西瓜 **17** watermelon	枣 **27** dates
杏 **7** apricot	菠萝 **18** pineapple	葡萄干 **28** raisins
油桃 **8** nectarine	葡萄柚 **19** grapefruit	坚果 **29** nuts
奇异果 **9** kiwi	柠檬 **20** lemon	覆盆子 **30** raspberries
木瓜 **10** papaya	青柠檬 **21** lime	蓝莓 **31** blueberries
芒果 **11** mango		草莓 **32** strawberries

[1–23]
A. This **apple** is delicious! Where did you get it?
B. At *Sam's Supermarket*.

[24–32]
A. These **grapes** are delicious! Where did you get them?
B. At *Franny's Fruit Stand*.

A. I'm hungry. Do we have any fruit?
B. Yes. We have ______s* and ______s.*

* *With 15–19, use:* We have ______ and ______.

A. Do we have any more ______s?†
B. No. I'll get some more when I go to the supermarket.

† *With 15–19, use:* Do we have any more ______?

What are your favorite fruits? Which fruits don't you like?

Which of these fruits grow where you live?

Name and describe other fruits you know.

VEGETABLES

蔬菜

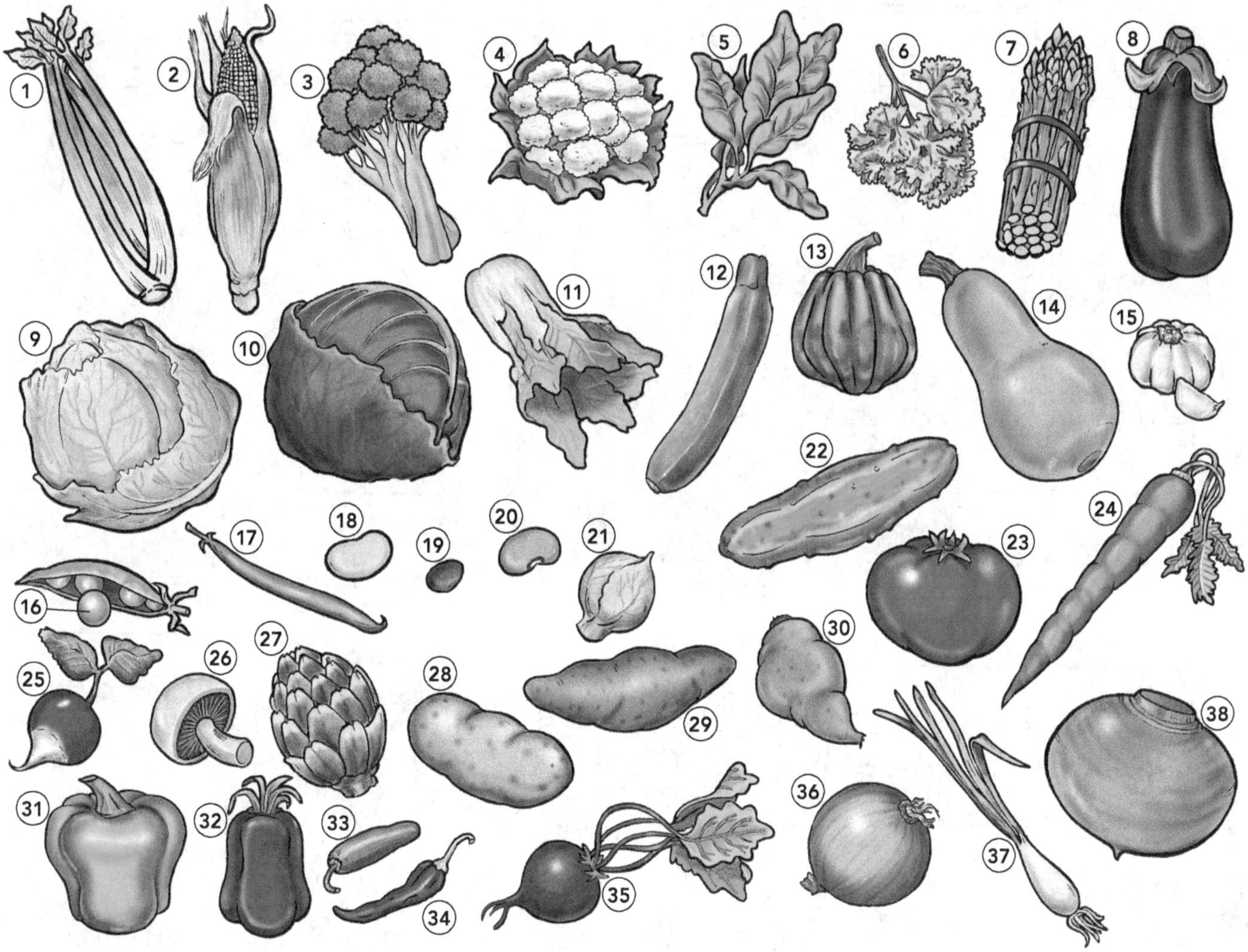

- 芹菜 **1** celery
- 玉米 **2** corn
- 西兰花 **3** broccoli
- 菜花 **4** cauliflower
- 菠菜 **5** spinach
- 香芹 **6** parsley
- 芦笋 **7** asparagus
- 茄子 **8** eggplant
- 生菜 **9** lettuce
- 卷心菜 **10** cabbage
- 小白菜/青江菜 **11** bok choy
- 意大利瓜 **12** zucchini
- 小青南瓜 **13** acorn squash
- 金瓜 **14** butternut squash
- 大蒜 **15** garlic
- 豌豆 **16** pea
- 四季豆 **17** string bean/ green bean
- 利马豆 **18** lima bean
- 黑豆 **19** black bean
- 芸豆/菜豆 **20** kidney bean
- 抱子甘蓝 **21** brussels sprout
- 黄瓜 **22** cucumber
- 蕃茄 **23** tomato
- 胡萝卜 **24** carrot
- 小红萝卜 **25** radish
- 蘑菇 **26** mushroom
- 洋蓟 **27** artichoke
- 马铃薯/土豆 **28** potato
- 白薯 **29** sweet potato
- 番薯/甜薯 **30** yam
- 青椒/甜椒 **31** green pepper/ sweet pepper
- 红椒 **32** red pepper
- 墨西哥辣椒 **33** jalapeño (pepper)
- 辣椒 **34** chili pepper
- 甜菜 **35** beet
- 洋葱 **36** onion
- 青葱 **37** scallion/ green onion
- 芜菁 **38** turnip

A. What do we need from the supermarket?
B. We need **celery*** and **peas**.†

* 1–15 † 16–38

A. How do you like the __[1–15]__/__[16–38]__s?
B. It's/They're delicious.

A. *Bobby*? Finish your vegetables!
B. But you KNOW I hate __[1–15]__/__[16–38]__s!
A. I know. But it's/they're good for you!

Which vegetables do you like?
Which vegetables don't you like?

Which of these vegetables grow where you live?

Name and describe other vegetables you know.

MEAT, POULTRY, AND SEAFOOD

肉类，家禽肉类，海鲜类

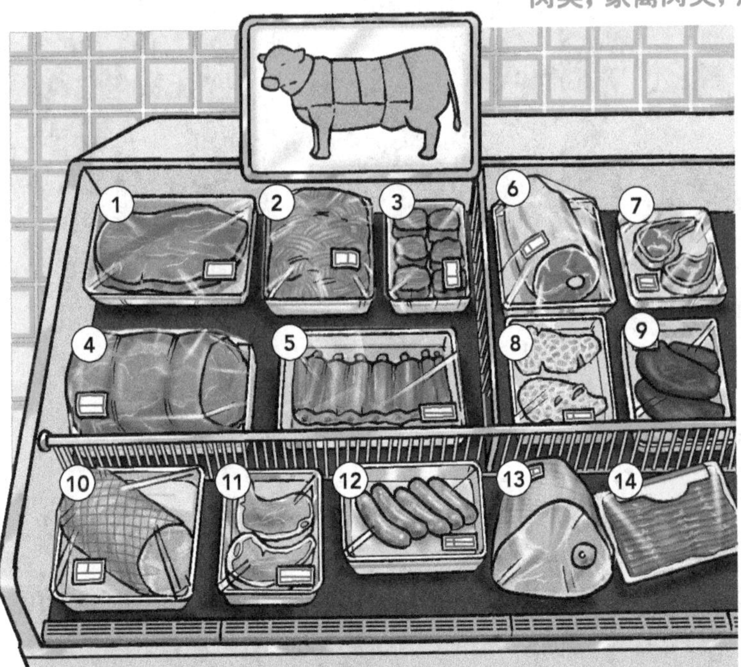

肉 **Meat**

牛排 **1** steak
绞牛肉 **2** ground beef
小块(红烧用)瘦牛肉 **3** stewing beef
烤牛肉 **4** roast beef
排骨 **5** ribs
小羊腿 **6** leg of lamb
小羊排 **7** lamb chops
可食用的动物肚 **8** tripe
肝脏 **9** liver
猪肉 **10** pork
猪排 **11** pork chops
香肠 **12** sausages
火腿 **13** ham
熏肉/培根 **14** bacon

家禽肉 **Poultry**

鸡 **15** chicken
鸡胸 **16** chicken breasts
鸡腿/鸡小腿 **17** chicken legs/drumsticks
鸡翅 **18** chicken wings
鸡大腿 **19** chicken thighs
火鸡 **20** turkey
鸭 **21** duck

海鲜 **Seafood**

鱼 FISH

鲑鱼 **22** salmon
比目鱼(大) **23** halibut
鳕鱼 **24** haddock
比目鱼/龙利 **25** flounder
鳟鱼 **26** trout
鲶鱼 **27** catfish
鳎鱼片 **28** filet of sole

贝类海产 SHELLFISH

虾 **29** shrimp
扇贝 **30** scallops
螃蟹 **31** crabs
蛤蜊 **32** clams
贻贝 **33** mussels
牡蛎/蚝 **34** oysters
龙虾 **35** lobster

A. I'm going to the supermarket. What do we need?
B. Please get some **steak**.
A. **Steak**? All right.

A. Excuse me. Where can I find ________?
B. Look in the ________ Section.
A. Thank you.

A. This/These ________ looks/look very fresh!
B. Let's get some for dinner.

Do you eat meat, poultry, or seafood?
Which of these foods do you like?

Which of these foods are popular in your cou

奶制品，果汁，饮料

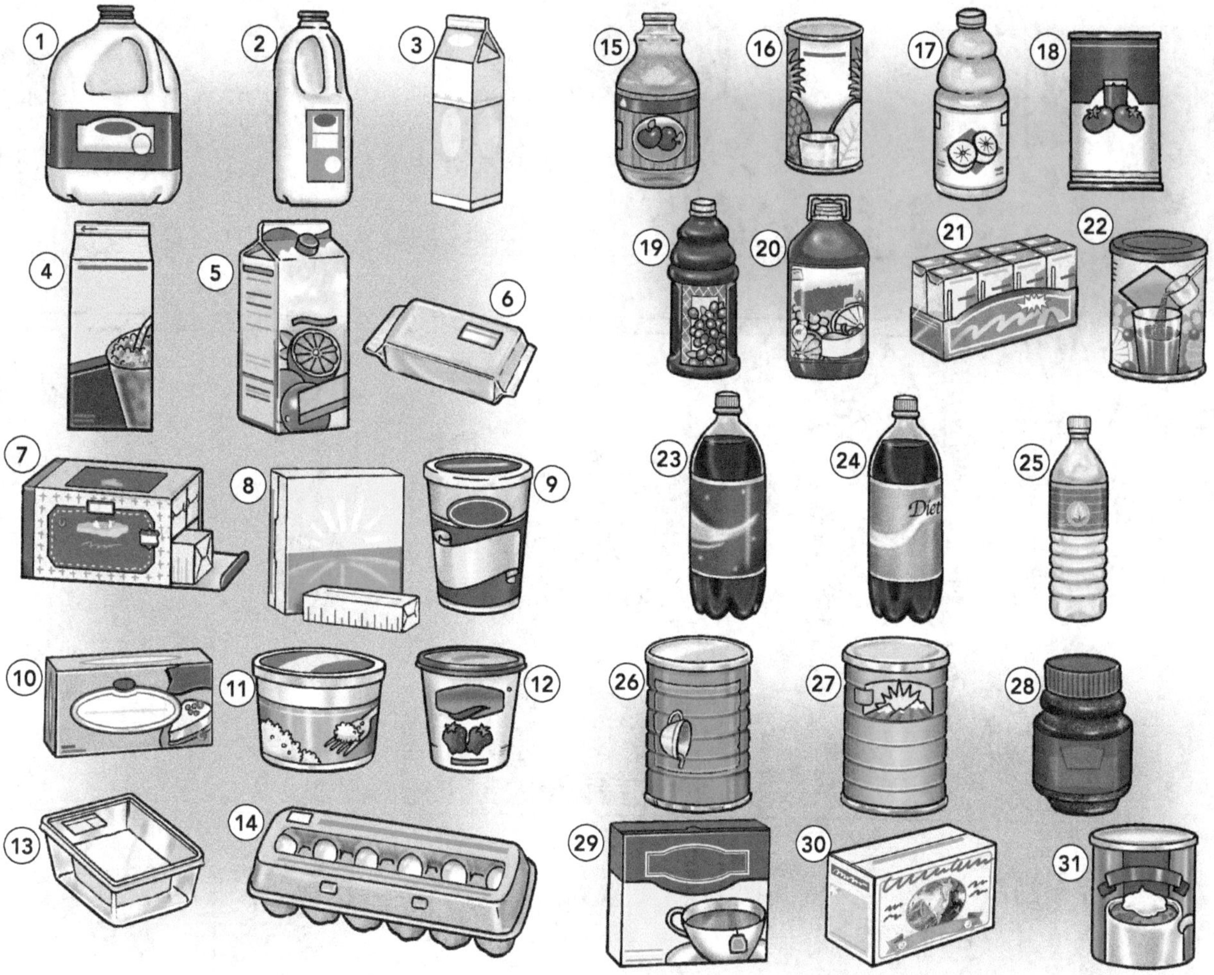

	Dairy Products 奶制品
1	milk 牛奶
2	low-fat milk 低脂牛奶
3	skim milk 脱脂牛奶
4	chocolate milk 巧克力牛奶
5	orange juice* 橙汁
6	cheese 乳酪
7	butter 奶油
8	margarine 人造黄油
9	sour cream 酸奶油
10	cream cheese 奶油乳酪
11	cottage cheese 卡迪吉乳酪/松软的白干酪
12	yogurt 酸奶
13	tofu* 豆腐
14	eggs 蛋

	Juices 果汁
15	apple juice 苹果汁
16	pineapple juice 菠萝汁
17	grapefruit juice 葡萄柚汁
18	tomato juice 蕃茄汁
19	grape juice 葡萄汁
20	fruit punch 综合果汁
21	juice paks 盒装果汁
22	powdered drink mix 即溶饮料粉

	Beverages 饮料
23	soda 汽水
24	diet soda 无糖汽水
25	bottled water 瓶装水

	Coffee and Tea 咖啡和茶
26	coffee 咖啡
27	decaffeinated coffee/decaf 无咖啡因咖啡
28	instant coffee 即溶咖啡
29	tea 茶
30	herbal tea 花草茶
31	cocoa/hot chocolate mix 可可/热巧克力混合料

* 橙汁和豆腐不是奶制品，但通常被放置在这个区域。

A. I'm going to the supermarket to get some **milk**. Do we need anything else?
B. Yes. Please get some **apple juice**.

A. Excuse me. Where can I find ________?
B. Look in the ________ Section.
A. Thanks.

A. Look! ________ is/are on sale this week!
B. Let's get some!

Which of these foods do you like?

Which of these foods are good for you?

Which brands of these foods do you buy?

DELI, FROZEN FOODS, AND SNACK FOODS

熟食，冷冻食品，休闲食品

熟食品 **Deli**

- 烤牛肉 1 roast beef
- 粗香肠 2 bologna
- 意大利香肠 3 salami
- 火腿 4 ham
- 火鸡 5 turkey
- 腌咸牛肉 6 corned beef
- 腌熏牛肉 7 pastrami
- 瑞士干酪 8 Swiss cheese
- 波萝伏洛干酪 9 provolone
- 美国干酪 10 American cheese
- 莫扎瑞拉乳酪（一种意大利干酪） 11 mozzarella
- 切达干酪（一种英国干酪） 12 cheddar cheese
- 马铃薯沙拉 13 potato salad
- 卷心菜沙拉 14 cole slaw
- 通心粉沙拉 15 macaroni salad
- 意粉沙拉 16 pasta salad
- 海鲜沙拉 17 seafood salad

冷冻食品 **Frozen Foods**

- 冰淇淋 18 ice cream
- 冷冻蔬菜 19 frozen vegetables
- 冷冻晚餐 20 frozen dinners
- 冷冻浓缩柠檬汁 21 frozen lemonade
- 冷冻浓缩橙汁 22 frozen orange juice

休闲食品 **Snack Foods**

- 土豆片 23 potato chips
- 玉米片 24 tortilla chips
- 椒盐脆饼 25 pretzels
- 坚果 26 nuts
- 爆玉米花 27 popcorn

A. Should we get some **roast beef**?
B. Good idea. And let's get some **potato salad**.

[1–17]
A. May I help you?
B. Yes, please. I'd like some ________.

[1–27]
A. Excuse me. Where is/are ________?
B. It's/They're in the ________ Section.

What kinds of snack foods are popular in your country?

Are frozen foods common in your country? What kinds of foods are in the Frozen Foods Section?

杂货

	Packaged Goods
包装食品	**Packaged Goods**
谷类早餐	1 cereal
饼干	2 cookies
薄片饼干	3 crackers
意大利通心面	4 macaroni
面条	5 noodles
意大利面	6 spaghetti
米饭	7 rice

	Canned Goods
罐头食品	**Canned Goods**
汤	8 soup
金枪鱼	9 tuna (fish)
罐头蔬菜	10 (canned) vegetables
水果罐头	11 (canned) fruit

	Jams and Jellies
果酱	**Jams and Jellies**
果酱	12 jam
果酱	13 jelly
花生酱	14 peanut butter

	Condiments
佐料/调味料	**Condiments**
蕃茄酱	15 ketchup
芥末酱	16 mustard
碎黄瓜酱	17 relish
酸黄瓜	18 pickles
橄榄	19 olives
盐	20 salt
胡椒	21 pepper
香料	22 spices
酱油	23 soy sauce
蛋黄酱	24 mayonnaise
炒菜油	25 (cooking) oil
橄榄油	26 olive oil
墨西哥辣酱	27 salsa
醋	28 vinegar
沙拉酱	29 salad dressing

	Baked Goods
焙烤食品	**Baked Goods**
面包	30 bread
小面包	31 rolls
英式松饼	32 English muffins
口袋饼	33 pita bread
蛋糕	34 cake

	Baking Products
焙烤用料	**Baking Products**
面粉	35 flour
糖	36 sugar
蛋糕粉	37 cake mix

A. I got **cereal** and **soup**. What else is on the shopping list?
B. **Ketchup** and **bread**.

A. Excuse me. I'm looking for ______.
B. It's/They're next to the _____.

A. Pardon me. I'm looking for ______.
B. It's/They're between the ______ and the ______.

Which of these foods do you like?

Which brands of these foods do you buy?

HOUSEHOLD SUPPLIES, BABY PRODUCTS, AND PET FOOD

家庭用品，婴儿用品，宠物食品

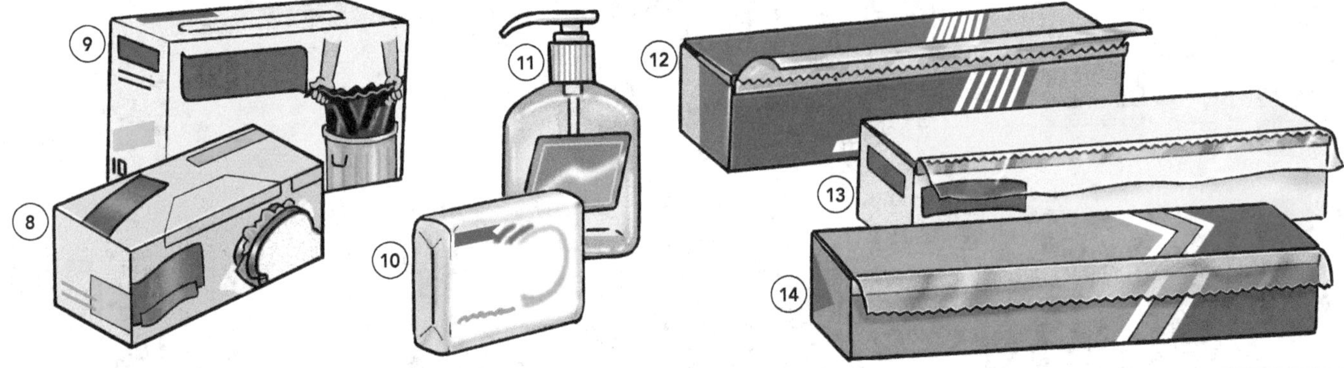

纸制品 **Paper Products**

餐巾纸 **1** napkins
纸杯 **2** paper cups
手巾纸 **3** tissues
吸管 **4** straws
纸盘 **5** paper plates
纸巾 **6** paper towels
卫生纸 **7** toilet paper

家庭用品 **Household Items**

三明治袋 **8** sandwich bags
垃圾袋 **9** trash bags
肥皂 **10** soap
液体肥皂 **11** liquid soap
铝箔纸 **12** aluminum foil
保鲜膜 **13** plastic wrap
蜡纸 **14** waxed paper

婴儿用品 **Baby Products**

婴儿麦片 **15** baby cereal
婴儿食品 **16** baby food
婴儿配方奶粉 **17** formula
湿巾 **18** wipes
即弃纸尿片 **19** (disposable) diapers

宠物食品 **Pet Food**

猫食 **20** cat food
狗食 **21** dog food

A. Excuse me. Where can I find **napkins**?
B. **Napkins**? Look in Aisle 4.

[7, 10–17, 20, 21]
A. We forgot to get ______!
B. I'll get it. Where is it?
A. It's in Aisle ______.

[1–6, 8, 9, 18, 19]
A. We forgot to get ______!
B. I'll get them. Where are they?
A. They're in Aisle ______.

What do you need from the supermarket? Make a complete shopping list!

THE SUPERMARKET

超级市场

通道 **1** aisle
购物者/顾客 **2** shopper/customer
购物篮 **3** shopping basket
结帐队伍 **4** checkout line
结帐柜台 **5** checkout counter
传送带 **6** conveyor belt
收银机 **7** cash register
购物推车 **8** shopping cart
口香糖 **9** (chewing) gum
糖果 **10** candy
减价优惠券 **11** coupons
收银员 **12** cashier
纸袋 **13** paper bag
装袋员 **14** bagger/packer
快速结帐队伍 **15** express checkout (line)
小报 **16** tabloid (newspaper)
杂志 **17** magazine
扫描机 **18** scanner
塑料袋 **19** plastic bag
蔬果区 **20** produce
经理 **21** manager
店员 **22** clerk
秤 **23** scale
铁罐回收机 **24** can-return machine
瓶子回收机 **25** bottle-return machine

[1–8, 11–19, 21–25]
A. This is a gigantic supermarket!
B. It is! Look at all the **aisle**s!

[9, 10, 20]
A. This is a gigantic supermarket!
B. It is. Look at all the **produce**!

Where do you usually shop for food? Do you go to a supermarket, or do you go to a small grocery store? Describe the place where you shop.

Describe the differences between U.S. supermarkets and food stores in your country.

CONTAINERS AND QUANTITIES

容器及数量

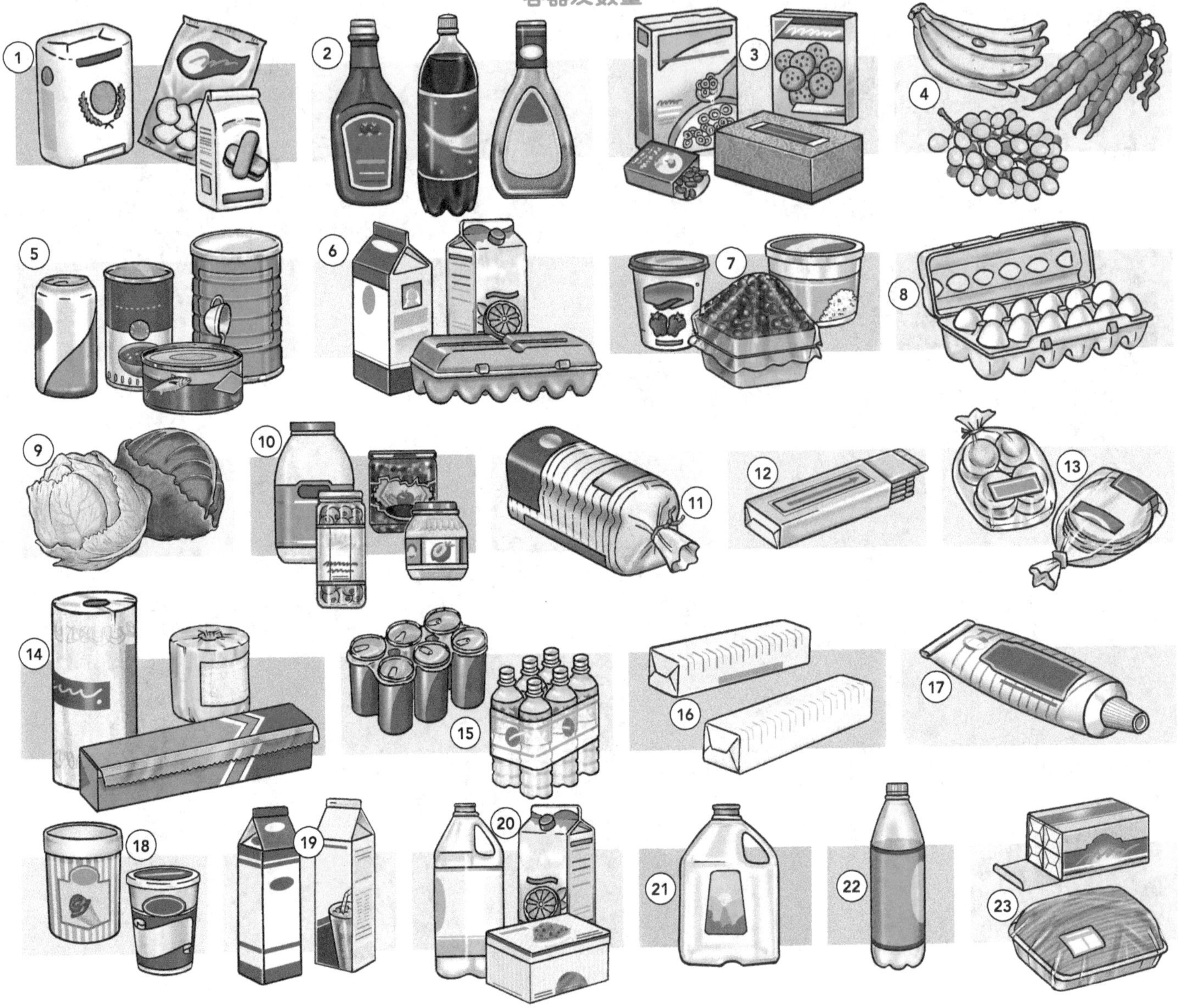

袋子	1	bag
瓶子	2	bottle
盒子	3	box
串/束	4	bunch
铁罐	5	can
纸盒	6	carton
容器	7	container
(一)打	8	dozen*
(一)颗	9	head
(一) 瓶	10	jar
(一)条－条(复数)	11	loaf–loaves
(一)包	12	pack
包装/(一)包	13	package
(一)卷	14	roll
半打	15	six-pack
(一)条	16	stick
软管/(一)条	17	tube
(一)品脱	18	pint
(一)夸脱	19	quart
半加仑	20	half-gallon
(一)加仑	21	gallon
(一)公升	22	liter
(一)磅	23	pound

* 应说 "a dozen eggs," 而不是 "a dozen of eggs"

A. Please get a **bag** of *flour* when you go to the supermarket.
B. A **bag** of *flour*? Okay.

A. Please get two **bottles** of *ketchup* when you go to the supermarket.
B. Two **bottles** of *ketchup*? Okay.

[At home]

A. What did you get at the supermarket?
B. I got ______, ______, and ______.

[In a supermarket]

A. Is this the express checkout line?
B. Yes, it is. Do you have more than eight items?
A. No. I only have ______, ______, and ______.

Open your kitchen cabinets and refrigerator. Make a list of all the things you find.

What do you do with empty bottles, jars, and cans? Do you recycle them, reuse them, or throw them away?

UNITS OF MEASURE

计量单位

茶匙 teaspoon
tsp.

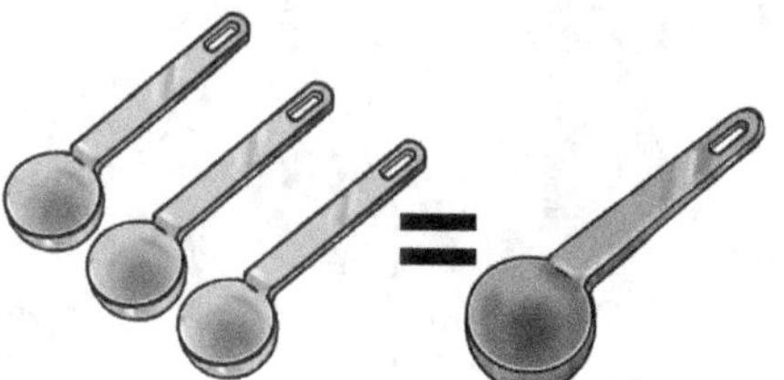
汤匙 tablespoon
Tbsp.

液体盎司 1 (fluid) ounce
1 fl. oz.

量杯 cup
c.
8 fl. ozs.

(一)品脱 pint
pt.
16 fl. ozs.

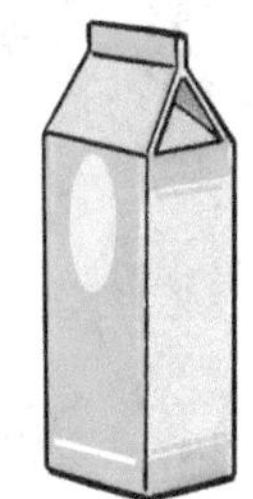
(一)夸脱 quart
qt.
32 fl. ozs.

(一)加仑 gallon
gal.
128 fl. ozs.

A. How much water should I put in?
B. The recipe says to add one _______ of water.

A. This fruit punch is delicious! What's in it?
B. Two _______s of apple juice, three _______s of orange juice, and a _______ of grape juice.

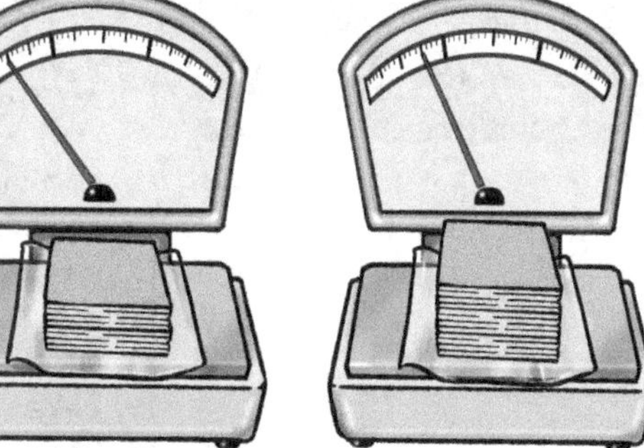

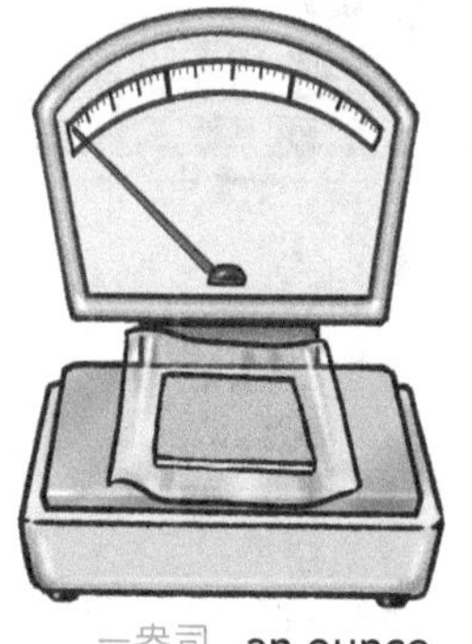
一盎司 an ounce
oz.

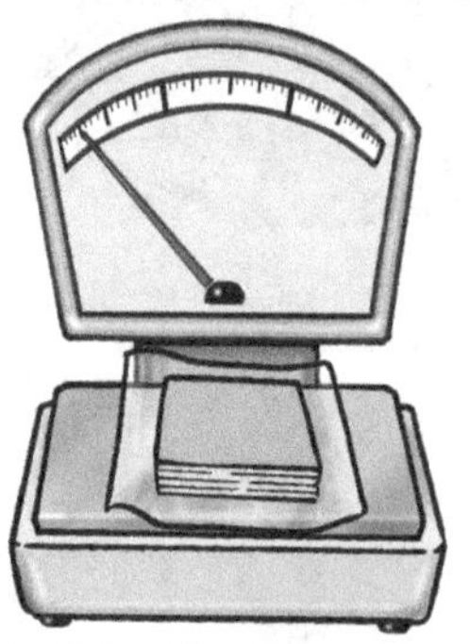
四分之一磅 a quarter of a pound
1/4 lb.
4 ozs.

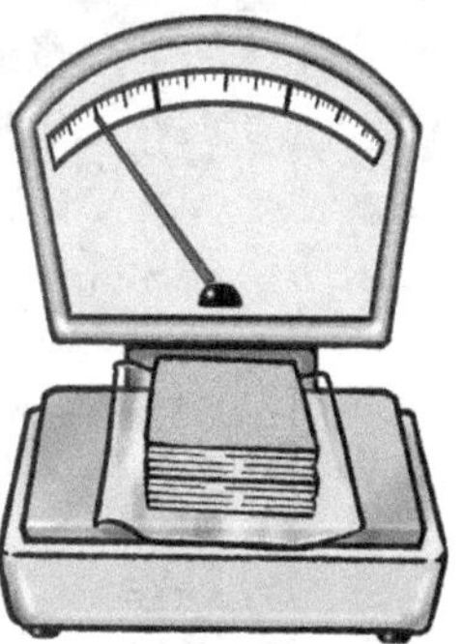
半磅 half a pound
1/2 lb.
8 ozs.

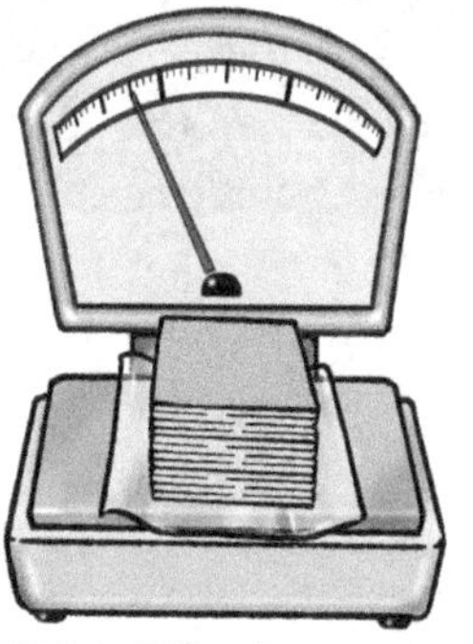
四分之三磅 three-quarters of a pound
3/4 lb.
12 ozs.

一磅 a pound
lb.
16 ozs.

A. How much roast beef would you like?
B. I'd like _______, please.
A. Anything else?
B. Yes. Please give me _______ of Swiss cheese.

A. This chili tastes very good! What did you put in it?
B. _______ of ground beef, _______ of beans, _______ of tomatoes, and _______ of chili powder.

食物制备及食谱

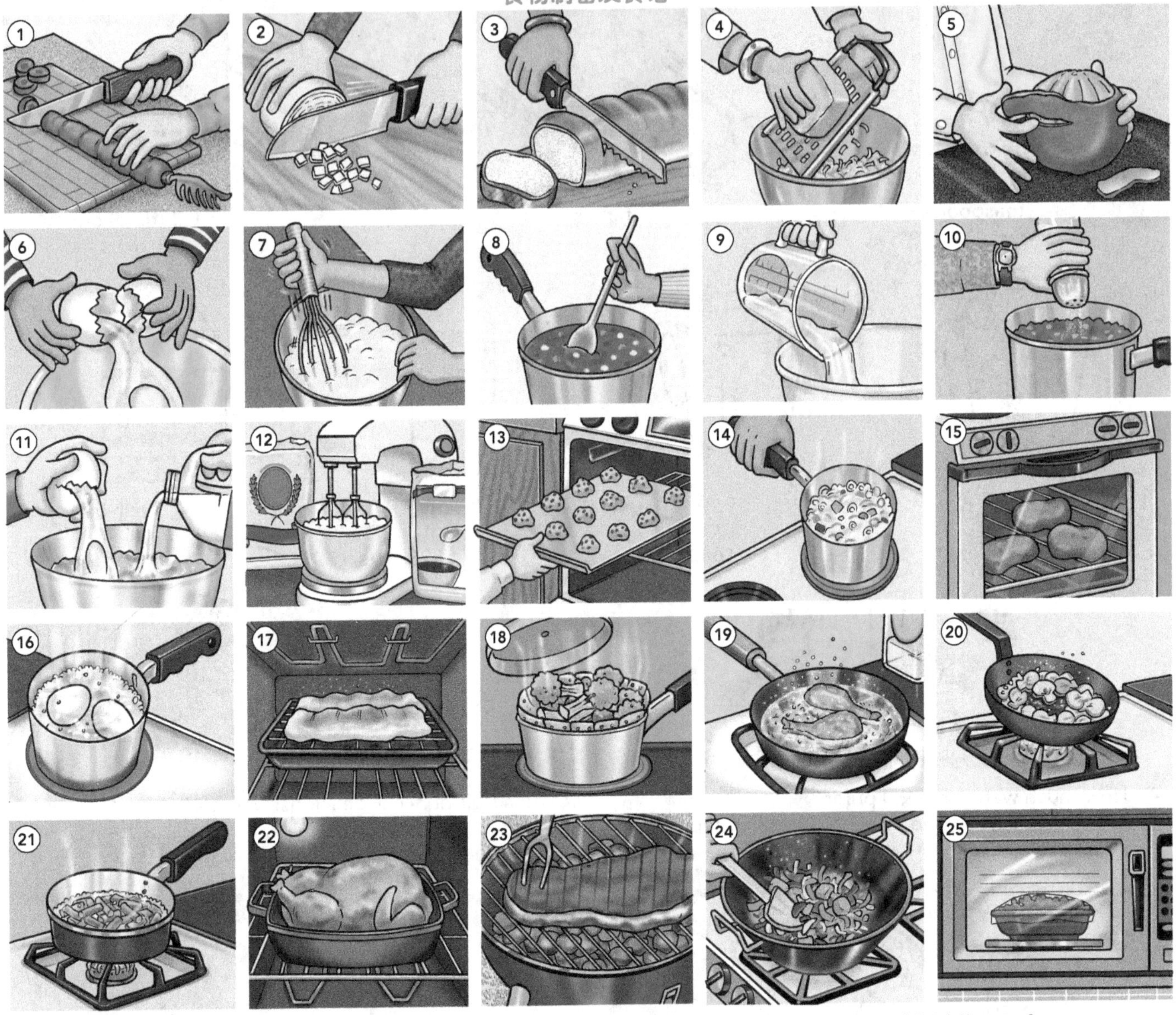

切	1 cut (up)	加	10 add	油炸/油煎	19 fry
切块	2 chop (up)	将____和____加在一起	11 combine ____ and ____	煎炒	20 saute
切片	3 slice	将____和____混合在一起	12 mix ____ and ____	煨/炖	21 simmer
擦碎	4 grate	将____放入____	13 put ____ in ____	烤	22 roast
剥皮	5 peel	烹调/煮	14 cook	用烤架烤	23 barbecue/grill
打(破)	6 break	烘烤	15 bake	炒	24 stir-fry
打(蛋等)	7 beat	水煮	16 boil	微波	25 microwave
搅拌	8 stir	烧烤	17 broil		
倒	9 pour	蒸	18 steam		

A. Can I help you?
B. Yes. Please **cut up** the vegetables.

[1–25]
A. What are you doing?
B. I'm ________ing the ....

[14–25]
A. How long should I ________ the ....?
B. ________ the .... for .... minutes/seconds.

What's your favorite recipe? Give instructions and use the units of measure on page 57. For example:

Mix a cup of flour and two tablespoons of sugar.
Add half a pound of butter.
Bake at 350° (degrees) for twenty minutes.

厨房器皿及用具

- 冰淇淋勺 **1** ice cream scoop
- 开罐器 **2** can opener
- 开瓶器 **3** bottle opener
- 蔬菜削皮器 **4** (vegetable) peeler
- 打蛋器 **5** (egg) beater
- 盖子 **6** lid/cover/top
- 锅子 **7** pot
- 平底煎锅 **8** frying pan/skillet
- 双层锅 **9** double boiler
- 炒菜锅 **10** wok
- 长柄杓 **11** ladle
- 过滤器 **12** strainer
- 煎铲 **13** spatula
- 蒸架 **14** steamer
- 刀子 **15** knife
- 大蒜钳 **16** garlic press
- 擦菜板 **17** grater
- 陶瓷烤盘 **18** casserole dish
- 烧烤盘 **19** roasting pan
- 烧烤架 **20** roasting rack
- 切肉刀 **21** carving knife
- 煮锅 **22** saucepan
- 沥水盆 **23** colander
- 厨房定时器 **24** kitchen timer
- 擀面棍 **25** rolling pin
- 派盘 **26** pie plate
- 水果刀 **27** paring knife
- 饼干烤盘 **28** cookie sheet
- 饼干模型 **29** cookie cutter
- 搅拌碗 **30** (mixing) bowl
- 搅拌器 **31** whisk
- 量杯 **32** measuring cup
- 量匙 **33** measuring spoon
- 蛋糕烤盘 **34** cake pan
- 木杓 **35** wooden spoon

A. Could I possibly borrow your **ice cream scoop**?
B. Sure. I'll be happy to lend you my **ice cream scoop**.
A. Thanks.

A. What are you looking for?
B. I can't find the ________.
A. Look in that drawer/in that cabinet/ on the counter/next to the ________/ ....

[A Commercial]
Come to *Kitchen World*! We have everything you need for your kitchen, from ________s and ________s, to ________s and ________s. Are you looking for a new ________? Is it time to throw out your old ________? Come to *Kitchen World* today! We have everything you need!

What kitchen utensils and cookware do you have in your kitchen?

Which things do you use very often?

Which things do you rarely use?

FAST FOOD

快餐

汉堡包	1	hamburger	冻酸奶	15	frozen yogurt
乳酪汉堡包	2	cheeseburger	奶昔	16	milkshake
热狗	3	hot dog	汽水	17	soda
鱼肉三明治	4	fish sandwich	盖子	18	lids
鸡肉三明治	5	chicken sandwich	纸杯	19	paper cups
炸鸡	6	fried chicken	吸管	20	straws
炸薯条	7	french fries	餐巾纸	21	napkins
墨西哥玉米片	8	nachos	塑料餐具	22	plastic utensils
墨西哥玉米饼	9	taco	蕃茄酱	23	ketchup
墨西哥卷饼	10	burrito	芥末酱	24	mustard
一片披萨饼	11	slice of pizza	蛋黄酱	25	mayonnaise
一碗墨西哥辣豆酱	12	bowl of chili	碎黄瓜酱	26	relish
沙拉	13	salad	沙拉酱	27	salad dressing
冰淇淋	14	ice cream			

A. May I help you?
B. Yes. I'd like a/an __[1–5, 9–17]__/ an order of __[6–8]__.

A. Excuse me. We're almost out of __[18–27]__.
B. I'll get some more from the supply room. Thanks for telling me.

Do you go to fast-food restaurants? Which ones? How often? What do you order?

Are there fast-food restaurants in your country? Are they popular? What foods do they have?

THE COFFEE SHOP AND SANDWICHES

咖啡店及三明治

甜甜圈 **1** donut
松糕 **2** muffin
百吉饼/硬面包圈 **3** bagel
小面包 **4** bun
丹麦面包 **5** danish/pastry
小圆面包 **6** biscuit
羊角面包 **7** croissant
鸡蛋 **8** eggs
煎松饼/煎薄饼 **9** pancakes
华夫饼 **10** waffles
土司面包 **11** toast
熏肉 **12** bacon
香肠 **13** sausages
自制炸薯块 **14** home fries
咖啡 **15** coffee
低咖啡因咖啡 **16** decaf coffee
茶 **17** tea
冰茶 **18** iced tea
浓缩柠檬汁 **19** lemonade
热巧克力 **20** hot chocolate
牛奶 **21** milk
鲔鱼三明治/金枪鱼三明治 **22** tuna fish sandwich
蛋沙拉三明治 **23** egg salad sandwich
鸡肉沙拉三明治 **24** chicken salad sandwich
火腿乳酪三明治 **25** ham and cheese sandwich
咸牛肉三明治 **26** corned beef sandwich
培根生菜蕃茄三明治/熏肉生菜蕃茄三明治 **27** BLT/bacon, lettuce, and tomato sandwich
烤牛肉三明治 **28** roast beef sandwich
白面包 **29** white bread
全麦面包 **30** whole wheat bread
口袋饼 **31** pita bread
裸麦粗面包 **32** pumpernickel
裸麦面包 **33** rye bread
(一个)小面包 **34** a roll
(一个)长条面包 **35** a submarine roll

A. May I help you?
B. Yes. I'd like a ____[1–7]____/an order of ____[8–14]____, please.
A. Anything to drink?
B. Yes. I'll have a small/medium-size/large/extra-large

____[15–21]____.

A. I'd like a ____[22–28]____ on ____[29–35]____, please.
B. What do you want on it?
A. Lettuce/tomato/mayonnaise/mustard/. . .

Do you like these foods? Which ones? Where do you get them? How often do you have them?

THE RESTAURANT

餐厅

领位 **A** seat the customers
倒水 **B** pour the water
帮客人点菜 **C** take the order
上菜 **D** serve the meal

女迎宾员 **1** hostess
迎宾员 **2** host
用餐者/顾客/顾客 **3** diner/patron/customer
雅座 **4** booth
桌子 **5** table
高脚椅 **6** high chair

幼儿加高座椅 **7** booster seat
菜单 **8** menu
面包篮 **9** bread basket
企台/侍者助手 **10** busperson
女服务生/上菜员 **11** waitress/server
服务生/上菜员 **12** waiter/server
沙拉吧 **13** salad bar
餐厅 **14** dining room
厨房 **15** kitchen
主厨 **16** chef

[4–9]
A. Would you like a **booth**?
B. Yes, please.

[10–12]
A. Hello. My name is *Julie*, and I'll be your **waitress** this evening.
B. Hello.

[1, 2, 13–16]
A. This restaurant has a wonderful **salad bar**.
B. I agree.

清理桌子 **E** clear the table
付账 **F** pay the check
付小费 **G** leave a tip
摆餐具 **H** set the table

洗碗室 **17** dishroom
洗碗机 **18** dishwasher
托盘 **19** tray
点心推车 **20** dessert cart
帐单 **21** check
小费 **22** tip
沙拉盘 **23** salad plate
面包奶油盘 **24** bread-and-butter plate
主餐盘 **25** dinner plate

汤碗 **26** soup bowl
水杯 **27** water glass
酒杯 **28** wine glass
茶杯 **29** cup
茶托/碟子 **30** saucer
餐巾 **31** napkin

银器 **silverware**
沙拉叉 **32** salad fork
主菜叉 **33** dinner fork
餐刀 **34** knife
茶匙 **35** teaspoon
汤匙 **36** soup spoon
奶油刀 **37** butter knife

[A–H]
A. Please _______.
B. All right. I'll _______ right away.

[23–37]
A. Excuse me. Where does the _______ go?
B. It goes
- to the left of the _______.
- to the right of the _______.
- on the _______.
- between the _______ and the _______.

[1, 2, 10–12, 16, 18]
A. Do you have any job openings?
B. Yes. We're looking for a _______.

[23–37]
A. Excuse me. I dropped my _______.
B. That's okay. I'll get you another _______ from the kitchen.

Tell about a restaurant you know. Describe the place and the people. (Is the restaurant large or small? How many tables are there? How many people work there? Is there a salad bar? . . .)

A RESTAURANT MENU

餐厅菜单

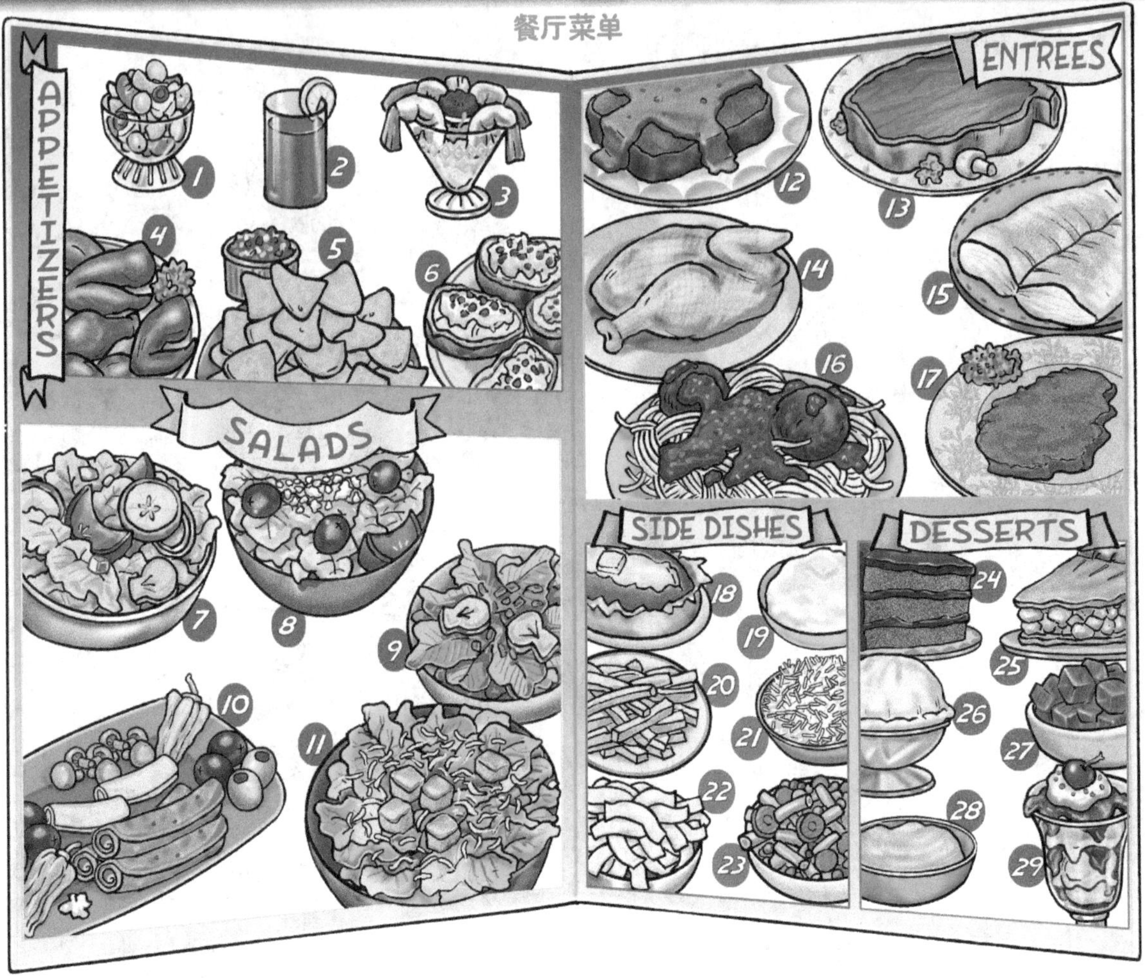

APPETIZERS

什锦水果 1 fruit cup/ fruit cocktail
蕃茄汁 2 tomato juice
鸡尾酒虾 3 shrimp cocktail
鸡翅 4 chicken wings
墨西哥玉米片 5 nachos
炸马铃薯皮 6 potato skins

SALADS

生菜沙拉/田园沙拉 7 tossed salad/ garden salad
希腊沙拉 8 Greek salad
菠菜沙拉 9 spinach salad
意大利开胃菜(一盘) 10 antipasto (plate)
凯萨沙拉 11 Caesar salad

ENTREES

肉糜面包 12 meatloaf
烤牛肉/顶级牛排 13 roast beef/ prime rib
烤鸡 14 baked chicken
烧烤鱼 15 broiled fish
肉丸意大利面 16 spaghetti and meatballs
小牛排 17 veal cutlet

SIDE DISHES

烤土豆(一个) 18 a baked potato
土豆泥 19 mashed potatoes
炸薯条 20 french fries
米饭 21 rice
面条 22 noodles
什锦蔬菜 23 mixed vegetables

DESSERTS

巧克力蛋糕 24 chocolate cake
苹果派 25 apple pie
冰淇淋 26 ice cream
果冻 27 jello
布丁 28 pudding
冰淇淋圣代 29 ice cream sundae

[Ordering dinner]

A. May I take your order?
B. Yes, please. For the appetizer, I'd like the ___[1–6]___.
A. And what kind of salad would you like?
B. I'll have the ___[7–11]___.
A. And for the main course?
B. I'd like the ___[12–17]___, please.
A. What side dish would you like with that?
B. Hmm. I think I'll have ___[18–23]___.

[Ordering dessert]

A. Would you care for some dessert?
B. Yes. I'll have ___[24–28]___/an ___[29]___.

Tell about the food at a restaurant you know. What's on the menu?

What are some typical foods on the menus of restaurants in your country?

COLORS

颜色

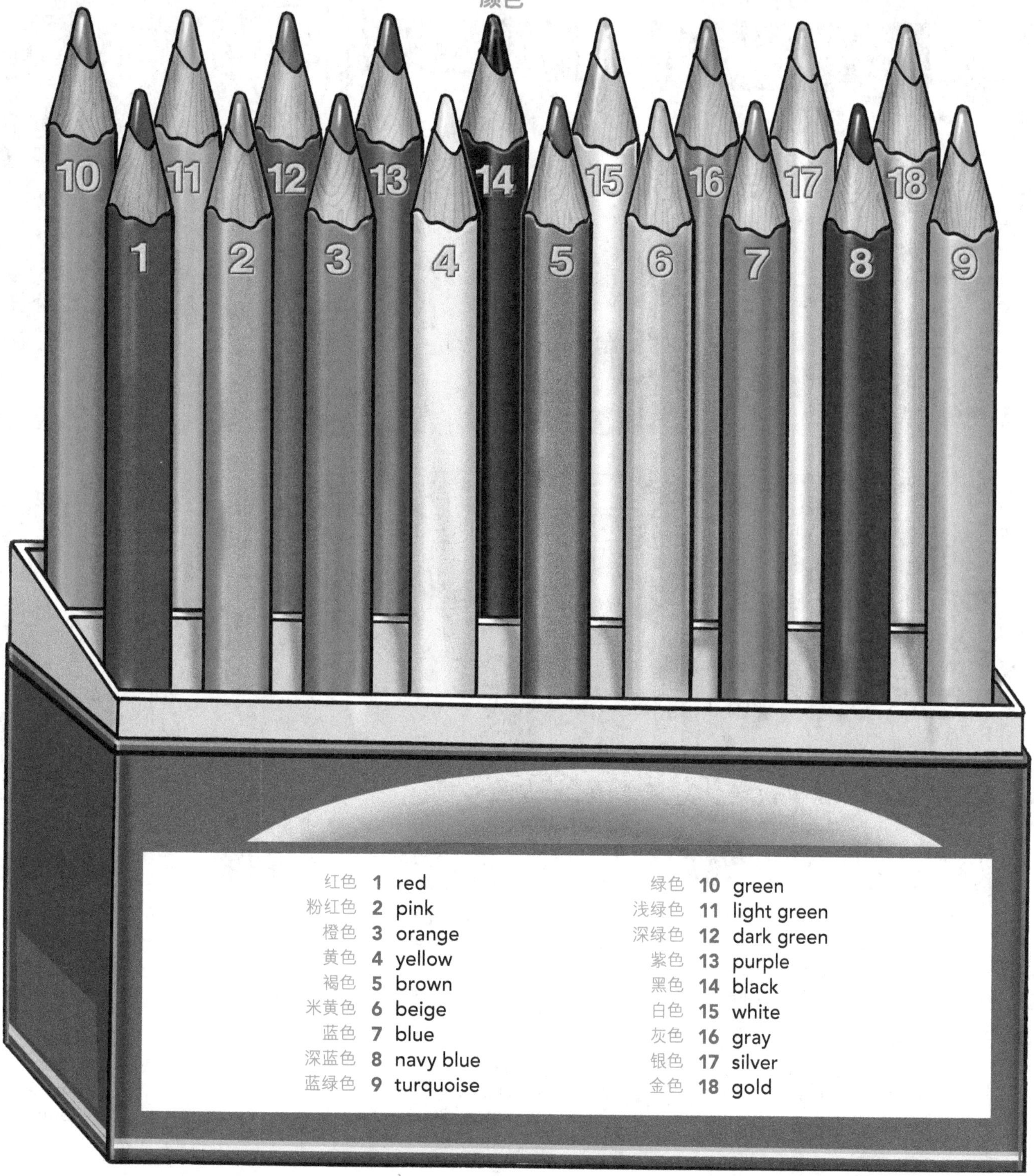

红色	1	red	绿色	10	green
粉红色	2	pink	浅绿色	11	light green
橙色	3	orange	深绿色	12	dark green
黄色	4	yellow	紫色	13	purple
褐色	5	brown	黑色	14	black
米黄色	6	beige	白色	15	white
蓝色	7	blue	灰色	16	gray
深蓝色	8	navy blue	银色	17	silver
蓝绿色	9	turquoise	金色	18	gold

A. What's your favorite color?
B. **Red.**

A. I like your ________ shirt.
You look very good in ________.
B. Thank you. ________ is my favorite color.

A. My TV is broken.
B. What's the matter with it?
A. People's faces are ________, the sky is ________, and the grass is ________!

Do you know the flags of different countries? What are the colors of flags you know?

What color makes you happy? What color makes you sad? Why?

CLOTHING

服装

女衬衫 1 blouse
裙子 2 skirt
衬衫 3 shirt
长裤/(宽松的)长裤 4 pants/slacks
运动衫 5 sport shirt
牛仔裤 6 jeans
带领针织衫/针织衫 7 knit shirt/jersey
连衣裙 8 dress
毛衣 9 sweater
夹克 10 jacket

轻便外套 11 sport coat/sport jacket/jacket
西装 12 suit
三件式西装 13 three-piece suit
领带 14 tie/necktie
制服 15 uniform
T恤衫 16 T-shirt
短裤 17 shorts
孕妇装 18 maternity dress
连身衣裤 19 jumpsuit
背心 20 vest

无袖背心裙 21 jumper
西装外套 22 blazer
束腰外衣 23 tunic
毛线裤袜 24 leggings
工作裤 25 overalls
高领毛衣 26 turtleneck
晚礼服 27 tuxedo
蝶形领结 28 bow tie
(女士的)晚礼服 29 (evening) gown

A. I think I'll wear my new **blouse** today.
B. Good idea!

A. I really like your ________.
B. Thank you.
A. Where did you get it/them?
B. At ....

A. Oh, no! I just ripped my ________!
B. What a shame!

What clothing items in this lesson do you wear?

What color clothing do you like to wear?

What do you wear at work or at school? at parties? at weddings?

外衣

外套 **1** coat
外套 **2** overcoat
帽子 **3** hat
夹克 **4** jacket
围巾 **5** scarf/muffler
毛衣外套 **6** sweater jacket
裤袜 **7** tights
鸭舌帽 **8** cap
皮夹克 **9** leather jacket
棒球帽 **10** baseball cap
风衣 **11** windbreaker
雨衣 **12** raincoat
雨帽 **13** rain hat
风雨衣 **14** trench coat
雨伞 **15** umbrella
斗篷/雨衣 **16** poncho
防雨夹克 **17** rain jacket
雨鞋 **18** rain boots
滑雪帽 **19** ski hat
滑雪夹克 **20** ski jacket
手套 **21** gloves
滑雪面罩 **22** ski mask
羽绒夹克 **23** down jacket
连指手套 **24** mittens
带帽的风雪大衣 **25** parka
太阳镜 **26** sunglasses
耳罩 **27** ear muffs
羽绒背心 **28** down vest

A. What's the weather like today?
B. It's cool/cold/raining/snowing.
A. I think I'll wear my ______.

[1–6, 8–17, 19, 20, 22, 23, 25, 28]
A. May I help you?
B. Yes, please. I'm looking for a/an ______.

[7, 18, 21, 24, 26, 27]
A. May I help you?
B. Yes, please. I'm looking for ______.

What do you wear outside when the weather is cool?/when it's raining?/when it's very cold?

SLEEPWEAR AND UNDERWEAR

睡衣及内衣

睡衣 **1** pajamas
(女)睡袍 **2** nightgown
长睡衫 **3** nightshirt
浴衣 **4** bathrobe/robe
拖鞋 **5** slippers
连身(包括脚)睡衣 **6** blanket sleeper
短袖内衣/汗衫/短袖圆领衫 **7** undershirt/T-shirt
(男)三角内裤/内裤 **8** (jockey) shorts/underpants/briefs

四角内裤 **9** boxer shorts/boxers
运动绷带/(男运动用的)护裆 **10** athletic supporter/jockstrap
长内衣裤 **11** long underwear/long johns
袜子 **12** socks
(女)三角内裤 **13** (bikini) panties
内裤 **14** briefs/underpants
胸罩 **15** bra

女用短袖衬衣 **16** camisole
短衬裙 **17** half slip
长衬裙 **18** (full) slip
长筒丝袜 **19** stockings
连裤袜 **20** pantyhose
袜裤 **21** tights
中筒丝袜 **22** knee-highs
中筒袜 **23** knee socks

A. I can't find my new ______.
B. Did you look in the bureau/dresser/closet?
A. Yes, I did.
B. Then it's/they're probably in the wash.

What sleepwear items do you wear? What sleepwear items do people in your family wear?

运动服装及鞋类

背心 **1** tank top
运动短裤 **2** running shorts
防汗带 **3** sweatband
慢跑衣裤/慢跑服/运动服 **4** jogging suit/running suit/warm-up suit
T恤衫 **5** T-shirt
弹力短裤/自行车短裤 **6** lycra shorts/bike shorts
较厚的长袖运动衫 **7** sweatshirt
较厚的运动裤 **8** sweatpants
罩衫 **9** cover-up

游泳衣/泳装 **10** swimsuit/bathing suit
游泳裤/泳装 **11** swimming trunks/swimsuit/bathing suit
(舞蹈、体操等穿的)紧身衣 **12** leotard

鞋子 **13** shoes
高跟鞋 **14** (high) heels
(女)无带便鞋 **15** pumps
休闲鞋 **16** loafers
运动鞋 **17** sneakers/athletic shoes
网球鞋 **18** tennis shoes
跑步鞋 **19** running shoes

高帮球鞋 **20** high-tops/high-top sneakers
凉鞋 **21** sandals
夹脚鞋 **22** thongs/flip-flops
靴子 **23** boots
工作靴 **24** work boots
登山靴 **25** hiking boots
牛仔靴 **26** cowboy boots
软皮鞋 **27** moccasins

[1–12]
A. Excuse me. I found this/these _______ in the dryer. Is it/Are they yours?
B. Yes. It's/They're mine. Thank you.

[13–27]
A. Are those new _______?
B. Yes, they are.
A. They're very nice.
B. Thanks.

Do you exercise? What do you do? What kind of clothing do you wear when you exercise?

What kind of shoes do you wear when you go to work or to school? when you exercise? when you relax at home? when you go out with friends or family members?

JEWELRY AND ACCESSORIES

珠宝及饰物

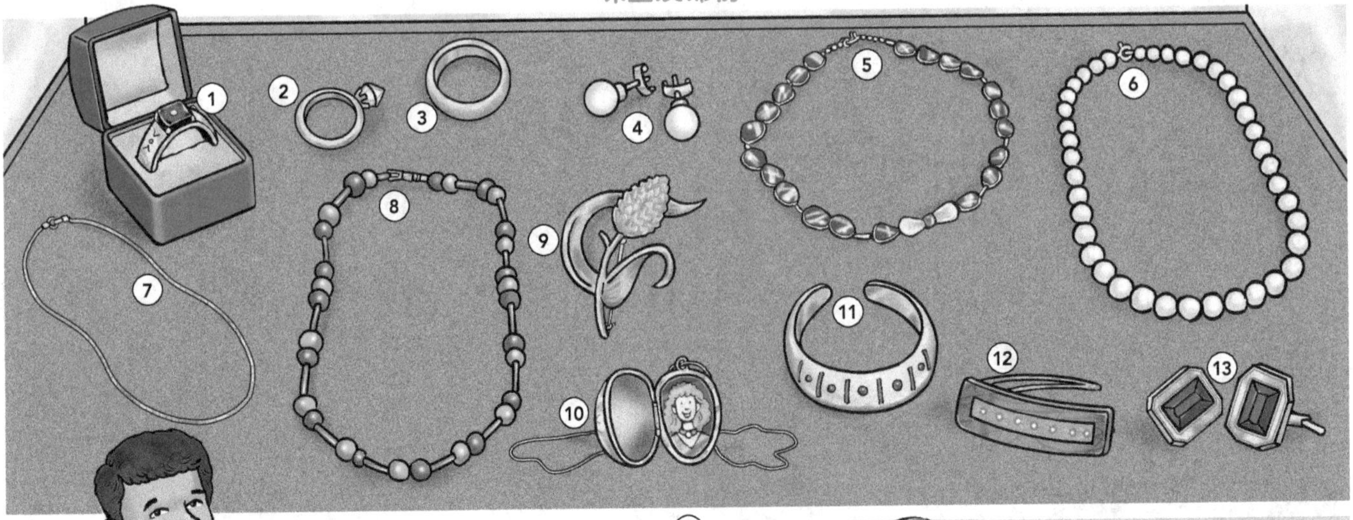

戒指	1	ring
订婚戒指	2	engagement ring
结婚戒指	3	wedding ring/wedding band
耳环	4	earrings
项链	5	necklace
珍珠项链	6	pearl necklace/pearls/ string of pearls
项链	7	chain
珠子项链	8	beads
胸针	9	pin/brooch
可存放照片的吊坠	10	locket
手镯	11	bracelet
条形发夹	12	barrette
袖扣	13	cuff links
吊裤带	14	suspenders
手表	15	watch/wrist watch
手帕	16	handkerchief
钥匙圈/钥匙链	17	key ring/key chain
零钱包	18	change purse
皮夹	19	wallet
皮带	20	belt
(女用)手提包	21	purse/handbag/pocketbook
肩背包	22	shoulder bag
大手提袋	23	tote bag
书包	24	book bag
背包	25	backpack
化妆包	26	makeup bag
公文包	27	briefcase

A. Oh, no! I think I lost my **ring**!
B. I'll help you look for it.

A. Oh, no! I think I lost my **earrings**!
B. I'll help you look for them.

[In a store]
A. Excuse me. Is this/Are these ________ on sale this week?
B. Yes. It's/They're half price.

[On the street]
A. Help! Police! Stop that man/woman!
B. What happened?!
A. He/She just stole my ________ and my ________!

Do you like to wear jewelry? What jewelry do you have?

In your country, what do men, women, and children use to carry their things?

DESCRIBING CLOTHING

描述衣物

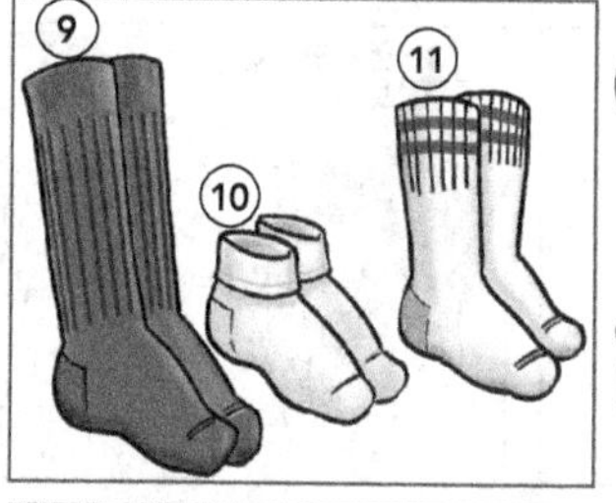

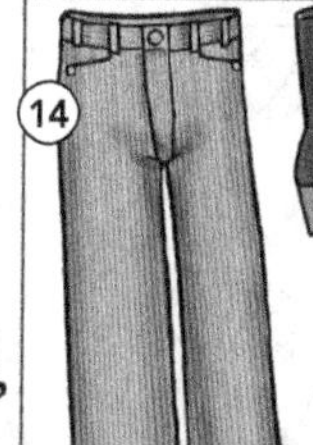

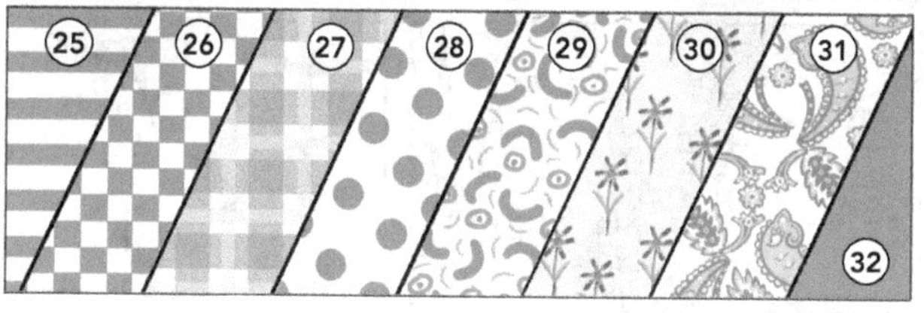

衣服类型 **Types of Clothing**

长袖衬衫 **1** long-sleeved shirt
短袖衬衫 **2** short-sleeved shirt
无袖衬衫 **3** sleeveless shirt
高领衬衫 **4** turtleneck (shirt)

V领毛衣 **5** V-neck sweater
无领有扣开襟的毛衣 **6** cardigan sweater
圆领毛衣 **7** crewneck sweater
高领毛衣 **8** turtleneck sweater

中筒袜 **9** knee-high socks
短筒袜 **10** ankle socks
短筒厚袜 **11** crew socks

穿孔耳环 **12** pierced earrings
夹式耳环 **13** clip-on earrings

材料种类 **Types of Material**

灯芯绒裤 **14** corduroy *pants*
皮靴 **15** leather *boots*
尼龙丝袜 **16** nylon *stockings*
棉质T恤衫 **17** cotton *T-shirt*
牛仔夹克 **18** denim *jacket*
法兰绒衬衫 **19** flannel *shirt*
聚酯女式短衫 **20** polyester *blouse*
亚麻连衣裙 **21** linen *dress*
丝围巾 **22** silk *scarf*
羊毛毛衣 **23** wool *sweater*
草帽 **24** straw *hat*

花样 **Patterns**

条纹 **25** striped
方格图案 **26** checked
格子花纹 **27** plaid
圆点花纹 **28** polka-dotted
有图案的/印花 **29** patterned/print
花卉图案 **30** flowered/floral
螺旋花纹图案 **31** paisley
纯蓝色 **32** solid *blue*

尺寸大小 **Sizes**

特小 **33** extra-small
小 **34** small
中 **35** medium
大 **36** large
特大 **37** extra-large

[1–24]
A. May I help you?
B. Yes, please. I'm looking for a *shirt*.*
A. What kind?
B. I'm looking for a *long-sleeved shirt*.

* *With 9–16:* I'm looking for ______.

[25–32]
A. How do you like this ______ tie/shirt/skirt?
B. Actually, I prefer that ______ one.

[33–37]
A. What size are you looking for?
B. ______.

Describe your favorite clothing items. For each item, tell about the color, the type of material, the size, and the pattern.

CLOTHING PROBLEMS AND ALTERATIONS

衣物问题及修改

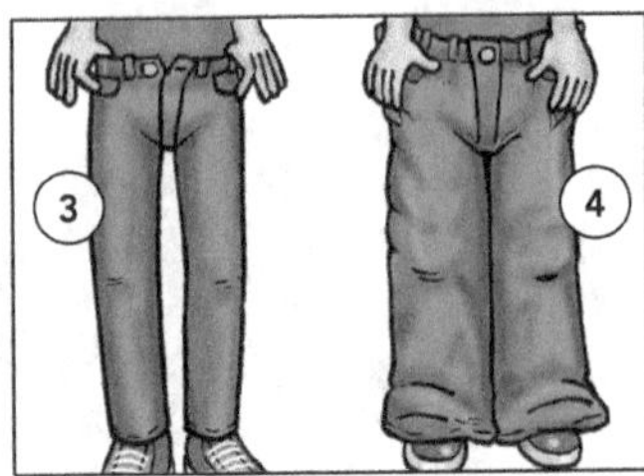
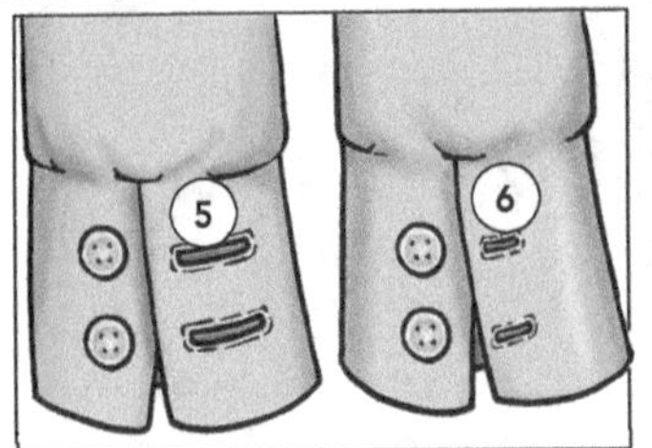
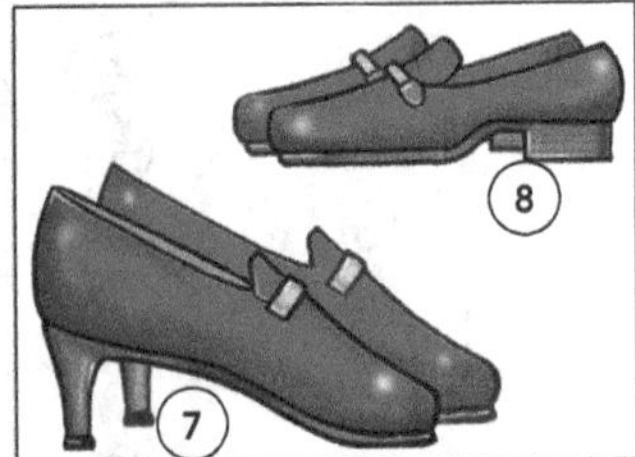
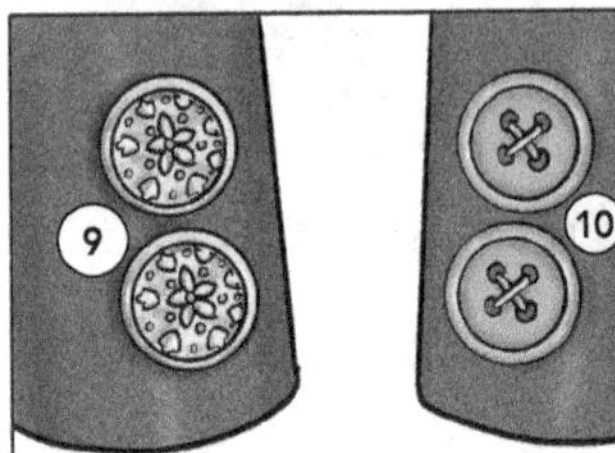

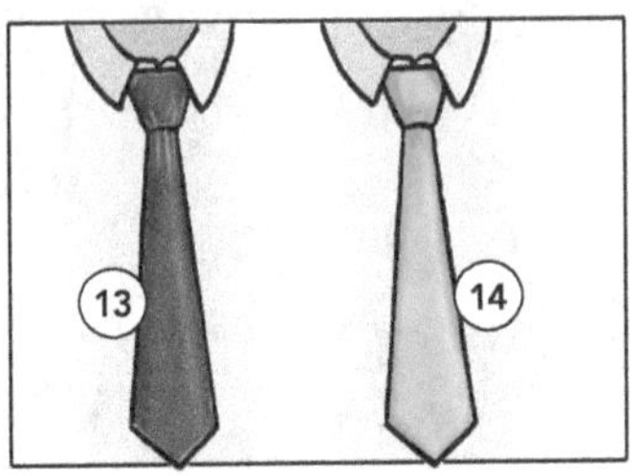
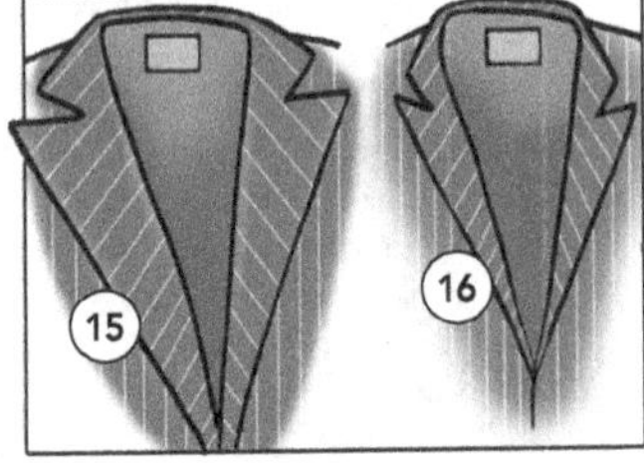
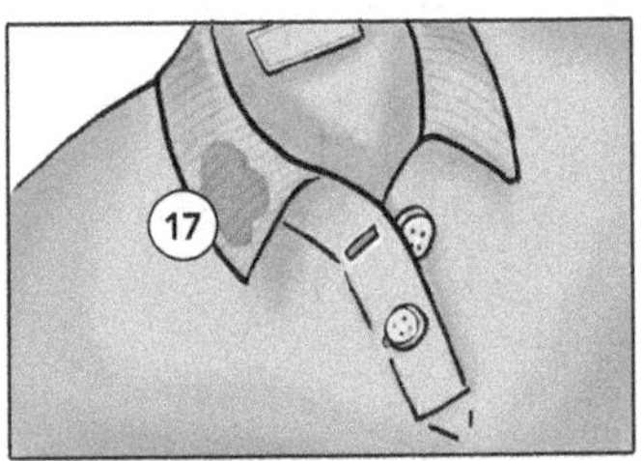
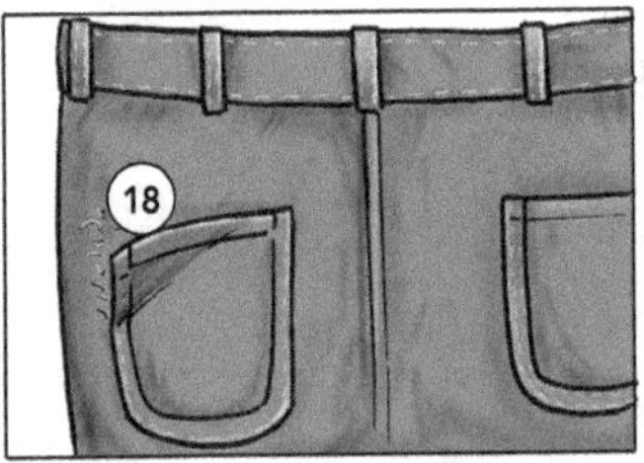
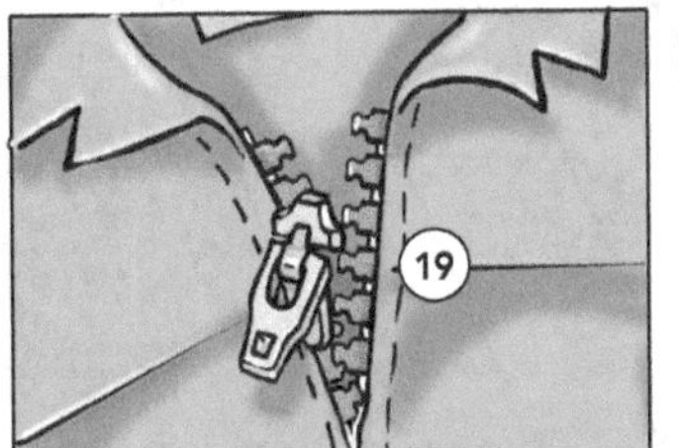
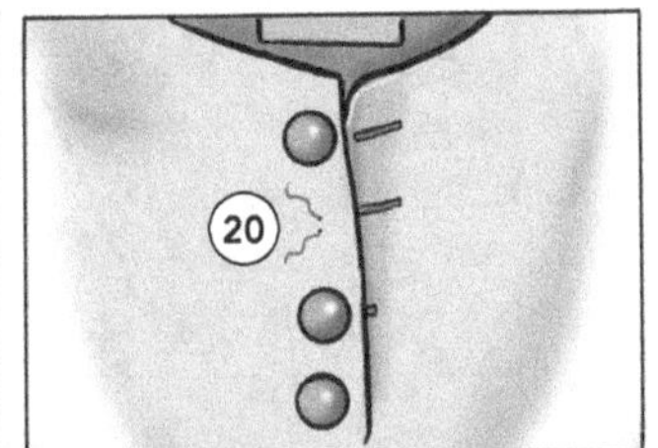
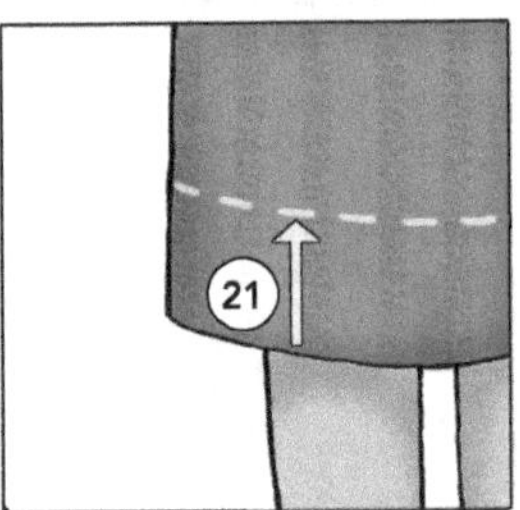

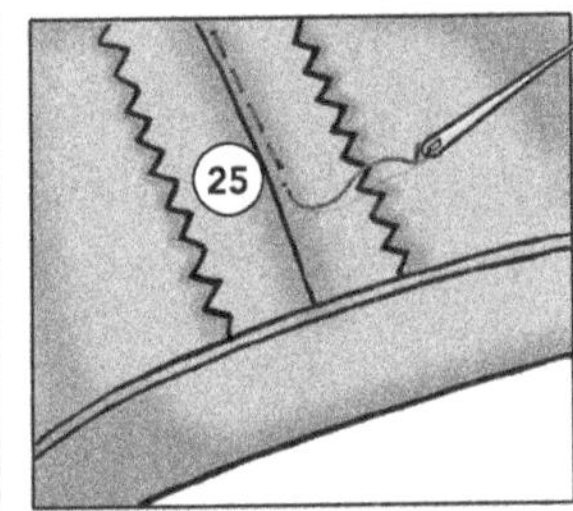

长－短 **1–2** long – short
紧－宽松 **3–4** tight – loose/baggy
大－小 **5–6** large/big – small
高－低 **7–8** high – low
华丽－朴素 **9–10** fancy – plain
重－轻 **11–12** heavy – light
深/暗－明亮 **13–14** dark – light
宽－窄 **15–16** wide – narrow

脏衣领 **17** stained *collar*
破了的口袋 **18** ripped/torn *pocket*
坏掉的拉炼 **19** broken *zipper*
掉了个钮扣 **20** missing *button*
缩短裙子 **21** shorten the *skirt*
放长袖子 **22** lengthen the *sleeves*
将夹克改小 **23** take in the *jacket*
将裤子改大 **24** let out the *pants*
修补接缝 **25** fix/repair the *seam*

[1–2]
A. Are the sleeves too **long**?
B. No. They're too **short**.

1–2 Are the sleeves too ________?
3–4 Are the pants too ________?
5–6 Are the buttonholes too ________?
7–8 Are the heels too ________?

9–10 Are the buttons too ________?
11–12 Is the coat too ________?
13–14 Is the color too ________?
15–16 Are the lapels too ________?

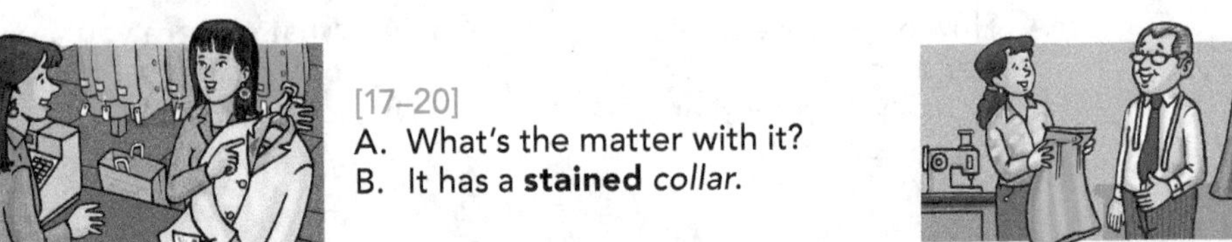

[17–20]
A. What's the matter with it?
B. It has a **stained** *collar*.

[21–25]
A. Please **shorten** the *skirt*.
B. **Shorten** the *skirt*? Okay.

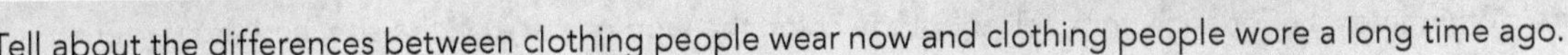

Tell about the differences between clothing people wear now and clothing people wore a long time ago.

洗衣服

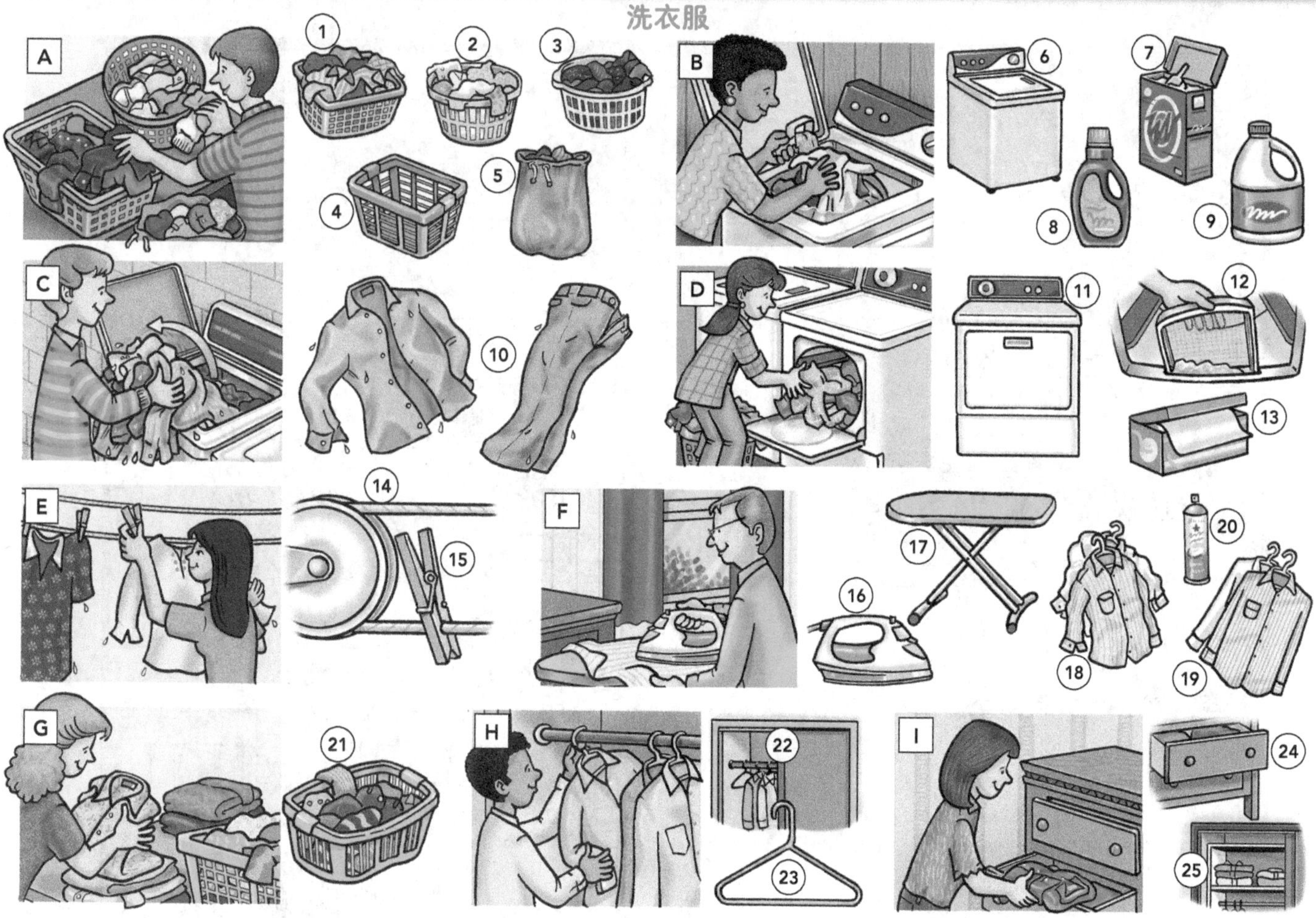

将要洗衣物分类	A	sort the laundry
将衣物放入洗衣机	B	load the washer
从洗衣机取出衣物	C	unload the washer
将衣物放入干衣机	D	load the dryer
将衣服挂上晒衣绳	E	hang clothes on the clothesline
烫衣服	F	iron
折叠洗好的衣物	G	fold the laundry
挂衣服	H	hang up clothing
收拾东西	I	put things away

待洗的衣物	1	laundry
浅色衣物	2	light clothing
深色衣物	3	dark clothing
洗衣篮	4	laundry basket
洗衣袋	5	laundry bag
洗衣机	6	washer/washing machine
洗衣粉	7	laundry detergent
衣物柔顺剂	8	fabric softener
漂白剂	9	bleach
湿衣物	10	wet clothing
干衣机	11	dryer
过滤网罩	12	lint trap
除静电纸	13	static cling remover
晒衣绳	14	clothesline
晒衣夹	15	clothespin
熨斗	16	iron
熨烫板	17	ironing board
皱折的衣物	18	wrinkled clothing
烫平的衣物	19	ironed clothing
熨喷浆	20	spray starch
干净衣物	21	clean clothing
衣橱	22	closet
衣架	23	hanger
抽屉	24	drawer
架子(单数)–架子(复数)	25	shelf–shelves

[A–I]
A. What are you doing?
B. I'm ________ing.

[4–6, 11, 14–17, 23]
A. Excuse me. Do you sell ________s?
B. Yes. They're at the back of the store.
A. Thank you.

[7–9, 13, 20]
A. Excuse me. Do you sell ________?
B. Yes. It's at the back of the store.
A. Thank you.

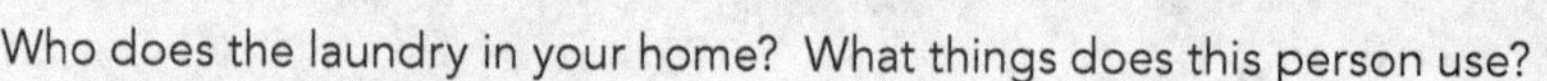

Who does the laundry in your home? What things does this person use?

THE DEPARTMENT STORE

百货公司

商店目录 1 (store) directory
珠宝专柜 2 Jewelry Counter
香水专柜 3 Perfume Counter
电扶梯 4 escalator
电梯 5 elevator
男士服装部 6 Men's Clothing Department
顾客取货区 7 customer pickup area
女士服装部 8 Women's Clothing Department
儿童服装部 9 Children's Clothing Department
家庭用品部 10 Housewares Department
家具部 11 Furniture Department/
Home Furnishings Department
家用电器部 12 Household Appliances Department
电子产品部 13 Electronics Department
顾客服务处 14 Customer Assistance Counter/
Customer Service Counter
男厕 15 men's room
女厕 16 ladies' room
饮水机 17 water fountain
点心贩卖部 18 snack bar
礼品包装柜台 19 Gift Wrap Counter

A. Excuse me. Where's the **store directory**?
B. It's over there, next to the **Jewelry Counter**.
A. Thanks.
B. You're welcome.

A. Excuse me. Do you sell *ties**?
B. Yes. You can find *ties** in the ___[6, 8–13]___ /at the ___[2, 3]___ on the first/second/third/fourth floor.
A. Thank you.

**ties/bracelets/dresses/toasters/. . .*

Describe a department store you know. Tell what is on each floor.

购物

A

B

C

D

E

F

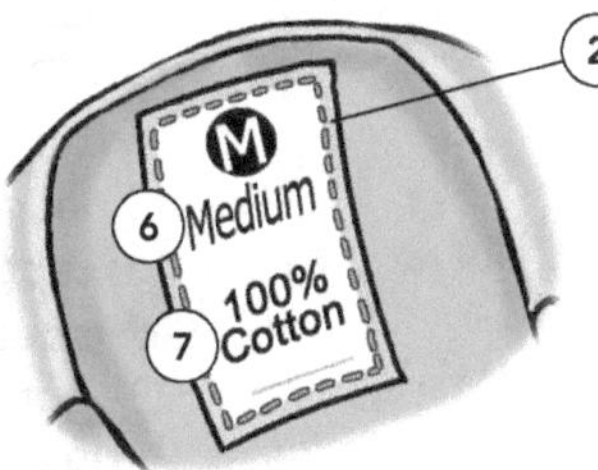

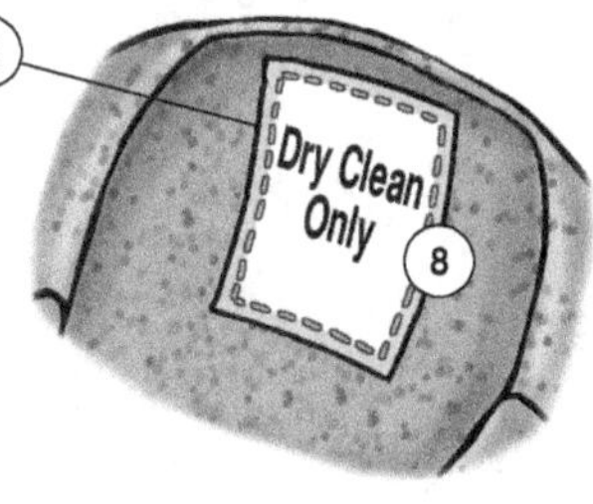

买	A	buy
退货	B	return
换货	C	exchange
试穿	D	try on
付钱	E	pay for
了解某项商品	F	get some information about

降价广告	1	sale sign
标签	2	label
价格标签	3	price tag
收据	4	receipt
折扣	5	discount
尺寸	6	size
材料	7	material

维护说明	8	care instructions
原价	9	regular price
特价	10	sale price
价格	11	price
销售税	12	sales tax
总额/总价格	13	total price

A. May I help you?
B. Yes, please. I want to ___[A–F]___ this item.
A. Certainly. I'll be glad to help you.

A. {What's the ___[5–7, 9–13]___? / What are the ___[8]___?
B. ________.
A. Are you sure?
B. Yes. Look at the ___[1–4]___!

Which stores in your area have sales? How often?

Tell about something you bought on sale.

VIDEO AND AUDIO EQUIPMENT

录像及音响设备

电视 **1** TV/television
等离子电视 **2** plasma TV
液晶电视 **3** LCD TV
背投电视 **4** projection TV
便携式电视 **5** portable TV
遥控器 **6** remote (control)
DVD/数字化视频光盘 **7** DVD
DVD播放机 **8** DVD player
录像带 **9** video/videocassette/videotape
录像机 **10** VCR/videocassette recorder
摄录像机 **11** camcorder/video camera
电池组 **12** battery pack
电池充电器 **13** battery charger
收音机 **14** radio
闹钟收音机 **15** clock radio
短波收音机 **16** shortwave radio
盒式录音机 **17** tape recorder/cassette recorder
麦克风 **18** microphone
立体声音响系统/音响系统 **19** stereo system/sound system
唱片 **20** record
唱盘 **21** turntable
激光唱片 **22** CD/compact disc
激光唱机 **23** CD player
调音器 **24** tuner
录音带 **25** (audio)tape/(audio)cassette
卡式录音座 **26** tape deck/cassette deck
喇叭 **27** speakers
手提式音响系统/手提录放音机 **28** portable stereo system/boombox
音乐光盘随身听 **29** portable/personal CD player
卡带随身听 **30** portable/personal cassette player
耳机 **31** headphones
随身数码音响播放器 **32** portable/personal digital audio player
视讯游戏系统 **33** video game system
视讯游戏 **34** video game
掌上游戏机 **35** hand-held video game

A. May I help you?
B. Yes, please. I'm looking for a **TV**.

* *With 27 & 31, use:* I'm looking for ______.

A. I like your new ______.
Where did you get it/them?
B. At ......*(name of store)*......

A. Which company makes the best ______?
B. In my opinion, the best ______ is/are made by ....

What video and audio equipment do you have or want?

In your opinion, which brands of video and audio equipment are the best?

TELEPHONES AND CAMERAS

电话及照相机

- 电话 **1** telephone/phone
- 无线电话 **2** cordless phone
- 移动电话/手机 **3** cell phone/cellular phone
- 电池 **4** battery
- 电池充电器 **5** battery charger
- 电话答录机 **6** answering machine
- 传呼机 **7** pager
- 电子记事本 **8** PDA/electronic personal organizer
- 传真机 **9** fax machine
- 袖珍型计算器 **10** (pocket) calculator
- 桌面计算器 **11** adding machine
- 稳压器 **12** voltage regulator
- 变压器 **13** adapter
- 35毫米照相机 **14** (35 millimeter) camera
- 镜头 **15** lens
- 胶卷 **16** film
- 变焦镜头 **17** zoom lens
- 数码相机 **18** digital camera
- 存储器磁盘 **19** memory disk
- 三脚架 **20** tripod
- 闪光灯 **21** flash (attachment)
- 相机盒 **22** camera case
- 幻灯机 **23** slide projector
- 电影屏幕 **24** (movie) screen

A. Can I help you?
B. Yes. I want to buy a **telephone**.*

* *With 16, use:* I want to buy ______.

A. Excuse me. Do you sell ______s?*
B. Yes. We have a large selection of ______s.

* *With 16, use the singular.*

A. Which ______ is the best?
B. This one here. It's made by .... *(company)*

What kind of telephone do you use?

Do you have a camera? What kind is it? What do you take pictures of?

Does anyone you know have an answering machine? When you call, what message do you hear?

COMPUTERS

计算机/电脑

电脑硬件 Computer Hardware

- 台式电脑 1 (desktop) computer
- 中央处理器 2 CPU/central processing unit
- 电脑显示器/电脑屏幕 3 monitor/screen
- 光盘驱动器 4 CD-ROM drive
- 光盘 5 CD-ROM
- 磁盘驱动器/磁盘机 6 disk drive
- 软盘 7 (floppy) disk
- 键盘 8 keyboard
- 鼠标 9 mouse
- 平面屏幕/液晶屏幕 10 flat panel screen/LCD screen
- 笔记本电脑 11 notebook computer
- 控制杆 12 joystick
- 轨迹球 13 track ball
- 调制解调器 14 modem
- 电涌保护器 15 surge protector
- 打印机 16 printer
- 扫描仪 17 scanner
- 连接线 18 cable

电脑软件 Computer Software

- 文档处理软件 19 word-processing program
- 试算表程序 20 spreadsheet program
- 教学软件程序 21 educational software program
- 电脑游戏 22 computer game

A. Can you recommend a good **computer**?
B. Yes. This **computer** here is excellent.

A. Is that a new ________?
B. Yes.
A. Where did you get it?
B. At ....*(name of store)*........

A. May I help you?
B. Yes, please. Do you sell ________s?
A. Yes. We carry a complete line of ________s.

Do you use a computer? When?

In your opinion, how have computers changed the world?

THE TOY STORE

玩具店

棋盘游戏 **1** board game
拼图游戏 **2** (jigsaw) puzzle
建筑玩具组合 **3** construction set
积木 **4** (building) blocks
皮球 **5** rubber ball
沙滩球 **6** beach ball
桶和铲 **7** pail and shovel
洋娃娃 **8** doll
洋娃娃衣服 **9** doll clothing
娃娃屋 **10** doll house
娃娃家具 **11** doll house furniture
活动玩偶 **12** action figure
毛绒玩具 **13** stuffed animal

火柴盒小汽车 **14** matchbox car
玩具卡车 **15** toy truck
玩具赛车组合 **16** racing car set
玩具火车组合 **17** train set
模型玩具组合 **18** model kit
科学实验组合 **19** science kit
对讲机组合 **20** walkie-talkie (set)
呼拉圈 **21** hula hoop
跳绳 **22** jump rope
吹泡泡肥皂水 **23** bubble soap
收藏卡 **24** trading cards
蜡笔 **25** crayons
彩色笔 **26** (color) markers

着色本 **27** coloring book
彩色美工用纸 **28** construction paper
颜料组合 **29** paint set
黏土 **30** (modeling) clay
贴纸 **31** stickers
脚踏车 **32** bicycle
三轮车 **33** tricycle
玩具拖车 **34** wagon
滑板 **35** skateboard
秋千 **36** swing set
游戏屋 **37** play house
充气游泳池 **38** kiddie pool/inflatable pool

A. Excuse me. I'm looking for (a/an) ________(s) for my *grandson*.*
B. Look in the next aisle.
A. Thank you.

* *grandson/granddaughter/. . .*

A. I don't know what to get my ....-year-old son/daughter for his/her birthday.
B. What about (a) ________?
A. Good idea! Thanks.

A. Mom/Dad? Can we buy this/these ________?
B. No, *Johnny*. Not today.

What toys are most popular in your country?

What were your favorite toys when you were a child?

THE BANK

银行

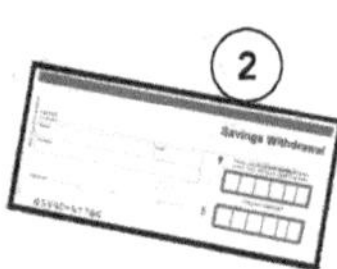

存款 **A** make a deposit
提款 **B** make a withdrawal
将支票兑换现金 **C** cash a check
买旅行支票 **D** get traveler's checks
开账户 **E** open an account
申请贷款 **F** apply for a loan
兑换货币 **G** exchange currency

存款单 **1** deposit slip
提款单 **2** withdrawal slip
支票 **3** check
旅行支票 **4** traveler's check
银行存折 **5** bankbook/passbook
金融卡/提款卡 **6** ATM card
信用卡 **7** credit card
银行保险库 **8** (bank) vault
保险箱 **9** safe deposit box
出纳员 **10** teller
警卫 **11** security guard
自动存取款机 **12** ATM (machine)/ cash machine
银行职员 **13** bank officer

[A–G]
A. Where are you going?
B. I'm going to the bank. I have to ______.

[5–7]
A. What are you looking for?
B. My ______. I can't find it anywhere!

[8–13]
A. How many ______s does the State Street Bank have?
B. ....

Do you have a bank account? What kind? Where? What do you do at the bank?

Do you ever use traveler's checks? When?

Do you have a credit card? What kind? When do you use it?

FINANCES
金融

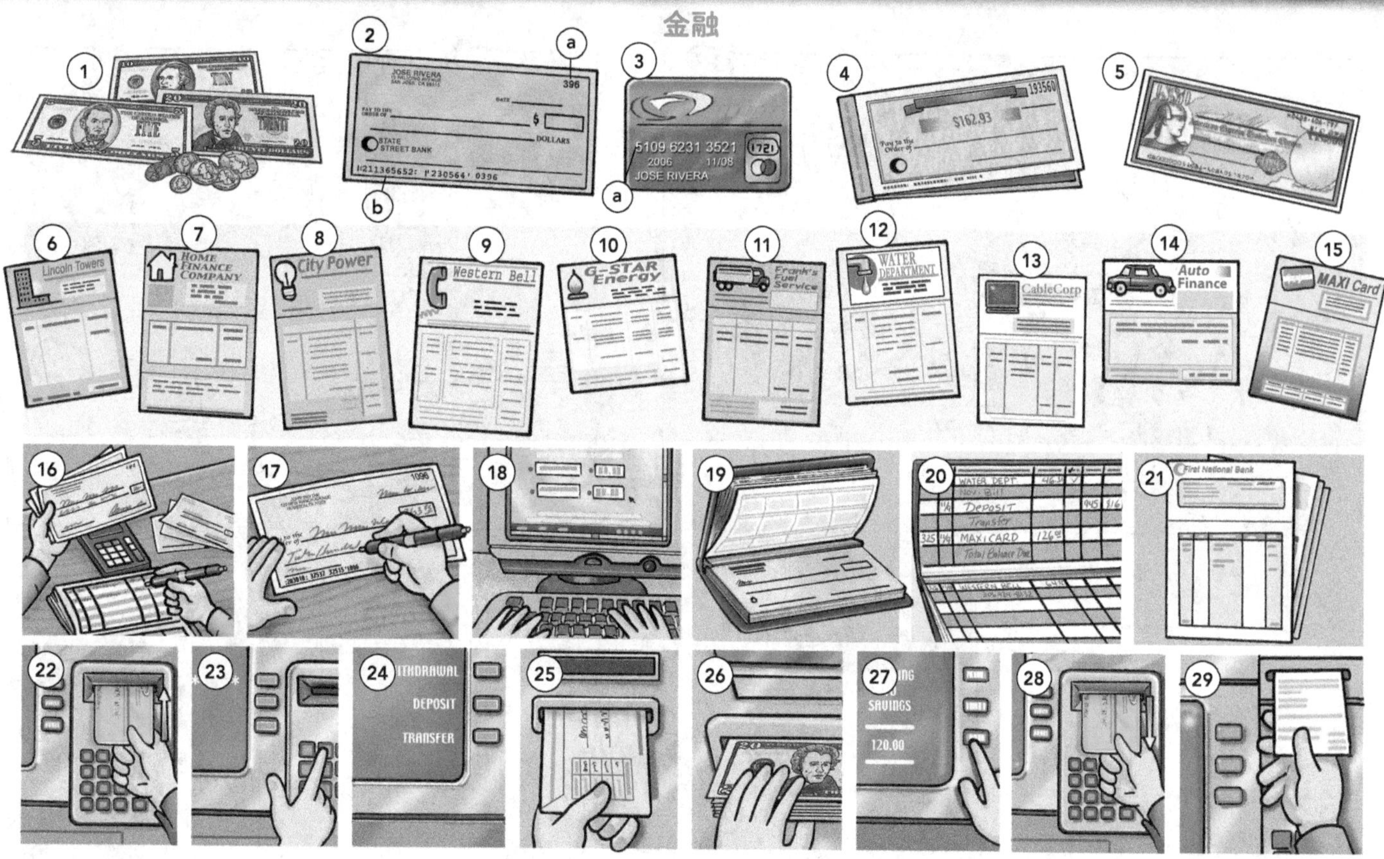

付款方式 Forms of Payment

- 现金 **1** cash
- 支票 **2** check
  - 支票号码 **a** check number
  - 帐户号码 **b** account number
- 信用卡 **3** credit card
  - 信用卡号码 **a** credit card number
- 汇票 **4** money order
- 旅行支票 **5** traveler's check

付款方式 Household Bills

- 房租 **6** rent
- 房屋贷款 **7** mortgage payment
- 电费单 **8** electric bill
- 电话帐单 **9** telephone bill
- 煤气帐单 **10** gas bill
- 燃油帐单/暖气费帐单 **11** oil bill/heating bill
- 水费单 **12** water bill
- 有线电视帐单 **13** cable TV bill
- 车贷 **14** car payment
- 信用卡帐单 **15** credit card bill

家庭理财 Family Finances

- 检查支票本是否收支平衡 **16** balance the checkbook
- 开支票 **17** write a check
- 使用网上银行 **18** bank online
- 支票本 **19** checkbook
- 支票登记簿 **20** check register
- 月结单 **21** monthly statement

使用自动存提款机 Using an ATM Machine

- 插入金融卡 **22** insert the ATM card
- 输入个人识别号码 **23** enter your PIN number/personal identification number
- 选择交易类型 **24** select a transaction
- 存款 **25** make a deposit
- 提取现金 **26** withdraw/get cash
- 转帐 **27** transfer funds
- 取出卡片 **28** remove your card
- 拿取交易收据/拿取收据 **29** take your transaction slip/receipt

A. Can I pay by __[1, 2]__/ with a __[3–5]__?
B. Yes. We accept __[1]__/ __[2–5]__s.

A. What are you doing?
B. I'm paying the __[6–15]__.
I'm __[16–18]__ing.
I'm looking for the __[19–21]__.

A. What should I do?
B. __[22–29]__.

What household bills do you receive?
How much do you pay for the different bills?

Who takes care of the finances in your household? What does that person do?

Do you use ATM machines?
If you do, how do you use them?

THE POST OFFICE

邮局

信 **1** letter
明信片 **2** postcard
航空邮简 **3** air letter/ aerogramme
包裹 **4** package/parcel
一等邮件 **5** first class
优先邮件 **6** priority mail
特快邮件 **7** express mail/ overnight mail
包裹邮件 **8** parcel post
挂号信 **9** certified mail
邮票 **10** stamp
整版邮票 **11** sheet of stamps

整卷邮票 **12** roll of stamps
邮票本 **13** book of stamps
汇票 **14** money order
地址变更登记表 **15** change-of-address form
入伍登记表格 **16** selective service registration form
护照申请表格 **17** passport application form
信封 **18** envelope
回邮地址 **19** return address
邮寄地址 **20** mailing address

邮政编码 **21** zip code
邮戳 **22** postmark
邮票/邮资 **23** stamp/ postage
投信口 **24** mail slot
邮局办事员 **25** postal worker/ postal clerk
秤 **26** scale
邮票自售机 **27** stamp machine
邮差 **28** letter carrier/ mail carrier
邮车 **29** mail truck
邮筒 **30** mailbox

[1–4]
A. Where are you going?
B. To the post office. I have to mail a/an ________.

[5–9]
A. How do you want to send it?
B. ________, please.

[10–17]
A. Next!
B. I'd like a ________, please.
A. Here you are.

[19–21, 23]
A. Do you want me to mail this letter?
B. Yes, thanks.
A. Oops! You forgot the ________!

How often do you go to the post office? What do you do there?

Tell about the postal system in your country.

图书馆

- 网上目录 **1** online catalog
- 卡片目录 **2** card catalog
- 作者 **3** author
- 书名 **4** title
- 借书证 **5** library card
- 复印机 **6** copier/ photocopier/ copy machine
- 书架 **7** shelves
- 儿童图书区 **8** children's section
- 儿童图书 **9** children's books
- 期刊阅览区 **10** periodical section
- 期刊 **11** journals
- 杂志 **12** magazines
- 报纸 **13** newspapers
- 视听资料区 **14** media section
- 磁带书 **15** books on tape
- 录音带 **16** audiotapes
- CD(复数) **17** CDs
- 录像带(复数) **18** videotapes
- 电脑软件 **19** (computer) software
- DVD(复数)/数字化视频光盘(复数) **20** DVDs
- 外语区 **21** foreign language section
- 外语书籍 **22** foreign language books
- 参考书阅览室 **23** reference section
- 缩微胶卷 **24** microfilm
- 缩微胶卷阅读机 **25** microfilm reader
- 词典 **26** dictionary
- 百科全书 **27** encyclopedia
- 地图集 **28** atlas
- 参考咨询台 **29** reference desk
- 图书馆参考资料咨询员 **30** (reference) librarian
- 借书处 **31** checkout desk
- 图书馆职员 **32** library clerk

[1, 2, 6–32]

A. Excuse me. Where's/Where are the ______?

B. Over there, at/near/next to the ______.

[8–23, 26–28]

A. Excuse me. Where can I find a/an [26–28] / [9, 11–13, 15–20, 22]?

B. Look in the [8, 10, 14, 21, 23] over there.

A. I'm having trouble finding a book.

B. Do you know the [3–4]?

A. Yes. ....

A. Excuse me. I'd like to check out this [26–28] /these [11–13].

B. I'm sorry. It/They must remain in the library.

Do you go to a library? Where? What does this library have?

Tell about how you use the library.

社区机构

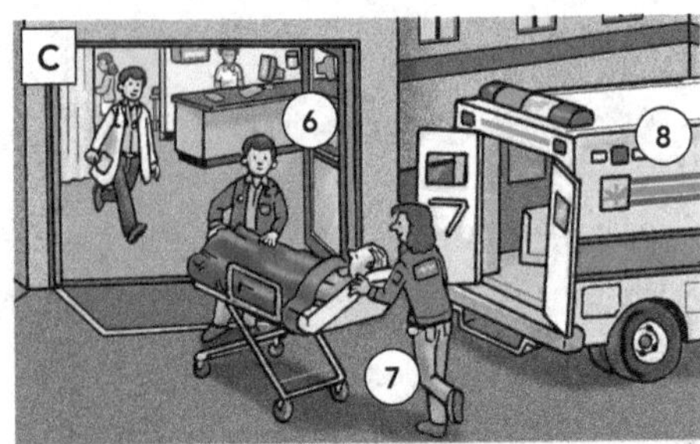

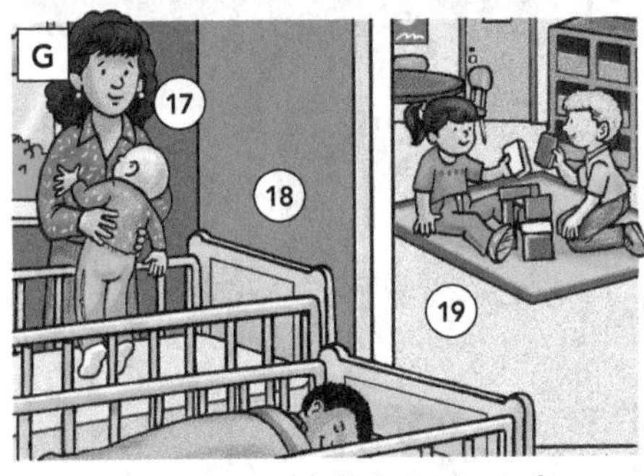

警察局 **A** police station
消防队 **B** fire station
医院 **C** hospital
市政厅 **D** town hall/city hall
活动中心 **E** recreation center
垃圾场 **F** dump
托儿所 **G** child-care center
老人中心 **H** senior center
教堂 **I** church
犹太教堂 **J** synagogue
清真寺/回教寺院 **K** mosque
庙 **L** temple

紧急事故接线员 **1** emergency operator
警察 **2** police officer
警车 **3** police car
救火车/消防车 **4** fire engine
救火员/消防员 **5** firefighter
急诊室 **6** emergency room
紧急救护技术员/医务助理 **7** EMT/paramedic
救护车 **8** ambulance
市长/镇长/市行政官 **9** mayor/city manager
会议室 **10** meeting room
体育馆 **11** gym
活动主任 **12** activities director
棋牌室 **13** game room
游泳池 **14** swimming pool
垃圾工 **15** sanitation worker
资源回收中心 **16** recycling center
育儿员 **17** child-care worker
育儿室 **18** nursery
娱乐室 **19** playroom
老人看护员 **20** eldercare worker/ senior care worker

[A–L]
A. Where are you going?
B. I'm going to the ________.

[1, 2, 5, 7, 12, 15, 17, 20]
A. What do you do?
B. I'm a/an ________.

[3, 4, 8]
A. Do you hear a siren?
B. Yes. There's a/an ________ coming up behind us.

What community institutions are in your city or town? Where are they located?

Which community institutions do you use? When?

犯罪行为及紧急事故

车祸	1	car accident
火	2	fire
爆炸	3	explosion
抢劫	4	robbery
入屋盗窃	5	burglary
在公共场所抢劫	6	mugging
绑架	7	kidnapping
迷失的孩子(单数)	8	lost child
劫车	9	car jacking
抢银行	10	bank robbery
攻击	11	assault
凶杀	12	murder
停电	13	blackout/ power outage
煤气泄漏	14	gas leak
主水管破裂	15	water main break
电线掉落	16	downed power line
化学品溢漏	17	chemical spill
火车出轨	18	train derailment
蓄意破坏公物	19	vandalism
帮派暴力	20	gang violence
酒后驾驶	21	drunk driving
贩卖毒品	22	drug dealing

[1–13]

A. I want to report a/an ________.
B. What's your location?
A. ....

[14–18]

A. Why is this street closed?
B. It's closed because of a ________.

[19–22]

A. I'm very concerned about the amount of ________ in our community.
B. I agree. ________ is a very serious problem.

Is there much crime in your community? Tell about it.

Have you ever experienced a crime or emergency? What happened?

身体

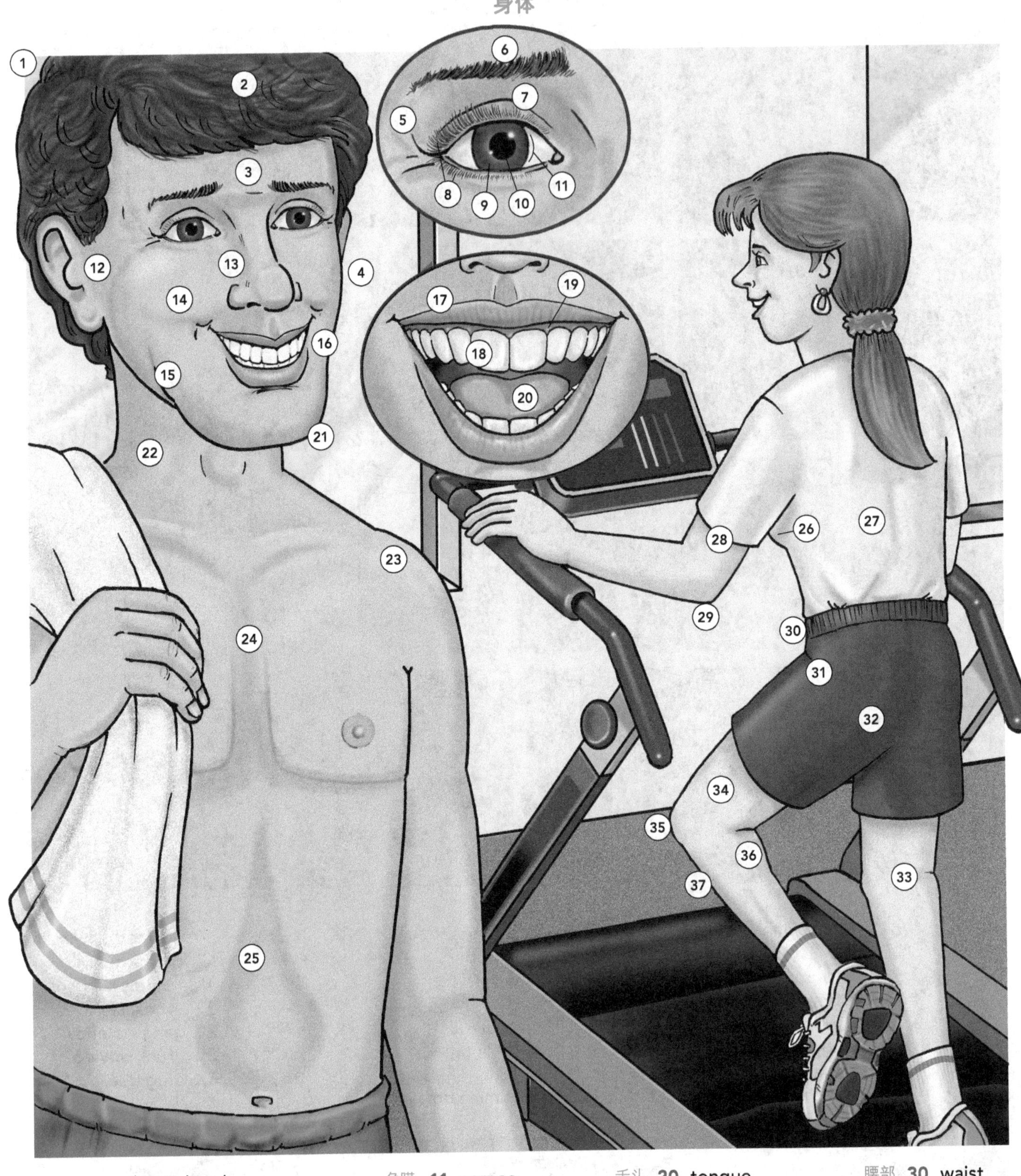

头 1 head
头发 2 hair
额头 3 forehead
脸 4 face
眼睛 5 eye
眉毛 6 eyebrow
眼皮/眼睑 7 eyelid
睫毛 8 eyelashes
(瞳孔外的)虹膜 9 iris
瞳孔 10 pupil

角膜 11 cornea
耳朵 12 ear
鼻子 13 nose
脸颊 14 cheek
下颌 15 jaw
嘴巴 16 mouth
嘴唇 17 lip
牙齿(单数)–牙齿(复数) 18 tooth–teeth
牙龈 19 gums

舌头 20 tongue
下巴 21 chin
颈/脖子 22 neck
肩膀 23 shoulder
胸 24 chest
腹部 25 abdomen
乳房 26 breast
背部 27 back
手臂 28 arm
手肘 29 elbow

腰部 30 waist
臀部 31 hip
屁股 32 buttocks
腿 33 leg
大腿 34 thigh
膝盖 35 knee
小腿 36 calf
胫/小腿 37 shin

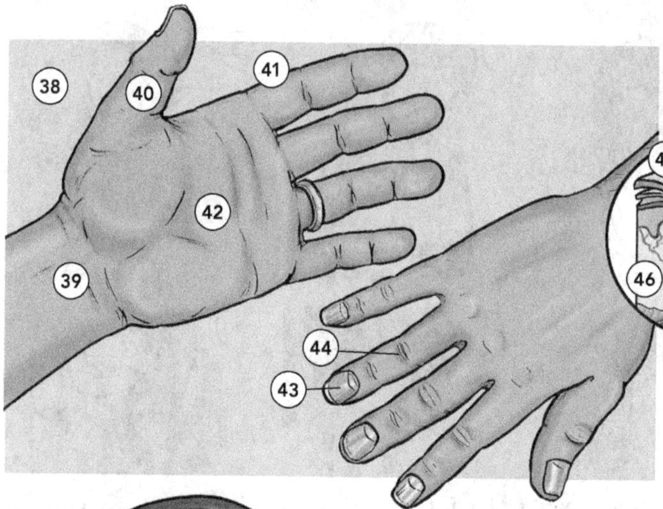

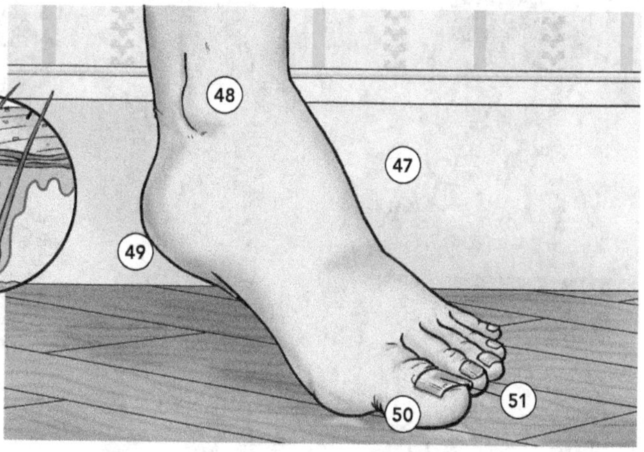

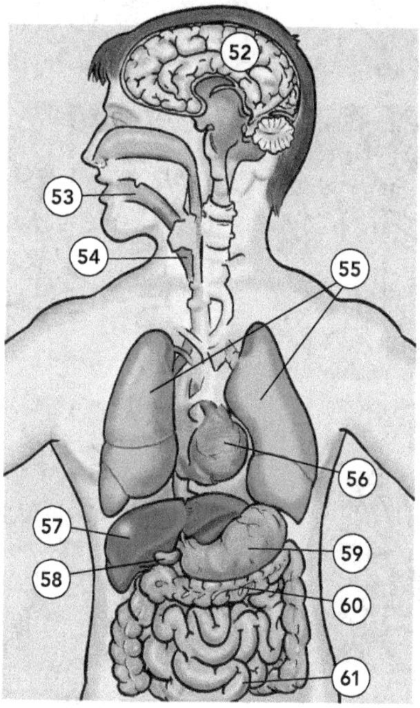

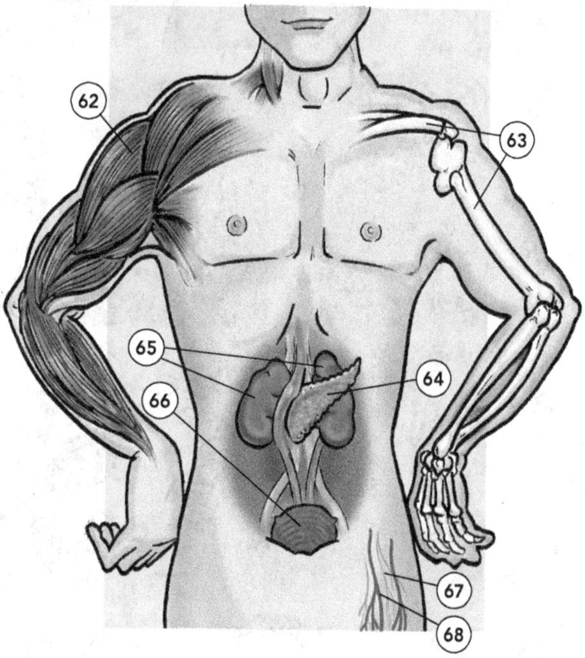

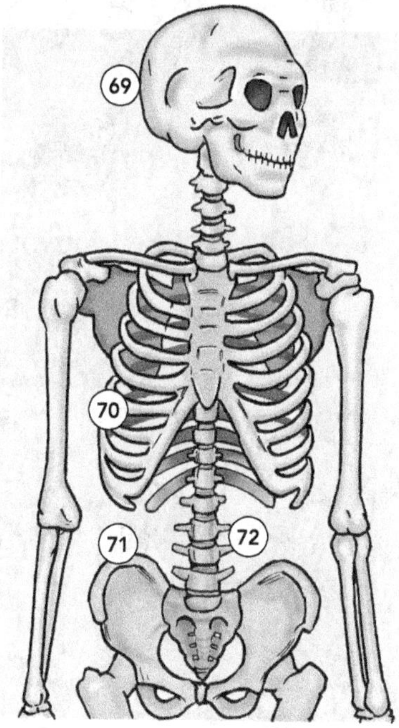

手 **38** hand
腕 **39** wrist
大姆指 **40** thumb
手指 **41** finger
手掌 **42** palm
手指甲 **43** fingernail
指关节 **44** knuckle
皮肤 **45** skin
神经 **46** nerve

脚(单数) **47** foot
足踝 **48** ankle
脚跟 **49** heel
脚指 **50** toe
脚指甲 **51** toenail
头脑 **52** brain
喉咙 **53** throat
食管/食道 **54** esophagus
肺 **55** lungs

心脏 **56** heart
肝脏 **57** liver
胆囊 **58** gallbladder
胃 **59** stomach
大肠 **60** large intestine
小肠 **61** small intestine
肌肉 **62** muscles
骨头 **63** bones
胰脏/胰腺 **64** pancreas

肾脏 **65** kidneys
膀胱 **66** bladder
静脉 **67** veins
动脉 **68** arteries
头骨 **69** skull
胸腔 **70** ribcage
骨盆 **71** pelvis
脊柱/脊髓 **72** spinal column/spinal cord

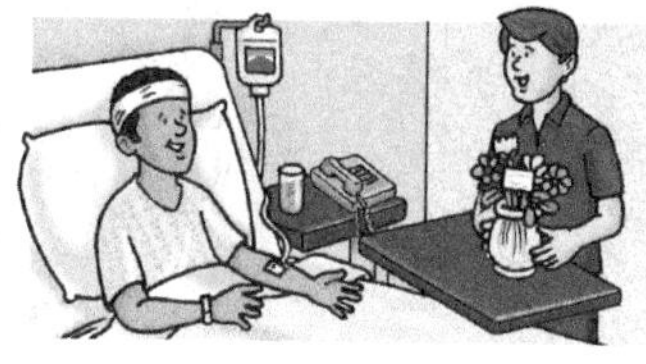

A. My doctor checked my **head** and said everything is okay.
B. I'm glad to hear that.

[1, 3–7, 12–29, 31–51]
A. Ooh!
B. What's the matter?
{My ________ hurts!
{My ________s hurt!

[52–72]
A. My doctor wants me to have some tests.
B. Why?
A. She's concerned about my ________.

Describe yourself as completely as you can.

Which parts of the body are most important at school? at work? when you play your favorite sport?

疾病，症状，伤情

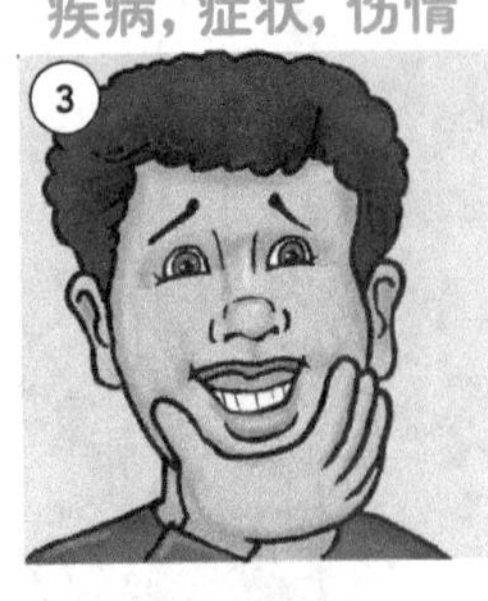

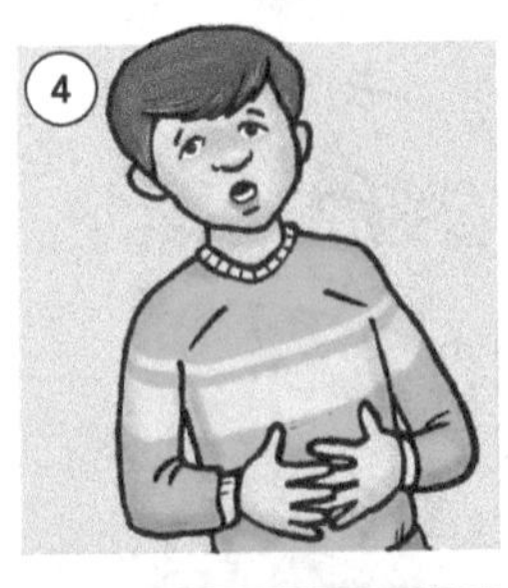

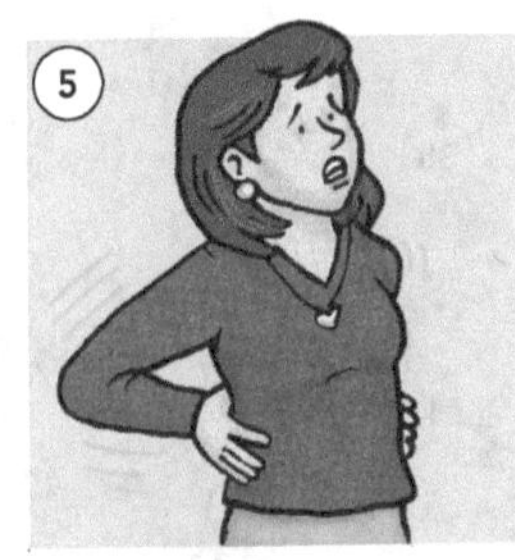

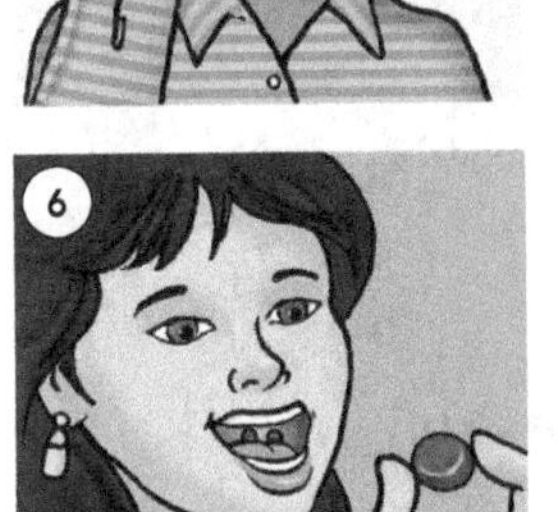

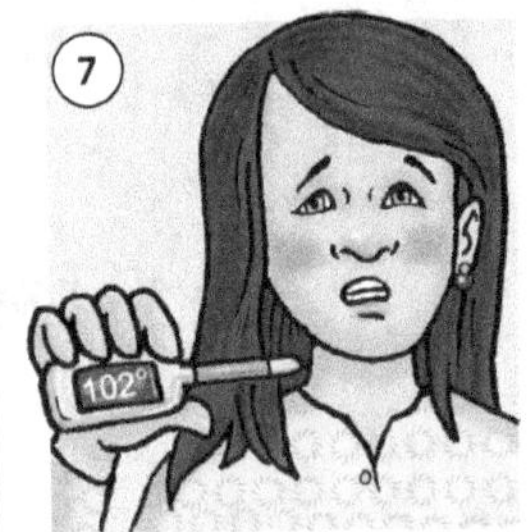

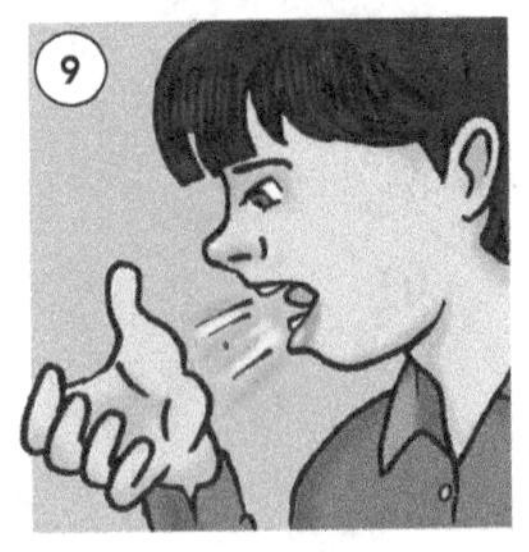

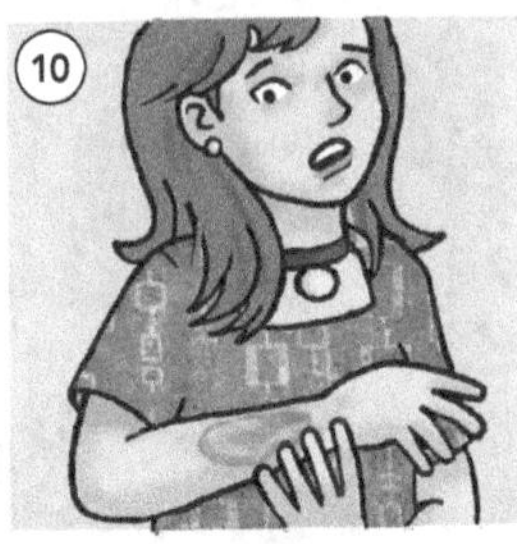

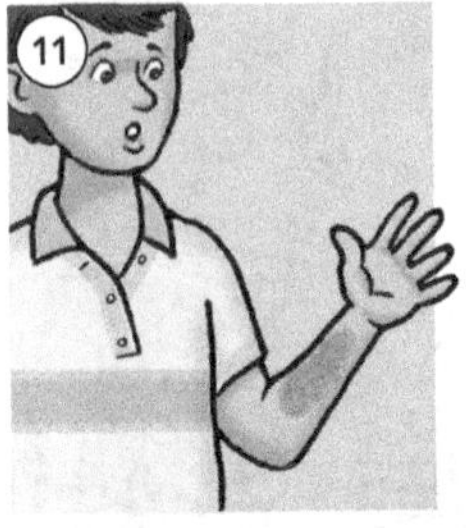

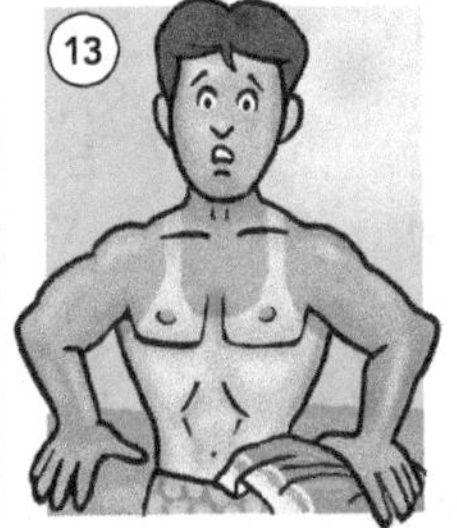

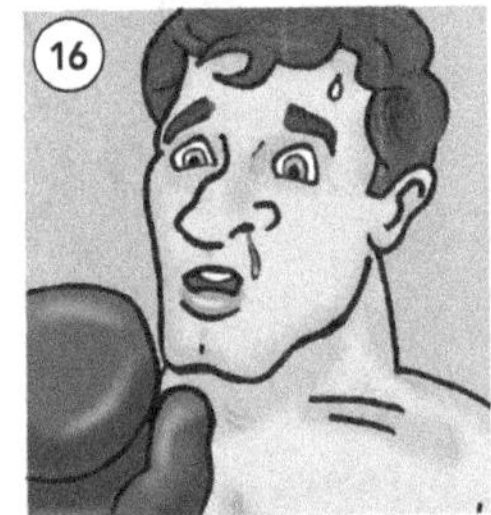

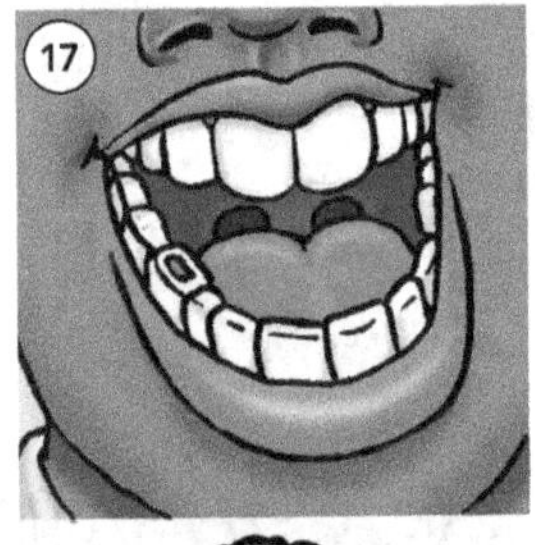

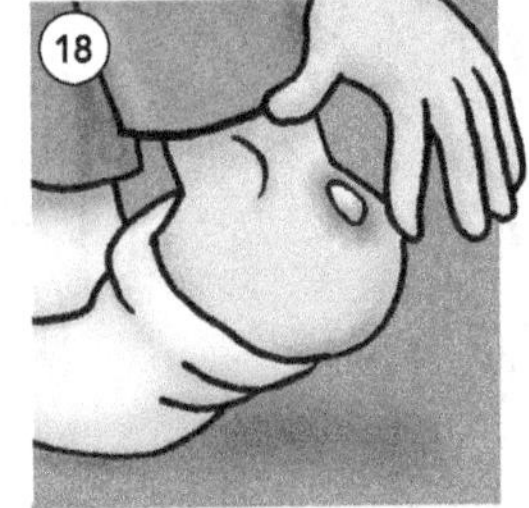

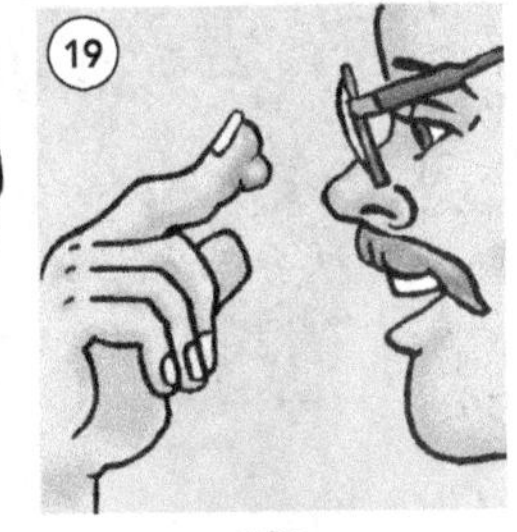

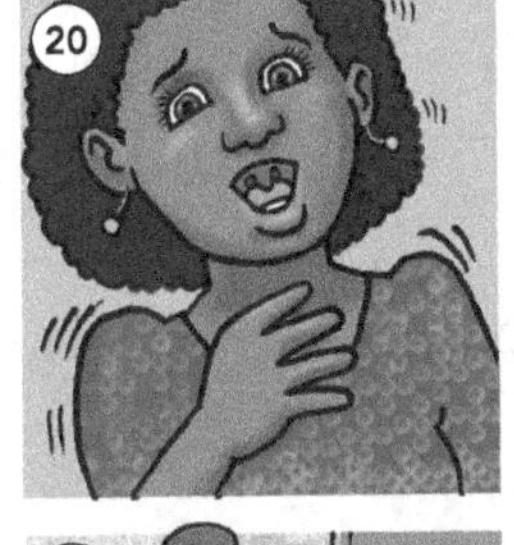

头痛 1 headache
耳朵痛 2 earache
牙痛 3 toothache
胃痛 4 stomachache
背痛 5 backache
喉咙痛 6 sore throat
发烧 7 fever/temperature
感冒 8 cold
咳嗽 9 cough

感染 10 infection
疹子 11 rash
虫咬 12 insect bite
晒伤 13 sunburn
颈僵硬 14 stiff neck
流鼻涕 15 runny nose
流鼻血 16 bloody nose
蛀牙 17 cavity
水泡 18 blister

疣 19 wart
打嗝 20 (the) hiccups
发冷 21 (the) chills
腹绞痛 22 cramps
腹泻 23 diarrhea
胸口痛 24 chest pain
气促/呼吸短促 25 shortness of breath
喉(头)炎 26 laryngitis

A. What's the matter?
B. I have a/an __[1–19]__.

A. What's the matter?
B. I have __[20–26]__.

昏厥	27	faint
晕眩	28	dizzy
恶心	29	nauseous
胀气	30	bloated
鼻塞	31	congested
精疲力竭	32	exhausted
咳嗽	33	cough
打喷嚏	34	sneeze
喘息	35	wheeze
打饱嗝	36	burp
呕吐	37	vomit/ throw up
流血	38	bleed
扭伤	39	twist
刮伤/抓伤	40	scratch
擦伤	41	scrape
使……瘀青	42	bruise
烫伤	43	burn
受伤(现在式)－受伤(过去式)	44	hurt–hurt
切(现在式)－切(过去式)	45	cut–cut
扭伤	46	sprain
使……脱臼	47	dislocate
折断(现在式)－折断(过去式)	48	break–broke
肿	49	swollen
痒	50	itchy

A. What's the problem?

B. I feel [27–30].
I'm [31–32].
I've been [33–38]ing a lot.

A. What happened?

B. I [39–45]ed my ....
I think I [46–48]ed my ....
My .... is/are [49–50].

A. How do you feel?

B. Not so good./Not very well./Terrible!

A. What's the matter?

B. ...., ..., and ....

A. I'm sorry to hear that.

Tell about the last time you didn't feel well. What was the matter?

Tell about a time you hurt yourself. What happened? How? What did you do about it?

What do you do when you have a cold? a stomachache? an insect bite? the hiccups?

FIRST AID
急救

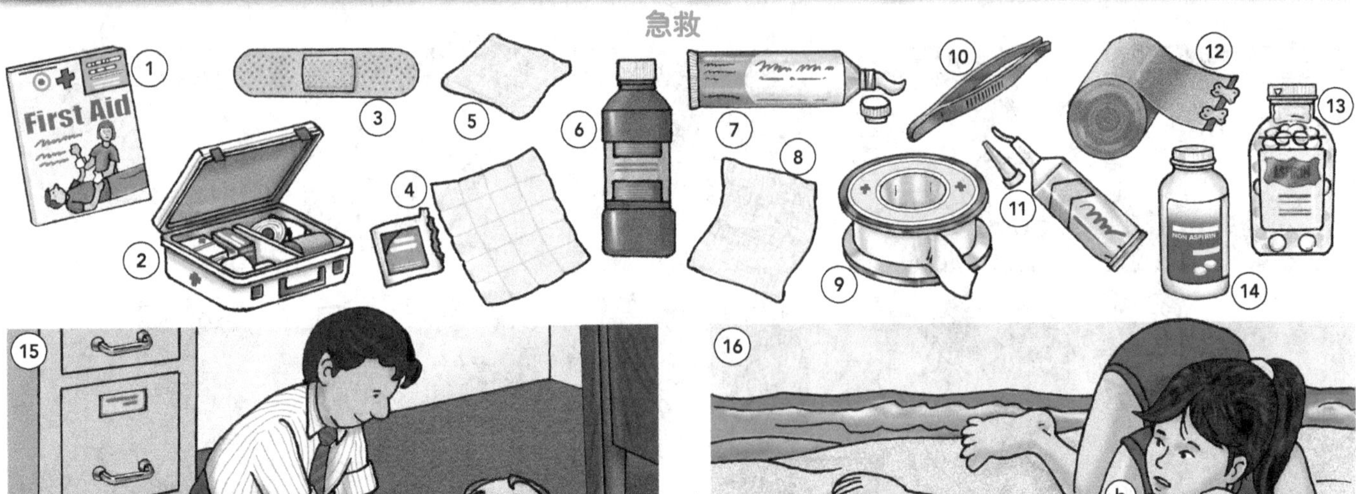

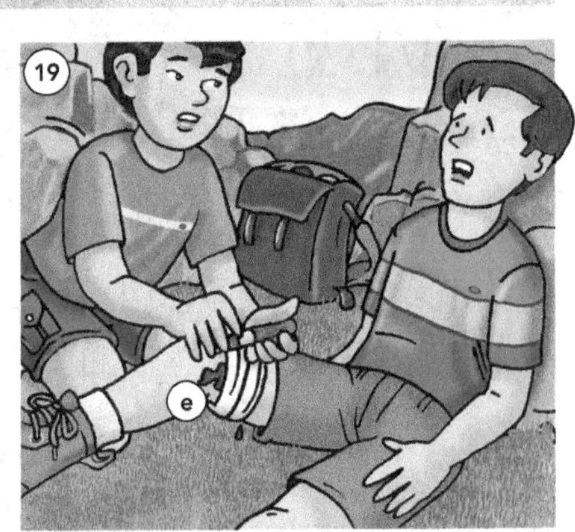

急救手册	1	first-aid manual	阿司匹林(解热镇痛药)	13	aspirin
急救箱	2	first-aid kit	不含阿司匹林的止痛药	14	non-aspirin pain reliever
护创胶布/OK绷带/绷带	3	(adhesive) bandage/ Band-Aid™	心肺复苏术	15	CPR (cardiopulmonary resuscitation)
消毒灭菌巾	4	antiseptic cleansing wipe	没有脉搏	a	has no pulse
消毒纱布垫	5	sterile (dressing) pad	人工呼吸	16	rescue breathing
双氧水	6	hydrogen peroxide	没有呼吸	b	isn't breathing
抗生素软膏	7	antibiotic ointment	海姆利克氏操作法(使堵住喉咙的异物吐出的急救措施)	17	the Heimlich maneuver
纱布	8	gauze	噎到	c	is choking
胶带	9	adhesive tape	夹板	18	splint
镊子	10	tweezers	手指断了	d	broke a finger
止痒霜剂	11	antihistamine cream	止血带	19	tourniquet
弹性绷带	12	elastic bandage/ Ace™ bandage	在流血	e	is bleeding

A. Do we have any [3–5, 12]s/ [6–11, 13, 14]?
B. Yes. Look in the first-aid kit.

A. Help! My friend [a–e]!
B. I can help!
I know how to do [15–17].
I can make a [18, 19].

Do you have a first-aid kit? If you do, what's in it? If you don't, where can you buy one?

Tell about a time when you gave or received first aid.

Where can a person learn first aid in your community?

急救与疾病

受伤 **1** hurt/injured
休克/惊愕 **2** in shock
不省人事 **3** unconscious
中暑 **4** heatstroke
冻伤 **5** frostbite
心脏病发作 **6** heart attack
过敏反应 **7** allergic reaction
吞下毒物 **8** swallow poison
药用过量 **9** overdose on drugs
摔倒(现在式)－摔倒(过去式) **10** fall–fell
触电（现在式）- 触电（过去式） **11** get–got an electric shock
流行性感冒 **12** the flu/influenza
耳朵发炎 **13** an ear infection

链球菌性喉炎 **14** strep throat
麻疹 **15** measles
腮腺炎 **16** mumps
水痘 **17** chicken pox
气喘 **18** asthma
癌症 **19** cancer
忧郁症 **20** depression
糖尿病 **21** diabetes
心脏病 **22** heart disease
高血压 **23** high blood pressure/
高血压 hypertension
结核病 **24** TB/tuberculosis
爱滋病 **25** AIDS*

* Acquired Immune Deficiency Syndrome

A. What happened?
B. My .... { is ___[1–3]___. / has ___[4–5]___. / is having a/an ___[6–7]___. / ___[8–11]___ed. }
A. What's your location?
B. ......(address)......

A. My .... is sick.
B. What's the matter?
A. He/She has ___[12–25]___.
B. I'm sorry to hear that.

Tell about a medical emergency that happened to you or someone you know.

Which illnesses in this lesson are you familiar with?

THE MEDICAL EXAM

健康检查

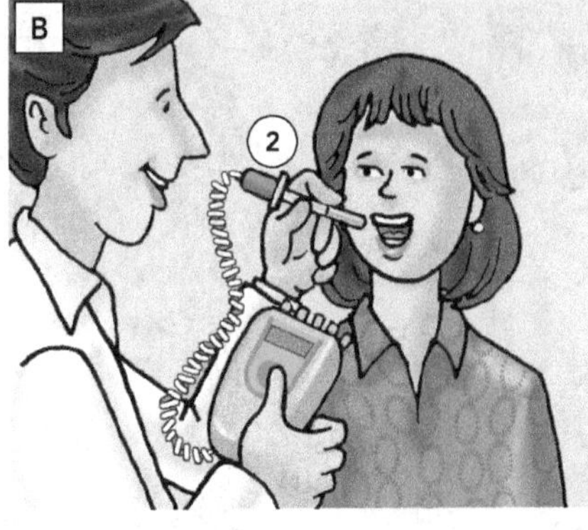

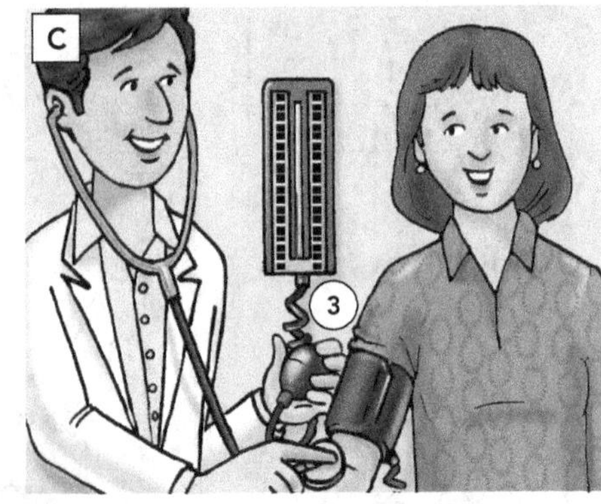

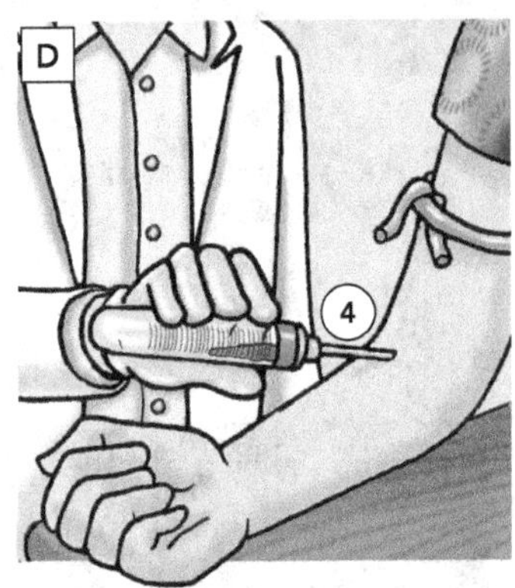

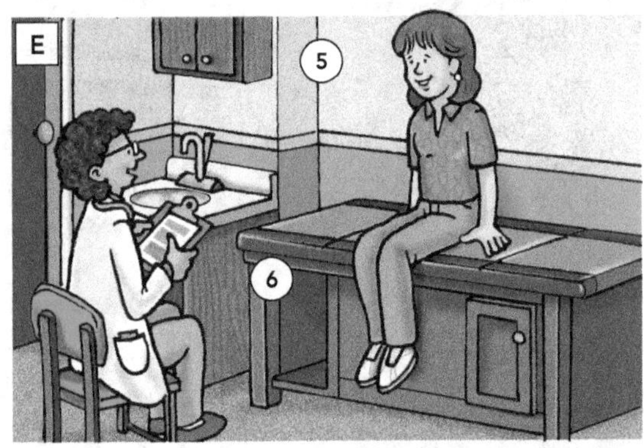

量你的身高体重 **A** measure *your* height and weight
量你的体温 **B** take *your* temperature
量你的血压 **C** check *your* blood pressure
抽血 **D** draw some blood
问你一些有关你身体状况的问题 **E** ask *you* some questions about *your* health
检查你的眼睛、耳朵、鼻子和喉咙 **F** examine *your* eyes, ears, nose, and throat
听你的心脏 **G** listen to *your* heart
照胸肺X光 **H** take a chest X-ray

秤 **1** scale
温度计 **2** thermometer
血压计 **3** blood pressure gauge
注射针/注射筒 **4** needle/syringe
检查室 **5** examination room
检查台 **6** examination table
视力检查表 **7** eye chart
听诊器 **8** stethoscope
X光机 **9** X-ray machine

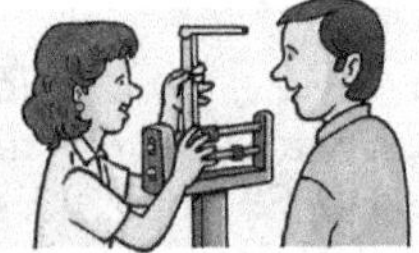

[A–H]
A. Now I'm going to **measure your height and weight.**
B. All right.

[A–H]
A. What did the doctor/nurse do during the examination?
B. She/He **measured my height and weight.**

[1–3, 5–9]
A. So, how do you like our new **scale?**
B. It's very nice, doctor.

How often do you have a medical exam? What does the doctor/nurse do?

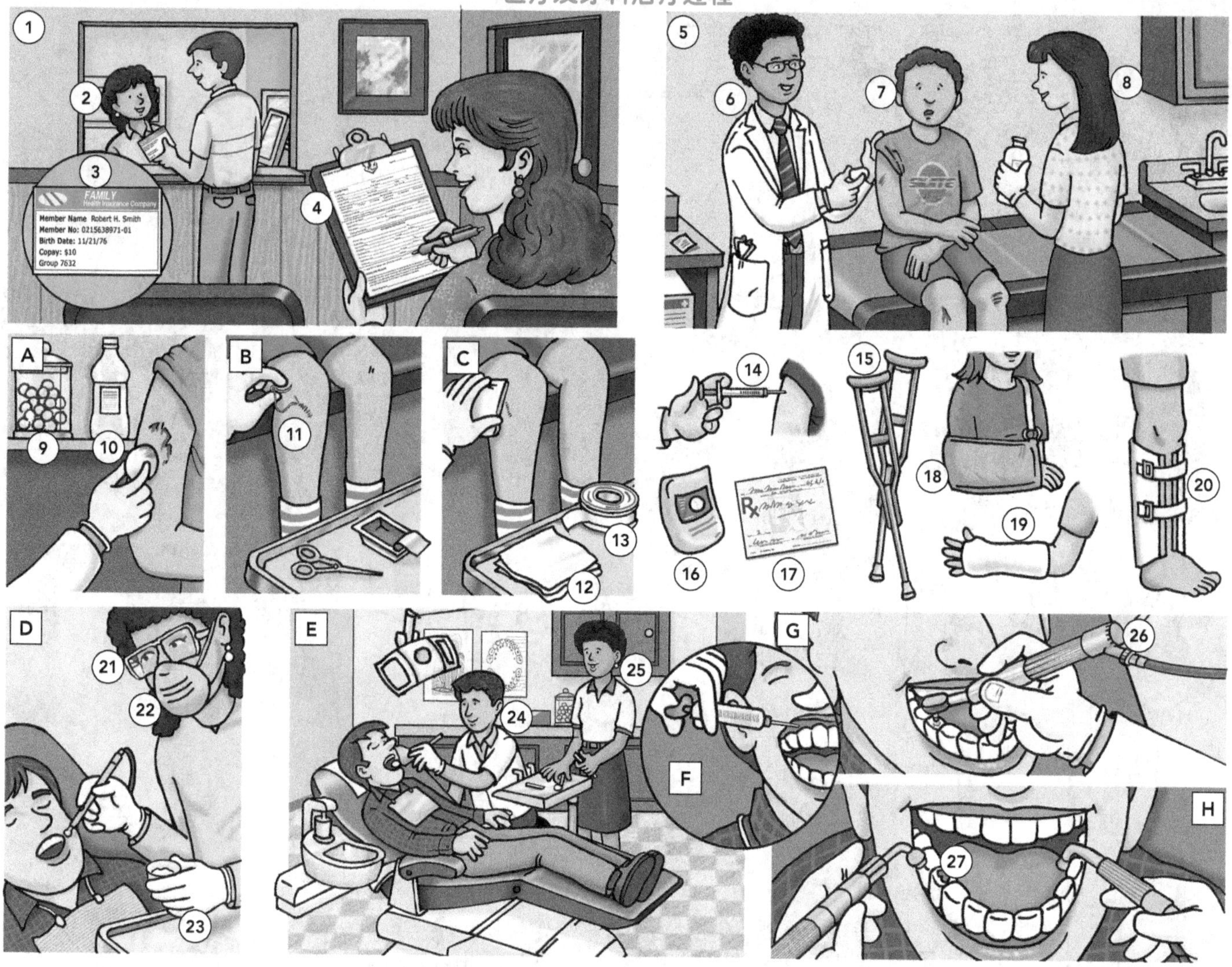

清洗伤口	A	clean the wound
闭合伤口	B	close the wound
包扎伤口	C	dress the wound
洗你的牙齿	D	clean *your* teeth
检查你的牙齿	E	examine *your* teeth
给你一针麻醉剂	F	give *you* a shot of anesthetic/ Novocaine™
钻蛀牙洞	G	drill the cavity
补牙	H	fill the tooth
候诊室	1	waiting room
接待员	2	receptionist
医保卡	3	insurance card
医疗病史表格	4	medical history form
检查室	5	examination room
医生	6	doctor/physician
病人	7	patient
护士	8	nurse
棉花球	9	cotton balls
酒精	10	alcohol
缝针	11	stitches
纱布	12	gauze
胶带	13	tape
打针	14	injection/shot
丁字形拐杖	15	crutches
冰袋	16	ice pack
处方	17	prescription
吊腕带	18	sling
固定用敷料/石膏	19	cast
矫形器/支具	20	brace
牙科卫生员	21	dental hygienist
口罩	22	mask
手套	23	gloves
牙医	24	dentist
牙科助理	25	dental assistant
牙医电钻	26	drill
补牙填充料	27	filling

A. Now I'm going to { ___[A–H]___.
give you (a/an) ___[14–17]___.
put your .... in a ___[18–20]___.

B. Okay.

A. I need { ___[9, 10, 12, 13, 23]___.
a ___[22, 26]___.

B. Here you are.

Tell about a personal experience you had with a medical or dental procedure.

MEDICAL ADVICE

医生指示

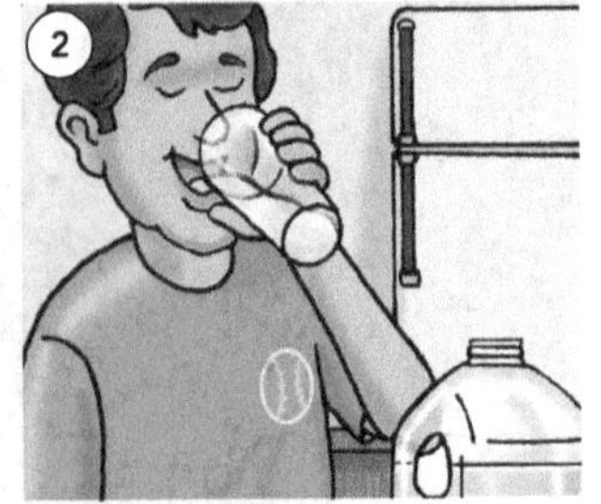

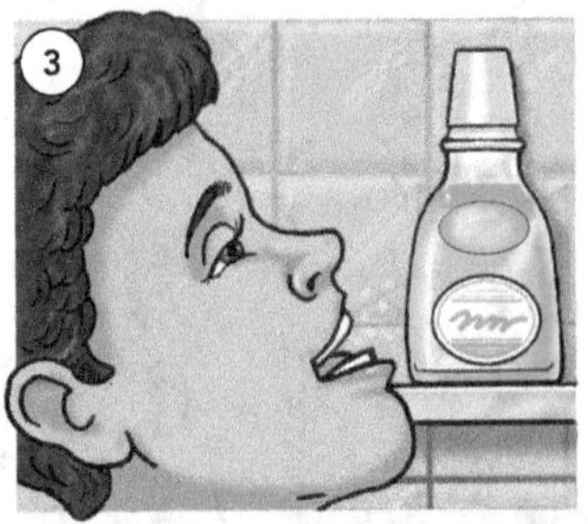

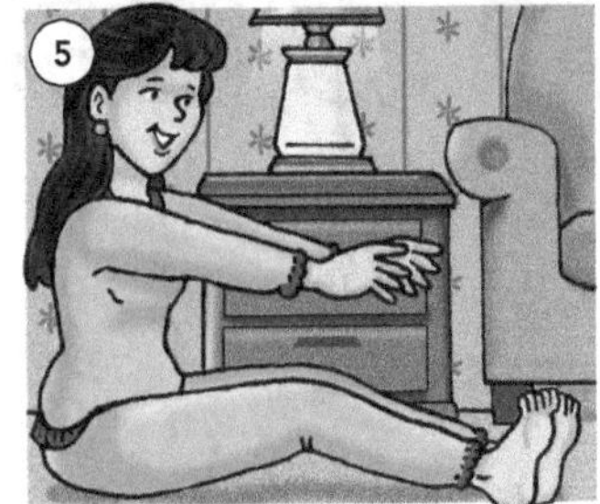

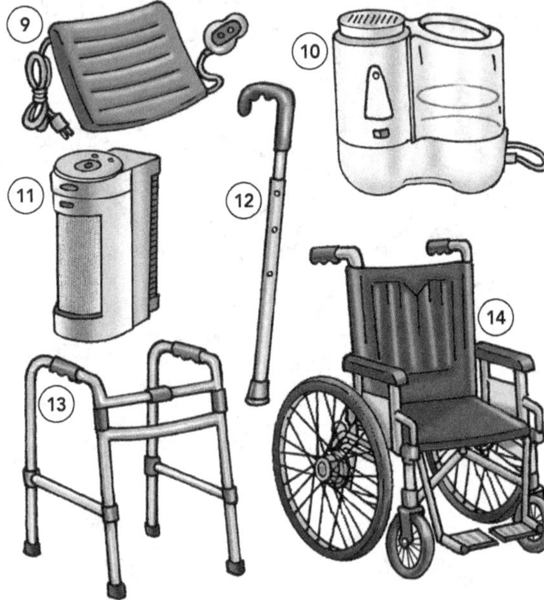

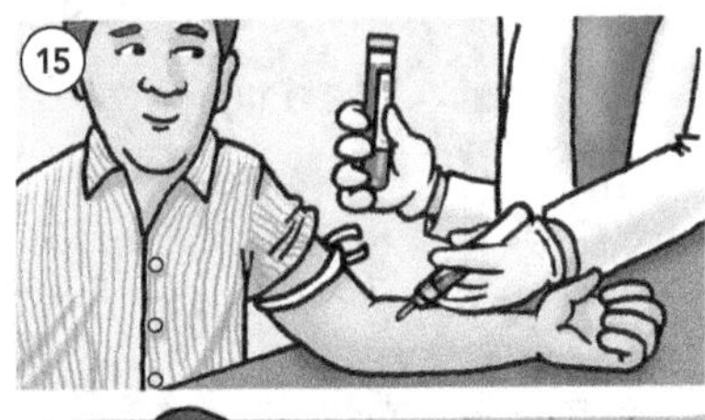

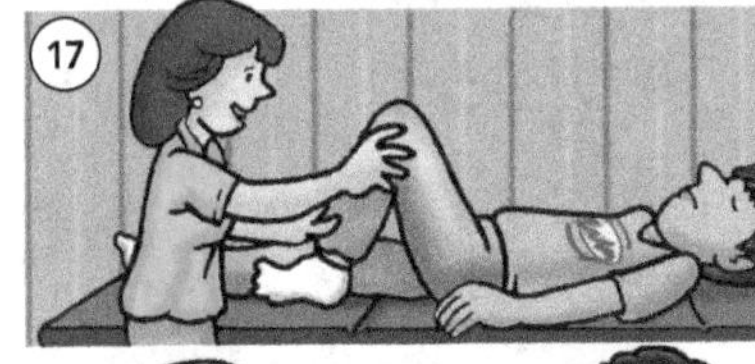

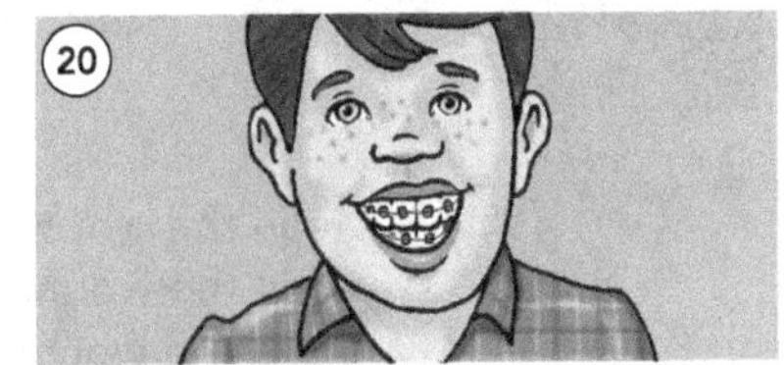

卧床休息 1 rest in bed
喝液体 2 drink fluids
漱口 3 gargle
控制饮食 4 go on a diet
做运动 5 exercise
服用维他命 6 take vitamins
看专科医生 7 see a specialist
针灸 8 get acupuncture
热敷垫 9 heating pad
增湿机 10 humidifier

空气清新机 11 air purifier
拐杖 12 cane
助行架 13 walker
轮椅 14 wheelchair
验血 15 blood work/blood tests
检查 16 tests
物理治疗 17 physical therapy
手术 18 surgery
咨询辅导 19 counseling
牙齿矫正器 20 braces

A. I think { you should __[1–8]__.
you should use a/an __[9–14]__.
you need __[15–20]__.

B. I see.

A. What did the doctor say?

B. The doctor thinks { I should __[1–8]__.
I should use a/an __[9–14]__.
I need __[15–20]__.

Tell about medical advice a doctor gave you. What did the doctor say? Did you follow the advice?

阿司匹林 **1** aspirin
感冒药片 **2** cold tablets
维他命/维生素 **3** vitamins
止咳糖浆 **4** cough syrup
不含阿司匹林的止痛药 **5** non-aspirin pain reliever
止咳糖 **6** cough drops
润喉糖 **7** throat lozenges
健胃药片/抗酸药片 **8** antacid tablets
鼻塞喷剂 **9** decongestant spray/ nasal spray
眼药水 **10** eye drops
软膏 **11** ointment
乳霜 **12** cream/creme
乳液 **13** lotion
药丸 **14** pill
药片 **15** tablet
胶囊 **16** capsule
椭圆形药片 **17** caplet
茶匙 **18** teaspoon
汤匙 **19** tablespoon

[1–13]
A. What did the doctor say?
B. { She/He told me to take ___[1–4]___/a ___[5]___.
  { She/He told me to use ___[6–13]___.

[14–19]
A. What's the dosage?
B. One ______ every four hours.

What medicines in this lesson do you have at home? What other medicines do you have?

What do you take or use for a fever? a headache? a stomachache? a sore throat? a cold? a cough?

Tell about any medicines in your country that are different from the ones in this lesson.

MEDICAL SPECIALISTS

医疗专家

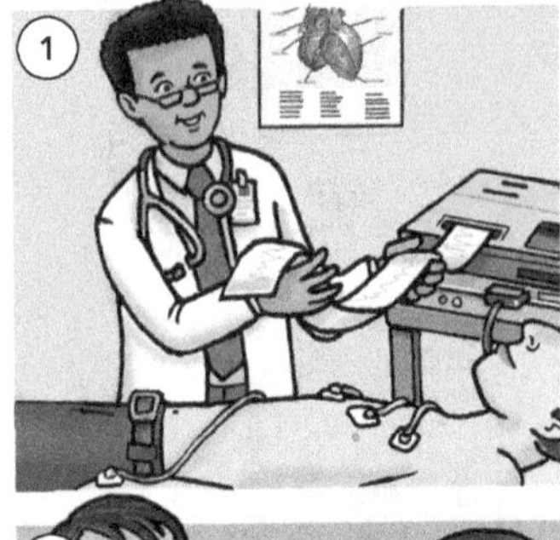

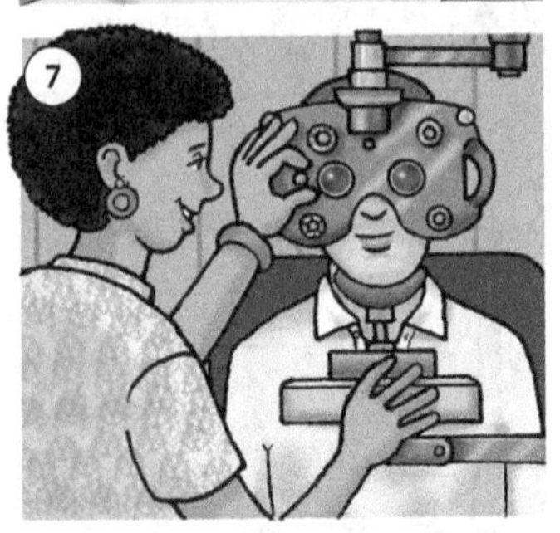
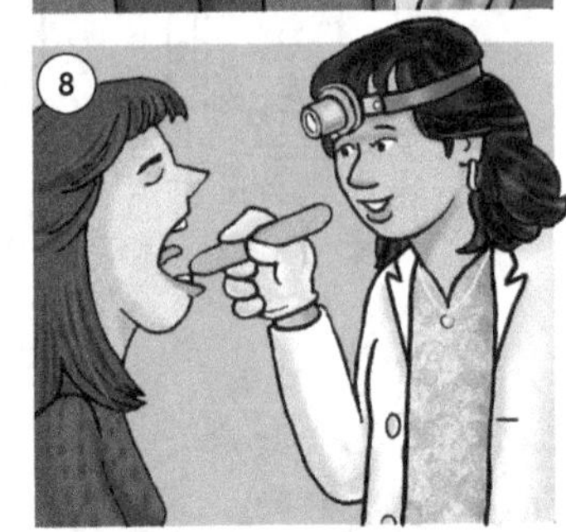

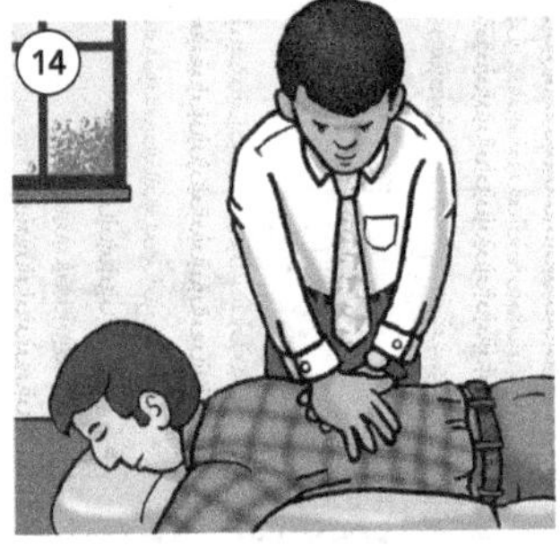
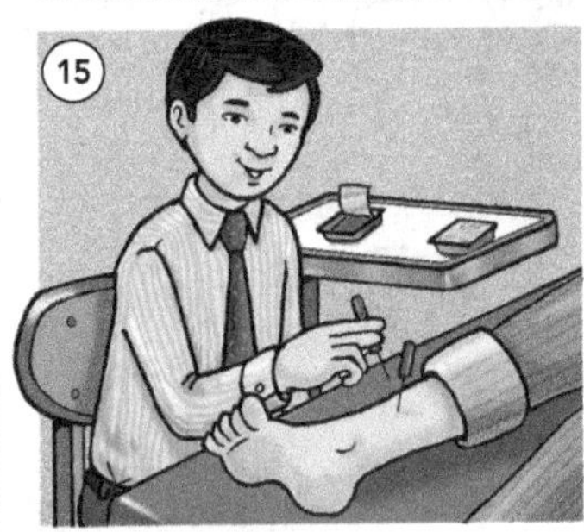
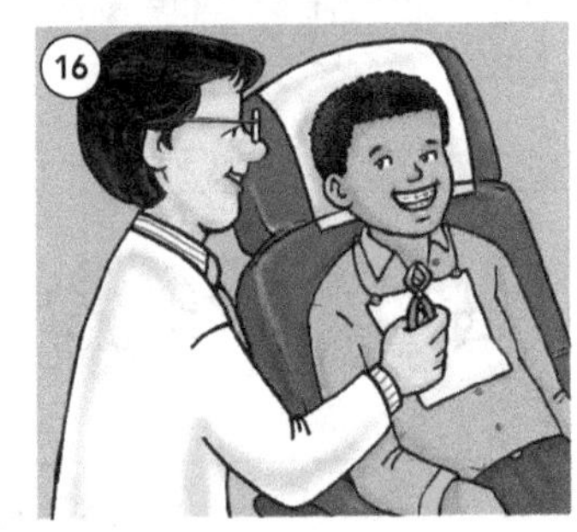

心脏科医师	1	cardiologist
妇产科医师	2	gynecologist
小儿科医师	3	pediatrician
老年科医师	4	gerontologist
过敏症专科医师	5	allergist
矫形外科医师	6	orthopedist
眼科医生	7	ophthalmologist
耳鼻喉科医生	8	ear, nose, and throat (ENT) specialist
听力检查师	9	audiologist
物理治疗师	10	physical therapist
咨询辅导员/治疗师	11	counselor/therapist
精神科医师	12	psychiatrist
肠胃科医生	13	gastroenterologist
脊椎指压治疗师	14	chiropractor
针灸医生	15	acupuncturist
牙齿矫正医生	16	orthodontist

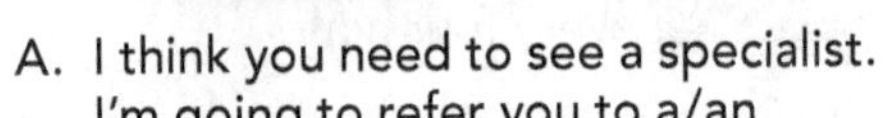

A. I think you need to see a specialist.
I'm going to refer you to a/an _______.
B. A/An _______?
A. Yes.

A. When is your next appointment with the _______?
B. It's at ......(time)...... on ......(date)......

Do you or members of your family see any of these medical specialists? Which ones?

医院

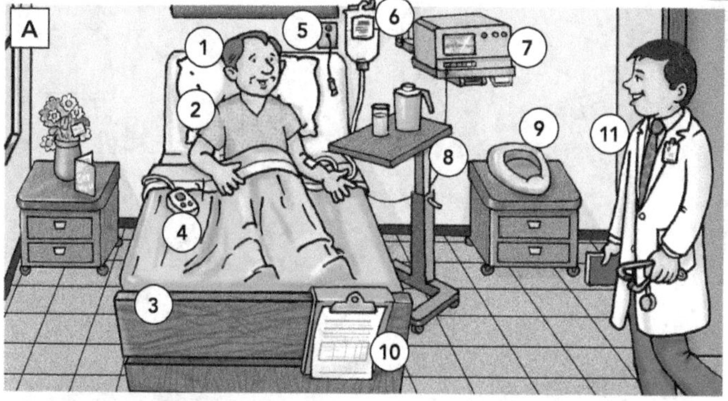

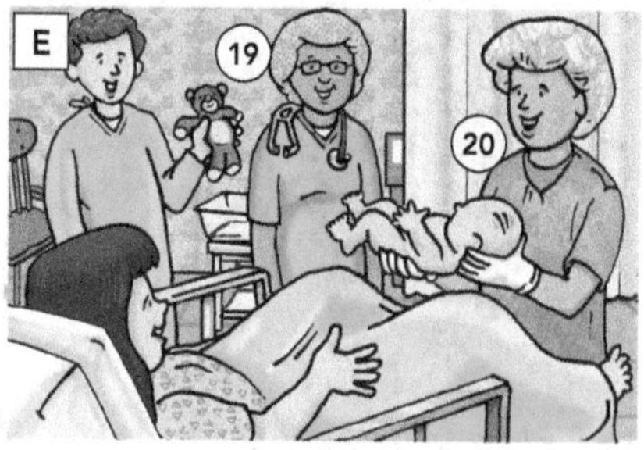

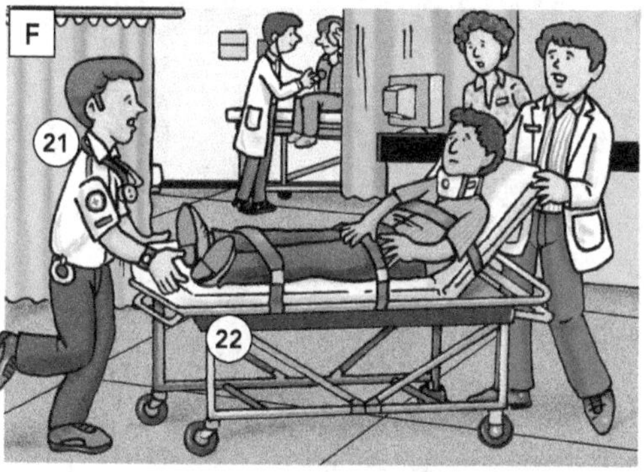

病房 **A patient's room**
- 病人 1 patient
- 住院服 2 hospital gown
- 病床 3 hospital bed
- 病床控制器 4 bed control
- 呼叫按钮/求助按钮 5 call button
- 静脉注射 6 I.V.
- 生命表征监测器 7 vital signs monitor
- 病床伸缩活动桌 8 bed table
- (床上用)便盆 9 bed pan
- 病历 10 medical chart
- 医生 11 doctor/physician

护士站 **B nurse's station**
- 护士 12 nurse
- 营养学专家 13 dietitian
- 护理员 14 orderly

手术室 **C operating room**
- 外科医生 15 surgeon
- 外科护士 16 surgical nurse
- 麻醉医师 17 anesthesiologist

等候室/候诊室 **D waiting room**
- 义工 18 volunteer

产房 **E birthing room / delivery room**
- 产科医师 19 obstetrician
- 助产士 20 midwife/nurse-midwife

急诊室 **F emergency room / ER**
- 紧急医疗技术人员 21 emergency medical technician/EMT
- 轮床 22 gurney

放射科 **G radiology department**
- X光技术员 23 X-ray technician
- 放射线技师 24 radiologist

检验室/化验室 **H laboratory / lab**
- 化验室技术员 25 lab technician

A. This is your ___[2–10]___.
B. I see.

A. Do you work here?
B. Yes. I'm a/an ___[11–21, 23–25]___.

A. Where's the ___[11–21, 23–25]___?
B. She's/He's { in the ___[A, C–H]___. / at the ___[B]___.

Tell about an experience you or a family member had in the hospital.

个人卫生

刷我的牙齿 **A brush *my* teeth**
牙刷 1 toothbrush
牙膏 2 toothpaste

用牙线清洁我的牙齿 **B floss *my* teeth**
牙线 3 dental floss

漱口 **C gargle**
漱口水 4 mouthwash

美白我的牙齿 **D whiten *my* teeth**
牙齿美白剂 5 teeth whitener

盆浴 **E bathe/take a bath**
香皂 6 soap
泡泡沐浴液 7 bubble bath

洗淋浴 **F take a shower**
浴帽 8 shower cap

洗我的头发 **G wash *my* hair**
洗发精 9 shampoo
润发乳 10 conditioner/rinse

弄干我的头发 **H dry *my* hair**
吹风机 11 hair dryer/blow dryer

梳我的头发 **I comb *my* hair**
尺梳 12 comb

梳我的头发 **J brush *my* hair**
梳子 13 (hair) brush

帮我的头发做造型 **K style *my* hair**
卷发棒 14 hot comb/curling iron
喷发定型剂 15 hairspray
发胶 16 hair gel
小发夹 17 bobby pin
条状发夹 18 barrette
发夹 19 hairclip

刮胡子 L **shave**
刮胡膏 20 shaving cream
刮胡刀 21 razor
刮胡刀片 22 razor blade
电动刮胡刀 23 electric shaver
止血笔 24 styptic pencil
刮胡后润肤液 25 aftershave (lotion)

修(涂)我的指甲 M **do *my* nails**
指甲锉 26 nail file
指甲砂锉 27 emery board
剪指甲刀 28 nail clipper
指甲刷 29 nail brush
剪刀 30 scissors

指甲油 31 nail polish
洗甲水 32 nail polish remover

涂抹 N **put on . . .**
防臭剂 33 deodorant
护手乳液 34 hand lotion
身体润肤乳液 35 body lotion
爽身粉 36 powder
古龙水/香水 37 cologne/perfume
防晒油 38 sunscreen

化妆 O **put on makeup**
腮红 39 blush/rouge
粉底 40 foundation/base
润肤露 41 moisturizer

粉饼 42 face powder
眼线笔 43 eyeliner
眼影 44 eye shadow
睫毛膏 45 mascara
眉笔 46 eyebrow pencil
口红 47 lipstick

擦亮我的鞋 P **polish *my* shoes**
鞋油 48 shoe polish
鞋带 49 shoelaces

[A–M, N (33–38), O, P]
A. What are you doing?
B. I'm ________ing.

[1, 8, 11–14, 17–19, 21–24, 26–30, 46, 49]
A. Excuse me. Where can I find ________(s)?
B. They're in the next aisle.

[2–7, 9, 10, 15, 16, 20, 25, 31–45, 47, 48]
A. Excuse me. Where can I find ________?
B. It's in the next aisle.

Which of these personal care products do you use?

You're going on a trip. Make a list of the personal care products you need to take with you.

婴儿护理

喂食	A	**feed**
婴儿食品	1	baby food
围兜	2	bib
奶瓶	3	bottle
奶嘴	4	nipple
奶粉	5	formula
液态维他命	6	(liquid) vitamins
换尿布	B	**change the baby's diaper**
纸尿片	7	disposable diaper
布尿片	8	cloth diaper
尿布别针	9	diaper pin
婴儿湿巾	10	(baby) wipes
婴儿爽身粉	11	baby powder
成长裤/训练裤	12	training pants
软膏	13	ointment
洗澡	C	**bathe**
婴儿洗发精	14	baby shampoo
棉花棒	15	cotton swab
婴儿润肤液	16	baby lotion
抱	D	**hold**
安抚奶嘴	17	pacifier
出牙咬环	18	teething ring
喂奶	E	**nurse**
穿衣服	F	**dress**
摇	G	**rock**
育儿中心	19	child-care center
幼儿保育员	20	child-care worker
摇椅	21	rocking chair
念书给……听	H	**read to**
小柜子	22	cubby
和……玩	I	**play with**
玩具	23	toys

A. What are you doing?

B. { I'm __[A, C–I]__ing the baby.
  { I'm __[B]__ing.

A. Do we need anything from the store?

B. Yes. We need some more { __[2–4, 7–9, 15, 17, 18]__s
  { __[1, 5, 6, 10–14, 16]__.

In your opinion, which are better: cloth diapers or disposable diapers? Why?

Tell about baby products in your country.

TYPES OF SCHOOLS

学校种类

幼儿园 **1** preschool/nursery school
小学 **2** elementary school
中学/初中 **3** middle school/junior high school
高中 **4** high school
成人学校 **5** adult school
职业学校 **6** vocational school/trade school
社区学院 **7** community college
学院 **8** college
大学 **9** university
研究生院 **10** graduate school
法学院 **11** law school
医学院 **12** medical school

A. Are you a student?
B. Yes. I'm in __[1–4, 8, 10–12]__.

A. Are you a student?
B. Yes. I go to a/an __[5–7, 9]__.

A. Is this apartment building near a/an ______?
B. Yes. ...*(name of school)*... is nearby.

A. Tell me about your previous education.
B. I went to ...*(name of school)*....
A. Did you like it there?
B. Yes. It was an excellent ______.

What types of schools are there in your community? What are their names, and where are they located?

What types of schools have you gone to? Where? When? What did you study?

学校

办公室	A	(main) office
校长室	B	principal's office
护理办公室	C	nurse's office
辅导室/训导处	D	guidance office
教室	E	classroom
走廊	F	hallway
衣物柜	a	locker
科学实验室	G	science lab
室内体育馆	H	gym/gymnasium
更衣间	a	locker room
跑道	I	track
露天看台	a	bleachers
运动场	J	field
大礼堂	K	auditorium
餐厅	L	cafeteria
图书馆	M	library
学校职员/学校秘书	1	clerk/ (school) secretary
校长	2	principal
驻校护士	3	(school) nurse
学生辅导顾问/训导员	4	(guidance) counselor
老师	5	teacher
副校长	6	assistant principal/ vice-principal
警卫人员	7	security officer
自然科学老师	8	science teacher
体育老师	9	P.E. teacher
教练	10	coach
管理员	11	custodian
餐厅工作人员	12	cafeteria worker
餐厅管理员	13	lunchroom monitor
学校图书管理员	14	(school) librarian

A. Where are you going?
B. I'm going to the ___[A–D, G–M]___.
A. Do you have a hall pass?
B. Yes. Here it is.

A. Where's the ___[1–14]___?
B. He's/She's in the ___[A–M]___.

Describe the school where you study English. Tell about the rooms, offices, and people.

Tell about differences between the school in this lesson and schools in your country.

学科

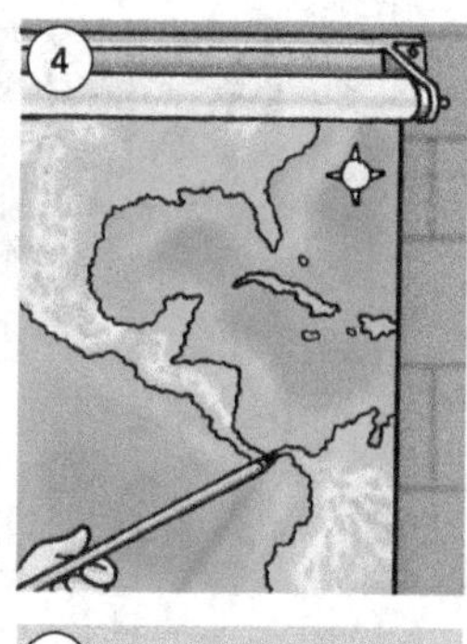

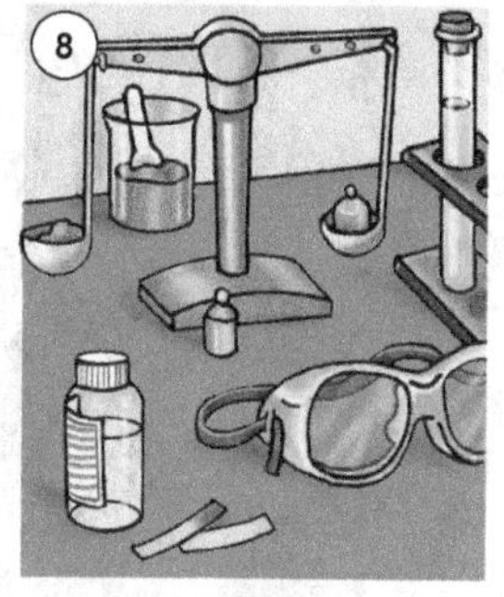

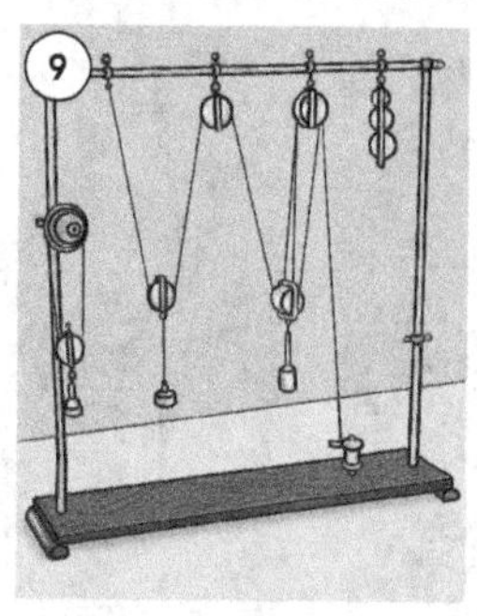

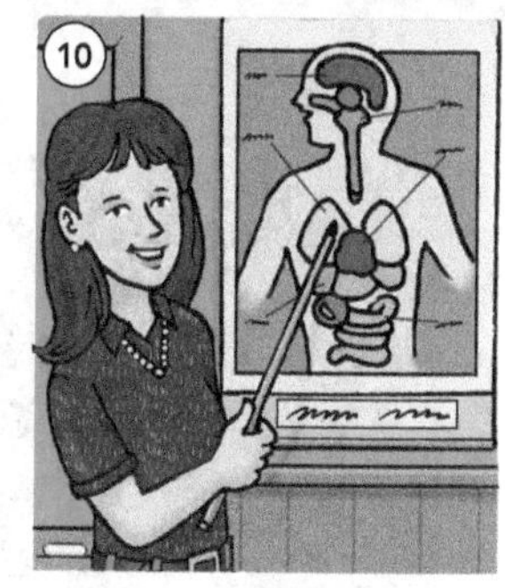

数学 **1** math/mathematics
英语 **2** English
历史 **3** history
地理 **4** geography
政府体制 **5** government
自然 **6** science
生物 **7** biology
化学 **8** chemistry
物理 **9** physics
健康教育 **10** health

电脑科学 **11** computer science
西班牙语 **12** Spanish
法语 **13** French
家政 **14** home economics
工艺课 **15** industrial arts/shop
商业教育 **16** business education
体育 **17** physical education/P.E.
驾驶班 **18** driver's education/driver's ed
艺术 **19** art
音乐 **20** music

A. What do you have next period?
B. **Math**. How about you?
A. **English**.
B. There's the bell. I've got to go.

What is/was your favorite subject? Why?

In your opinion, what's the most interesting subject? the most difficult subject? Why do you think so?

EXTRACURRICULAR ACTIVITIES

课外活动

乐队 **1** band
管弦乐团 **2** orchestra
合唱团 **3** choir/chorus
戏剧表演 **4** drama
(美式)橄榄球 **5** football
啦啦队 **6** cheerleading/pep squad
学生会 **7** student government
社区服务 **8** community service
校报 **9** school newspaper
学校年册 **10** yearbook
文学杂志 **11** literary magazine
影音小组 **12** A.V. crew
辩论社 **13** debate club
电脑社 **14** computer club
国际社 **15** international club
国际象棋社 **16** chess club

A. Are you going home right after school?

B. { No. I have ___[1–6]___ practice.
No. I have a ___[7–16]___ meeting.

What extracurricular activities do/did you participate in?

Which extracurricular activities in this lesson are there in schools in your country? What other activities are there?

Arithmetic 算数

2+1=3 8-3=5 4x2=8 10÷2=5

加法 addition	减法 subtraction	乘法 multiplication	除法 division
2 **plus** 1 **equals*** 3.	8 **minus** 3 **equals*** 5.	4 **times** 2 **equals*** 8.	10 **divided by** 2 **equals*** 5.

You can also say:* **is

A. How much is *two plus one?*
B. *Two plus one* equals/is *three.*

Make conversations for the arithmetic problems above and others.

Fractions 分数

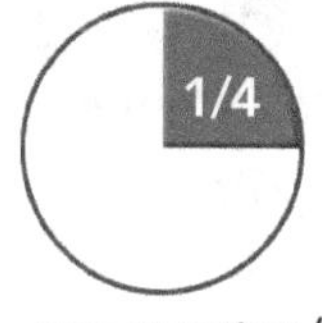

one quarter/ one fourth

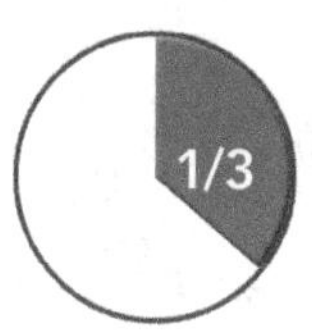

one third

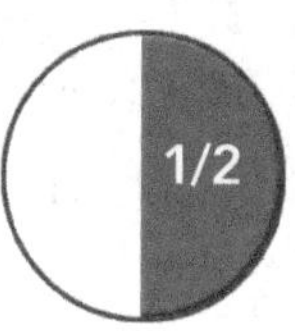

one half/ half

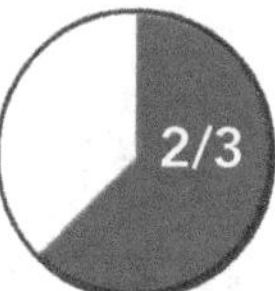

two thirds

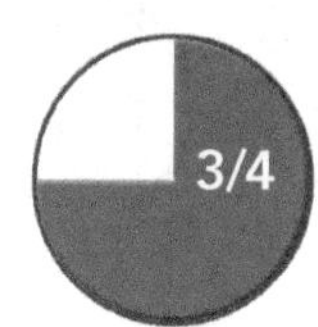

three quarters/ three fourths

A. Is this on sale?
B. Yes. It's ________ off the regular price.

A. Is the gas tank almost empty?
B. It's about ________ full.

Percents 百分比

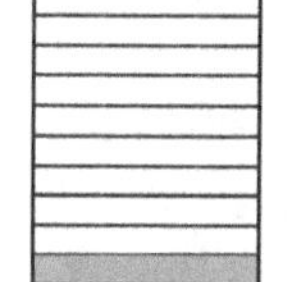
10% ten percent

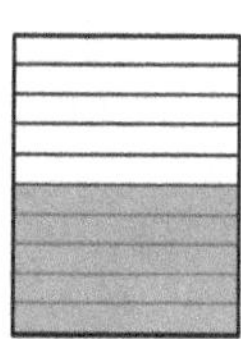
50% fifty percent

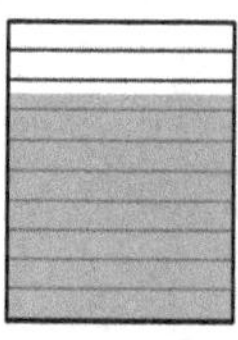
75% seventy-five percent

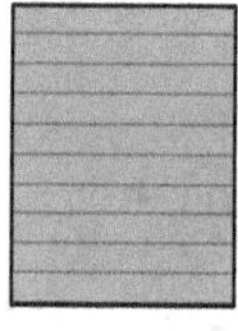
100% one-hundred percent

A. How did you do on the test?
B. I got ________ percent of the answers right.

A. What's the weather forecast?
B. There's a ________ percent chance of rain.

Types of Math 数学种类

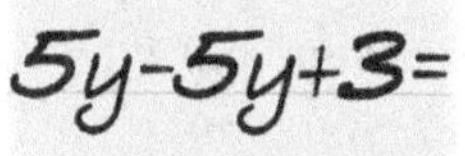

algebra
代数

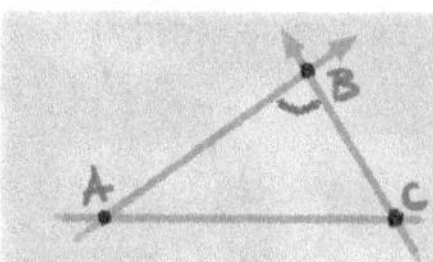

geometry
几何

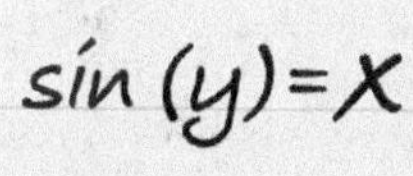

trigonometry
三角

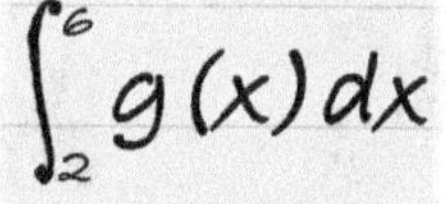

calculus
微积分

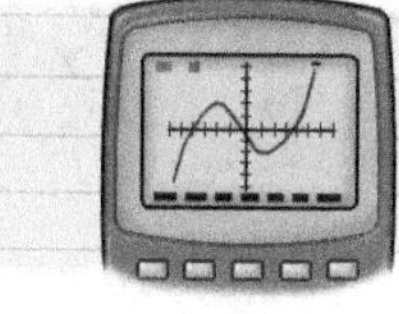
statistics
统计学

A. What math course are you taking this year?
B. I'm taking ________.

Are you good at math?

What math courses do/did you take in school?

Tell about something you bought on sale. How much off the regular price was it?

Research and discuss: What percentage of people in your country live in cities? live on farms? work in factories? vote in general elections?

MEASUREMENTS AND GEOMETRIC SHAPES

测量及几何形状

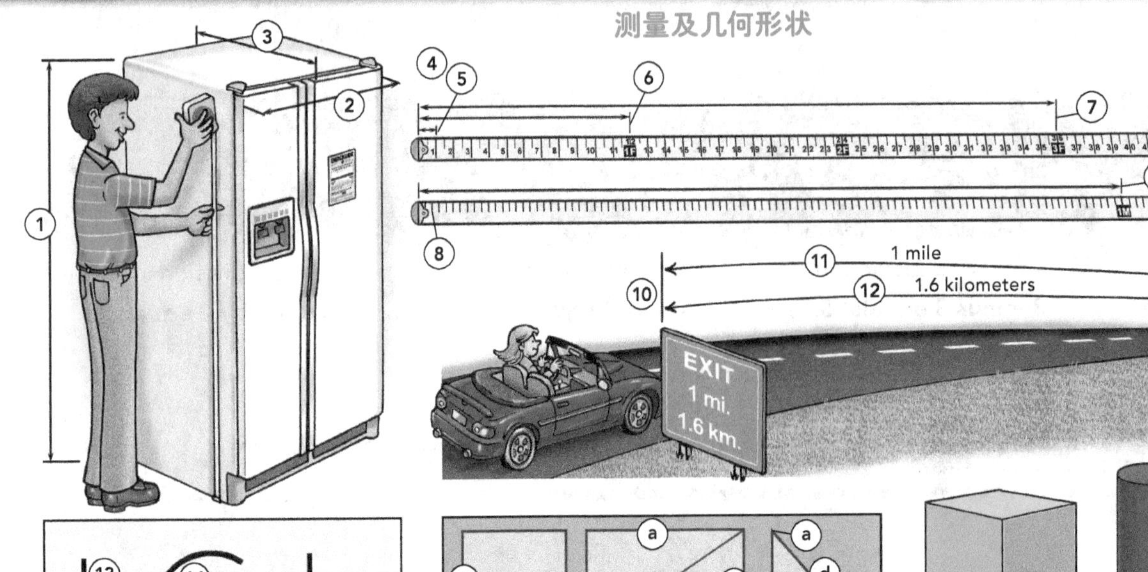

测量 Measurements

- 高度 **1** height
- 宽度 **2** width
- 深度 **3** depth
- 长度 **4** length
- 英寸 **5** inch
- 英尺（单数）-（复数） **6** foot–feet
- 码 **7** yard
- 厘米 **8** centimeter
- 米 **9** meter
- 距离 **10** distance
- 英里 **11** mile
- 公里 **12** kilometer

线 Lines

- 直线 **13** straight line
- 曲线 **14** curved line
- 平行线 **15** parallel lines
- 垂直线 **16** perpendicular lines

几何形状 Geometric Shapes

- 正方形 **17** square
  - 边 **a** side
- 长方形 **18** rectangle
  - 长 **a** length
  - 宽 **b** width
  - 对角线 **c** diagonal
- 直角三角形 **19** right triangle
  - 顶点 **a** apex
  - 直角 **b** right angle
  - 底边 **c** base
  - 直角三角形的斜边 **d** hypotenuse
- 等腰三角形 **20** isosceles triangle
  - 锐角 **a** acute angle
  - 钝角 **b** obtuse angle
- 圆形 **21** circle
  - 中心 **a** center
  - 半径 **b** radius
  - 直径 **c** diameter
  - 圆周 **d** circumference
- 椭圆 **22** ellipse/oval

立体图形 Solid Figures

- 立方体 **23** cube
- 圆柱体 **24** cylinder
- 球体 **25** sphere
- 圆锥体 **26** cone
- 三角椎体 **27** pyramid

[1–9]
A. What's the ______[1–4]?
B. .... ______[5–9](s).

[11–12]
A. What's the distance?
B. .... ______(s).

1 inch (1")	=	2.54 centimeters (cm)
1 foot (1')	=	0.305 meters (m)
1 yard (1 yd.)	=	0.914 meters (m)
1 mile (mi.)	=	1.6 kilometers (km)

[17–22]
A. Who can tell me what shape this is?
B. I can. It's a/an ______.

[23–27]
A. Who knows what figure this is?
B. I do. It's a/an ______.

[13–27]
A. This painting is magnificent!
B. Hmm. I don't think so. It just looks like a lot of ______s and ______s to me!

Types of Sentences & Parts of Speech 句子种类及词性

A Students(1) study(2) in(3) the(4) new(5) library.

B Do they(6) study hard(7)?

C Read page nine.

D This cake is fantastic!

叙述的	A	declarative	名词	1	noun	形容词	5	adjective
疑问的	B	interrogative	动词	2	verb	代词	6	pronoun
祈使的	C	imperative	介词	3	preposition	副词	7	adverb
感叹的	D	exclamatory	冠词	4	article			

A. What type of sentence is this?
B. It's a/an __[A–D]__ sentence.

A. What part of speech is this?
B. It's a/an __[1–7]__.

Punctuation Marks & the Writing Process 标点符号及写作过程

句点	8	period	激发构思	16	brainstorm ideas
问号	9	question mark	整理我的构思	17	organize *my* ideas
感叹号	10	exclamation point	写初稿	18	write a first draft
逗点	11	comma	题目	a	title
撇号	12	apostrophe	段落	b	paragraph
引号	13	quotation marks	修改	19	make corrections/revise/edit
冒号	14	colon	得到意见反馈	20	get feedback
分号	15	semi-colon	写完成稿/重写	21	write a final copy/rewrite

A. Did you find any mistakes?
B. Yes. You forgot to put a/an __[8–15]__ in this sentence.

A. Are you working on your composition?
B. Yes. I'm __[16–21]__ing.

文学与写作

虚构小说	1	fiction
长篇小说	2	novel
短篇故事	3	short story
诗歌/诗	4	poetry/poems
非虚构小说	5	non-fiction
传记	6	biography
自传	7	autobiography
文章/短文	8	essay
调查报告	9	report
杂志文章	10	magazine article
报纸文章	11	newspaper article
社论	12	editorial
信	13	letter
明信片	14	postcard
纸签/便条	15	note
邀请函	16	invitation
感谢函	17	thank-you note
备忘录	18	memo
电子邮件	19	e-mail
即时通讯	20	instant message

A. What are you doing?

B. I'm writing { ______[1, 4, 5]______. / a/an ______[2, 3, 6–20]______.

What kind of literature do you like to read?
What are some of your favorite books?
Who is your favorite author?

Do you like to read newspapers and magazines? Which ones do you read?

Do you sometimes send or receive letters, postcards, notes, e-mail, or instant messages? Tell about the people you communicate with, and how.

地理

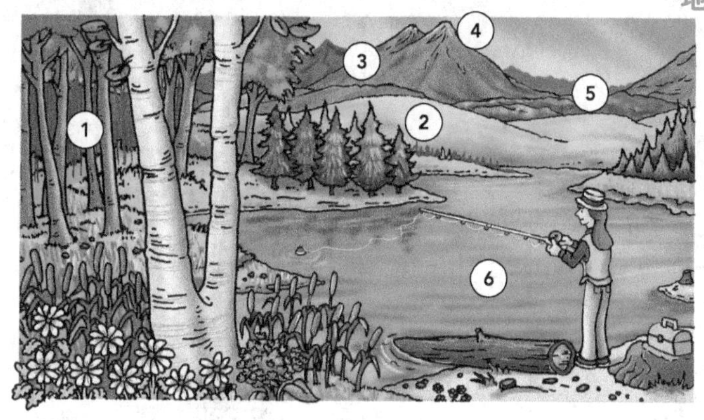

森林 1 forest/woods
山丘 2 hill
山脉 3 mountain range
山峰 4 mountain peak
山谷 5 valley
湖 6 lake
平原 7 plains
草地 8 meadow
小溪 9 stream/brook
池塘 10 pond
高原 11 plateau
峡谷 12 canyon
沙丘 13 dune/sand dune
沙漠 14 desert
丛林 15 jungle
海岸 16 seashore/shore
海湾 17 bay
海洋 18 ocean
岛屿 19 island
半岛 20 peninsula
雨林 21 rainforest
河流 22 river
瀑布 23 waterfall

A. Isn't this a beautiful ________?!
   Aren't these beautiful ________s?!
B. Yes. It's/They're magnificent!

Tell about the geography of your country. Describe the different geographic features.

Have you seen some of the geographic features in this lesson? Which ones? Where?

科学

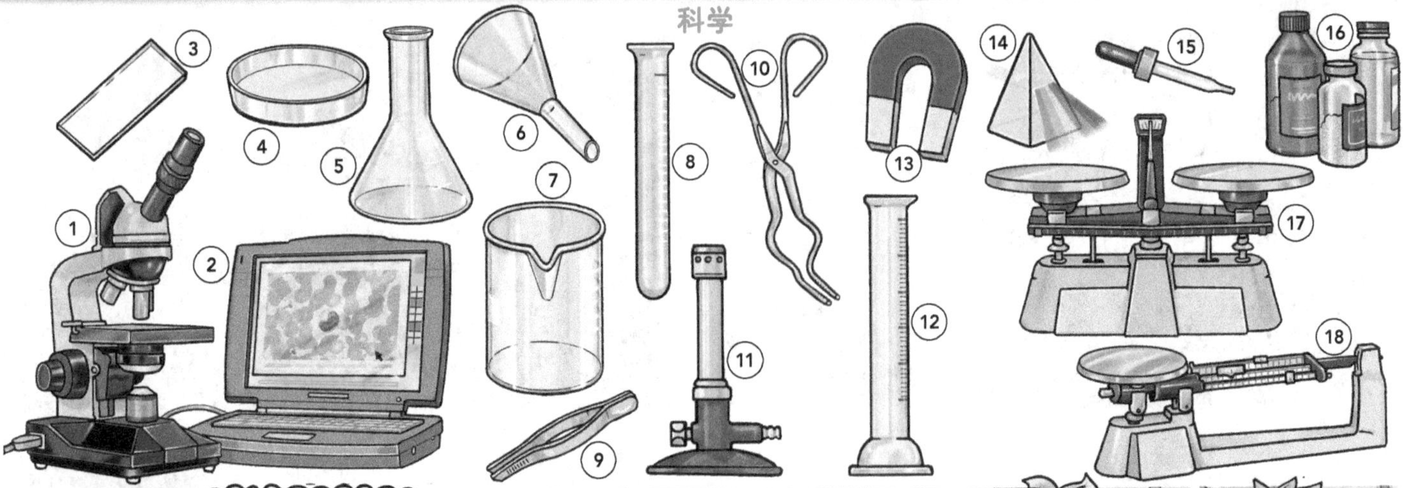

What happens to a plant without sunlight?

If a plant doesn't get sunlight, then it will die.

If a plant doesn't get sunlight, then it...

科学实验设备 **Science Equipment**

显微镜	1	microscope
电脑	2	computer
(显微镜用)载波片/载片	3	slide
(做细菌培养的)有盖培养皿	4	Petri dish
(实验用)烧瓶/长颈瓶	5	flask
漏斗	6	funnel
烧杯	7	beaker
试管	8	test tube
镊子	9	forceps
坩埚钳	10	crucible tongs
本生灯	11	Bunsen burner
玻璃刻度量筒	12	graduated cylinder
磁铁	13	magnet
棱镜	14	prism
滴管	15	dropper
化学品	16	chemicals
天平	17	balance
秤	18	scale

科学方法 **The Scientific Method**

陈述疑问	A	state the problem
提出假设	B	form a hypothesis
拟定研究步骤	C	plan a procedure
执行研究步骤	D	do a procedure
观察/记录观察	E	make/record observations
作出结论	F	draw conclusions

A. What do we need to do this procedure?
B. We need a/an/the ____[1–18]____.

A. How is your experiment coming along?
B. I'm getting ready to ____[A–F]____.

Do you have experience with the scientific equipment in this lesson? Tell about it.

What science courses do/did you take in school?

Think of an idea for a science experiment.
What question about science do you want to answer? State the problem.
What do you think will happen in the experiment? Form a hypothesis.
How can you test your hypothesis? Plan a procedure.

宇宙

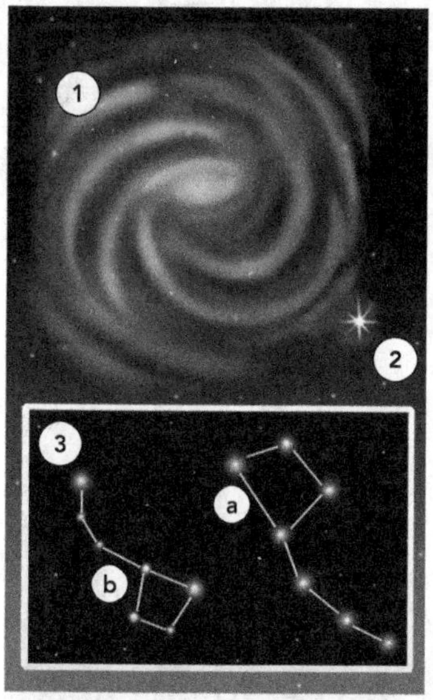

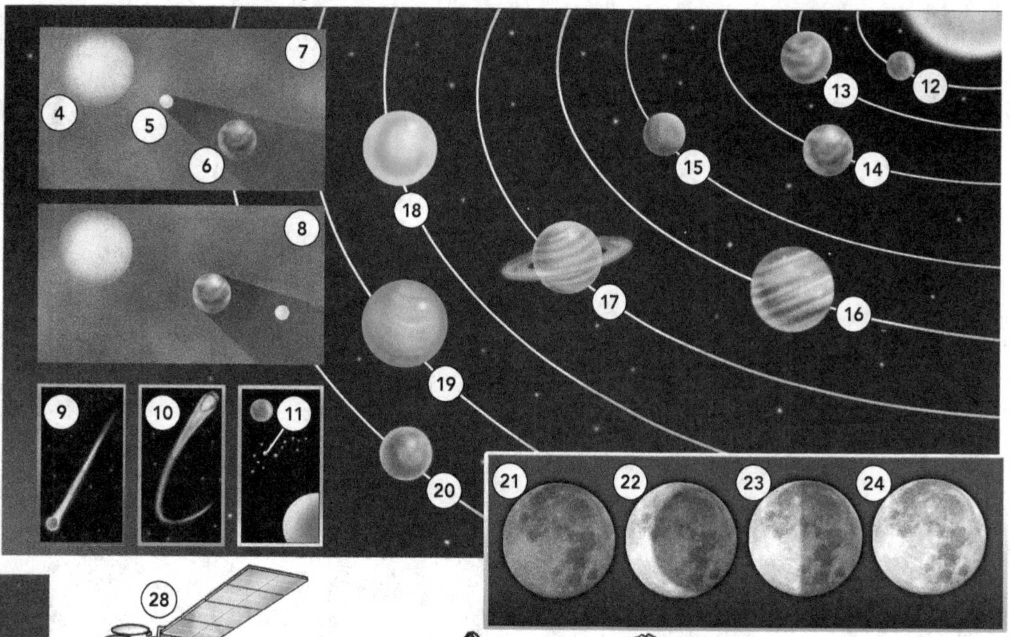

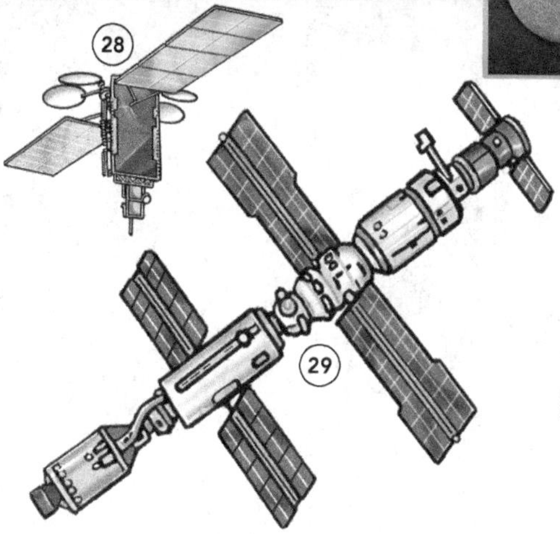

宇宙		**The Universe**
银河系/星系	**1**	galaxy
星星	**2**	star
星座	**3**	constellation
北斗七星	**a**	The Big Dipper
小熊座	**b**	The Little Dipper
太阳系		**The Solar System**
太阳	**4**	sun
月球	**5**	moon
行星	**6**	planet
日蚀	**7**	solar eclipse
月蚀	**8**	lunar eclipse
流星	**9**	meteor
彗星	**10**	comet
小行星	**11**	asteroid
水星	**12**	Mercury
金星	**13**	Venus
地球	**14**	Earth
火星	**15**	Mars
木星	**16**	Jupiter
土星	**17**	Saturn
天王星	**18**	Uranus
海王星	**19**	Neptune
冥王星	**20**	Pluto
新月	**21**	new moon
娥眉月	**22**	crescent moon
弦月	**23**	quarter moon
满月	**24**	full moon
天文学		**Astronomy**
天文台/观测所	**25**	observatory
(单筒)望远镜	**26**	telescope
天文学家	**27**	astronomer
太空探索		**Space Exploration**
卫星	**28**	satellite
太空站	**29**	space station
宇航员	**30**	astronaut
幽浮/不明飞行物体	**31**	U.F.O./ Unidentified Flying Object/ flying saucer

[1–24]
A. Is that (a/an/the) ________?
B. I'm not sure. I think it might be (a/an/the) ________.

[28–30]
A. Is the ________ ready for tomorrow's launch?
B. Yes. "All systems are go!"

Pretend you are an astronaut traveling in space. What do you see?

Draw and name a constellation you are familiar with.

Do you think space exploration is important? Why?

Have you ever seen a U.F.O.? Do you believe there is life in outer space? Why?

职业 1

会计 **1** accountant
男演员 **2** actor
女演员 **3** actress
建筑师 **4** architect
艺术家 **5** artist
装配工 **6** assembler
保姆 **7** babysitter
面包师傅 **8** baker

理发师 **9** barber
砌砖匠/石匠 **10** bricklayer/mason
商人 **11** businessman
女商人 **12** businesswoman
屠夫 **13** butcher
木匠 **14** carpenter
收银员 **15** cashier
主厨/厨师 **16** chef/cook

育儿中心工作人员 **17** child day-care worker
电脑软件工程师 **18** computer software engineer
建筑工人 **19** construction worker
清洁工 **20** custodian/janitor
客服人员 **21** customer service representative
数据输入员 **22** data entry clerk

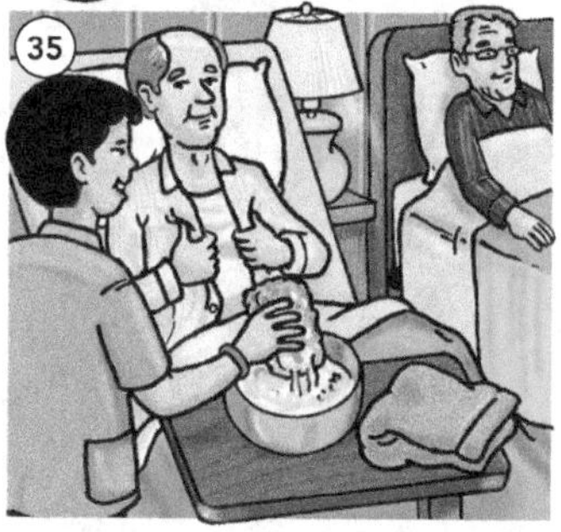

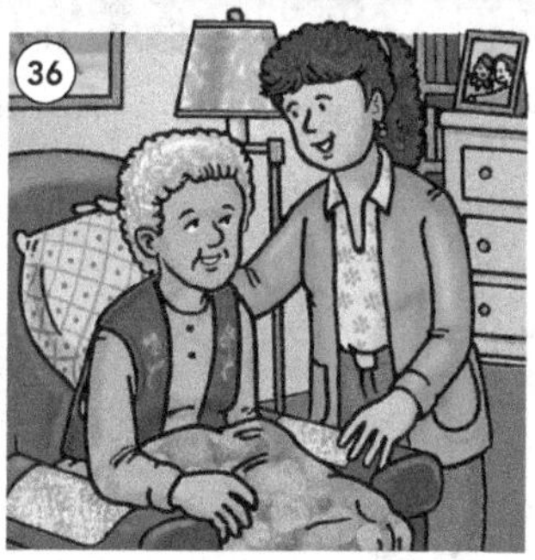

送货员	23	delivery person
码头工人	24	dockworker
工程师	25	engineer
工厂工人	26	factory worker
农夫	27	farmer
消防员	28	firefighter
渔夫	29	fisher
餐饮服务人员	30	food-service worker
工头/领班	31	foreman
园丁/庭院设计师	32	gardener/landscaper
制衣工人	33	garment worker
美发师	34	hairdresser
护理人员	35	health-care aide/ attendant
家庭医护人员/ 家庭护理人员	36	home health aide/ home attendant
家庭主妇(夫)	37	homemaker
管家/饭店客房清洁员	38	housekeeper

A. What do you do?
B. I'm an **accountant**. How about you?
A. I'm a **carpenter**.

[At a job interview]

A. Are you an experienced ________?
B. Yes. I'm a very experienced ________.

A. How long have you been a/an ________?
B. I've been a/an ________ for .... months/years.

Which of these occupations do you think are the most interesting? the most difficult? Why?

职业 2

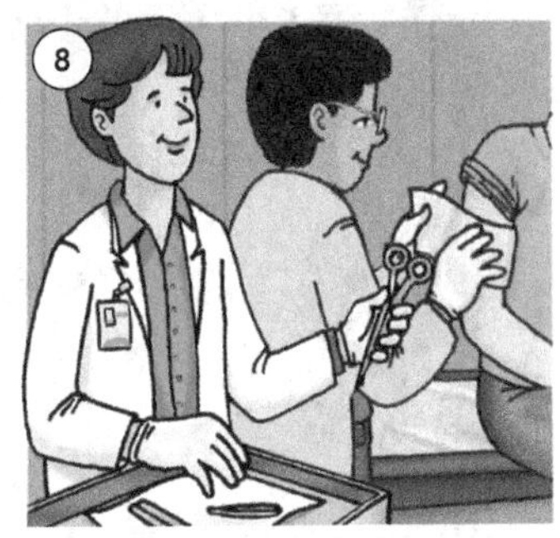

新闻记者 1 journalist/reporter
律师 2 lawyer
机床操作工 3 machine operator
邮差/邮递员 4 mail carrier/letter carrier
经理 5 manager
指甲修饰师 6 manicurist
汽车修理工 7 mechanic
医疗助理员 8 medical assistant/physician assistant
快递人员 9 messenger/courier
搬运工人 10 mover
音乐家 11 musician
油漆工人 12 painter
药剂师 13 pharmacist
摄影师 14 photographer
飞行员 15 pilot
警察 16 police officer
邮局办事员 17 postal worker
接待员 18 receptionist
修理人员 19 repairperson
推销员 20 salesperson

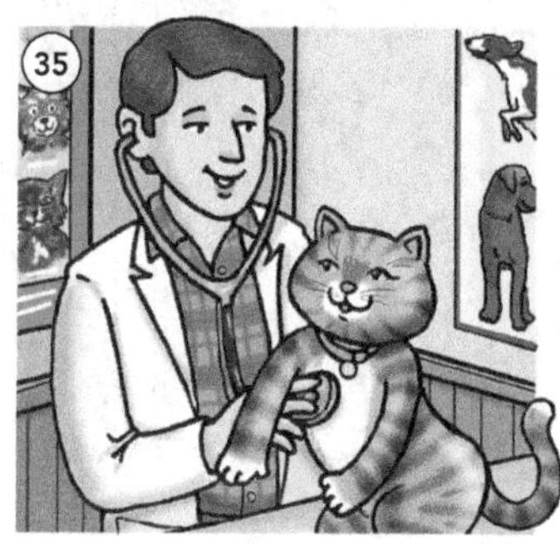

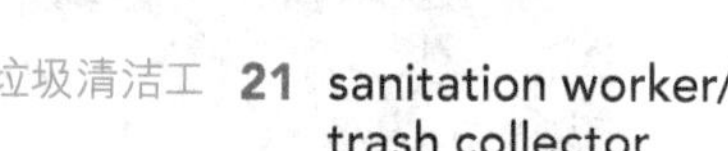

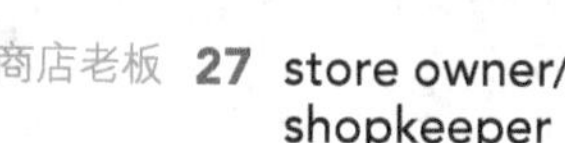

垃圾清洁工 **21** sanitation worker/trash collector
秘书 **22** secretary
警卫 **23** security guard
军人 **24** serviceman
女军人 **25** servicewoman
仓库管理员 **26** stock clerk
商店老板 **27** store owner/shopkeeper
主管/督导人员 **28** supervisor
裁缝 **29** tailor
老师/教师 **30** teacher/instructor
电话销售员 **31** telemarketer
翻译员/口译员 **32** translator/interpreter
旅行社 **33** travel agent
卡车司机 **34** truck driver
兽医 **35** veterinarian/vet
服务生 **36** waiter/server
女服务生/服务生 **37** waitress/server
焊接工 **38** welder

A. What's your occupation?
B. I'm a **journalist**.
A. A **journalist**?
B. Yes. That's right.

A. Are you still a ________?
B. No. I'm a ________.
A. Oh. That's interesting.

A. What kind of job would you like in the future?
B. I'd like to be a ________.

Do you work? What's your occupation?

What are the occupations of people in your family?

工作技能与活动

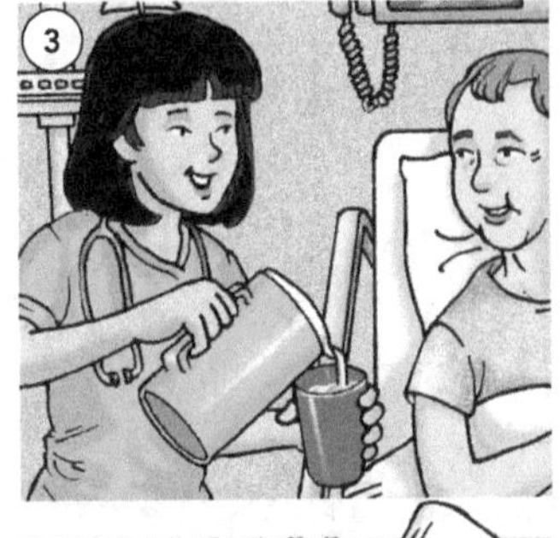

表演 1 act
装配零件 2 assemble *components*
协助病人 3 assist *patients*
烘烤 4 bake
建造物品 5 build *things*/construct *things*
清扫 6 clean
烹调/煮 7 cook
送披萨饼 8 deliver *pizzas*
设计建筑物 9 design *buildings*
绘(图) 10 draw
开卡车 11 drive *a truck*
归档 12 file
开飞机 13 fly *an airplane*
种菜 14 grow *vegetables*
守卫大楼 15 guard *buildings*
经营餐厅 16 manage *a restaurant*
除草 17 mow *lawns*
操作机器 18 operate *equipment*
油漆 19 paint
弹钢琴 20 play the *piano*

烹调食物 **21** prepare *food*
修理东西 **22** repair *things*/fix *things*
卖车 **23** sell *cars*
上菜 **24** serve *food*
缝纫 **25** sew
唱歌 **26** sing
说西班牙语 **27** speak *Spanish*
监督人员 **28** supervise *people*

照顾老人 **29** take care of *elderly people*
盘点/点清存货 **30** take inventory
教 **31** teach
翻译 **32** translate
打字 **33** type
使用收银机 **34** use *a cash register*
洗碗盘 **35** wash *dishes*
写作 **36** write

A. Can you **act**?
B. Yes, I can.

A. Do you know how to ________?
B. Yes. I've been ________ing for years.

A. Tell me about your skills.
B. I can ________, and I can ________.

Tell about your job skills.
What can you do?

JOB SEARCH

求职

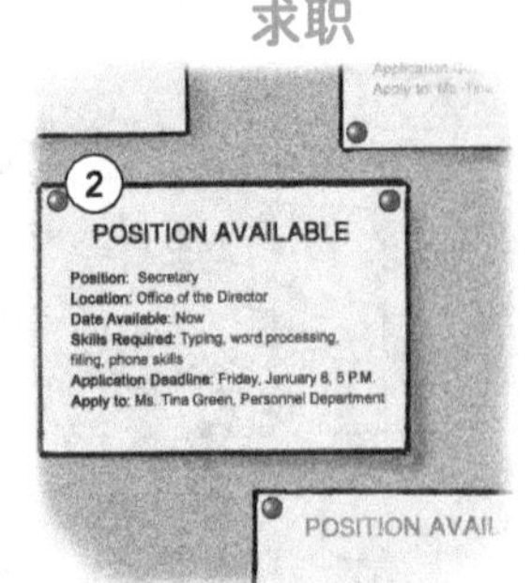

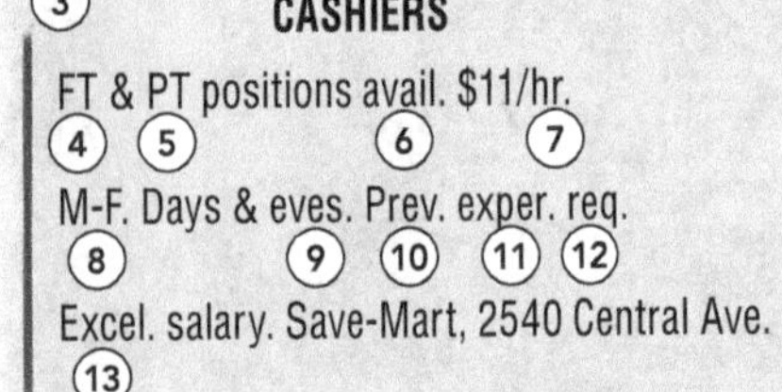

各类招聘广告 Types of Job Ads

- 招聘广告 **1** help wanted sign
- 招聘广告 **2** job notice/ job announcement
- 分类广告/招聘广告 **3** classified ad/want ad

招聘广告缩略语 Job Ad Abbreviations

- 全职 **4** full-time
- 兼职 **5** part-time
- 有空缺 **6** available
- 小时 **7** hour
- 星期一至星期五 **8** Monday through Friday
- 晚上 **9** evenings
- 以前的 **10** previous
- 经验 **11** experience
- 必须的 **12** required
- 相当好的 **13** excellent

求职 Job Search

- 应征 **A** respond to an ad
- 查询信息 **B** request information
- 要求面试 **C** request an interview
- 准备履历 **D** prepare a resume
- 穿著适宜 **E** dress appropriately
- 填写申请表格 **F** fill out an application (form)
- 前往面试 **G** go to an interview
- 谈谈你具备的技能与资格 **H** talk about your skills and qualifications
- 描述你的经验 **I** talk about your experience
- 询问有关薪资问题 **J** ask about the salary
- 询问有关福利的问题 **K** ask about the benefits
- 写感谢函 **L** write a thank-you note
- 被录用 **M** get hired

A. How did you find your job?
B. I found it through a ___[1–3]___.

A. How was your job interview?
B. It went very well.
A. Did you ___[D–F, H–M]___?
B. Yes, I did.

Tell about a job you are familiar with. What are the skills and qualifications required for the job? What are the hours? What is the salary?

Tell about how people you know found their jobs.

Tell about your own experience with a job search or a job interview.

工作场所

- 接待处 **A** reception area
- 会议室 **B** conference room
- 收发室 **C** mailroom
- 办公区 **D** work area
- 办公室 **E** office
- 办公用品储藏室 **F** supply room
- 储藏室 **G** storage room
- 员工休息室 **H** employee lounge
- 衣架 **1** coat rack
- 衣橱 **2** coat closet
- 接待员 **3** receptionist
- 会议桌 **4** conference table
- 说明图版 **5** presentation board
- 邮用秤 **6** postal scale
- 邮资仪 **7** postage meter
- 办公室助理 **8** office assistant
- 信箱 **9** mailbox
- 小隔间 **10** cubicle
- 转椅 **11** swivel chair
- 打字机 **12** typewriter
- 桌面计算器 **13** adding machine
- 复印机 **14** copier/photocopier
- 碎纸机 **15** paper shredder
- 切纸机 **16** paper cutter
- 档案管理员 **17** file clerk
- 档案柜 **18** file cabinet
- 秘书 **19** secretary
- 电脑桌 **20** computer workstation
- 雇主/老板/主管 **21** employer/boss
- 行政助理 **22** administrative assistant
- 办公室经理 **23** office manager
- 用品柜 **24** supply cabinet
- 储藏柜 **25** storage cabinet
- 自动售货机 **26** vending machine
- 饮水机 **27** water cooler
- 咖啡机 **28** coffee machine
- 留言栏 **29** message board
- 帮……留话 **a** take a message
- 作介绍/报告 **b** give a presentation
- 将信件分类 **c** sort the mail
- 复印/影印 **d** make copies
- 归档 **e** file
- 打一封信 **f** type a letter

[A–H]
A. Where's ....(name)..........?
B. He's/She's in the _____.

[1–29]
A. What do you think of the new _____?
B. He's/She's/It's very nice.

[a–f]
A. What's ....(name).......... doing?
B. He's/She's _____ing.

Describe a workplace you are familiar with. Tell about the rooms, the areas, and the employees.

OFFICE SUPPLIES AND EQUIPMENT

办公室用品及设备

书桌 **1** desk
订书机 **2** stapler
文件盘 **3** letter tray/ stacking tray
旋转卡片目录 **4** rotary card file
桌垫 **5** desk pad
预约簿 **6** appointment book
夹纸笔记板 **7** clipboard
记事本 **8** note pad/ memo pad
电动削铅笔机 **9** electric pencil sharpener
桌历/台历 **10** desk calendar
便签粘贴纸 **11** Post-It note pad
万用记事本/ 个人记事本 **12** organizer/ personal planner
橡皮筋 **13** rubber band
曲别针 **14** paper clip
订书针 **15** staple
图钉 **16** thumbtack
长头图钉 **17** pushpin
黄页长便笺本 **18** legal pad
文件夹 **19** file folder
索引卡 **20** index card
信封 **21** envelope
印有信头的信纸 **22** stationery/ letterhead (paper)
气泡信封 **23** mailer
邮件标签 **24** mailing label
打字机色带 **25** typewriter cartridge
墨水匣 **26** ink cartridge
橡皮图章 **27** rubber stamp
印台 **28** ink pad
胶棒 **29** glue stick
胶水 **30** glue
橡胶胶水 **31** rubber cement
修正液 **32** correction fluid
透明胶带 **33** cellophane tape/ clear tape
包装胶带 **34** packing tape/ sealing tape

A. My desk is a mess!
I can't find my [2–12] !
B. Here it is next to your [2–12] .

A. Could you get some more [13–21, 23–29] s/ [22, 30–34] from the supply room?
B. Some more [13–21, 23–29] s/ [22, 30–34] ? Sure. I'd be happy to.

Which supplies and equipment do you use? What do you use them for?

Which supplies in this lesson do you have at home? at school?

THE FACTORY

工厂

打卡钟(上下班计时钟) **1** time clock
工时卡 **2** time cards
衣物间 **3** locker room
装配线 **4** (assembly) line
工厂工人 **5** (factory) worker
工作站 **6** work station
生产线主管 **7** line supervisor
质量监督员 **8** quality control supervisor

机器 **9** machine
传送带 **10** conveyor belt
仓库 **11** warehouse
包装员 **12** packer
铲车/叉架起货机 **13** forklift
载货用电梯 **14** freight elevator
工会公告 **15** union notice
意见箱 **16** suggestion box

运输部 **17** shipping department
运务员 **18** shipping clerk
搬运货物的手推车 **19** hand truck/dolly
装卸台 **20** loading dock
财务科 **21** payroll office
人事室 **22** personnel office

A. Excuse me. I'm a new employee. Where's/Where are the ______?
B. Next to/Near/In/On the ______.

A. Have you seen *Tony*?
B. Yes. *He's* in/on/at/next to/near the ______.

Are there any factories where you live? What kind? What are the working conditions there?

What products do factories in your country produce?

THE CONSTRUCTION SITE

建筑工地

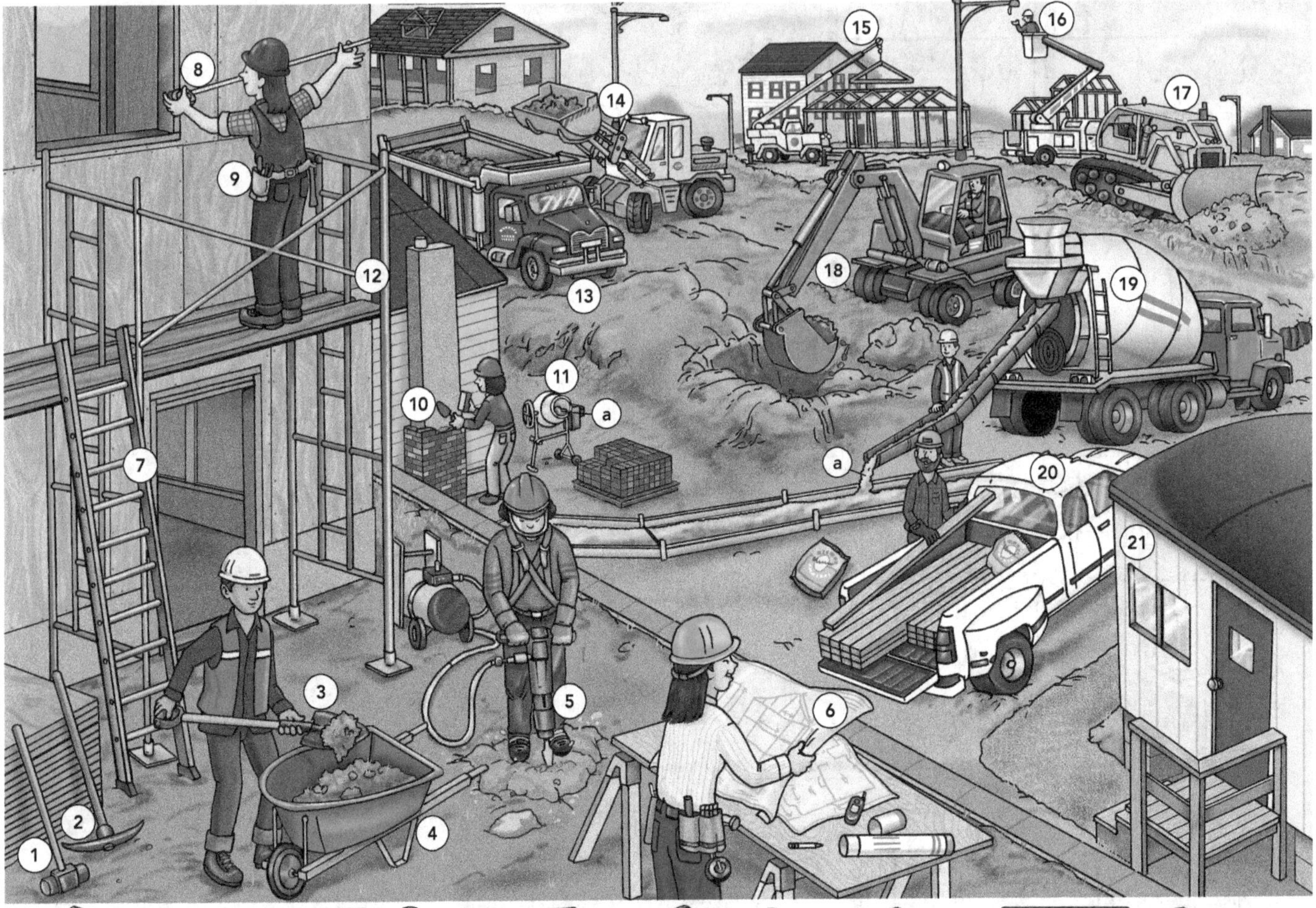

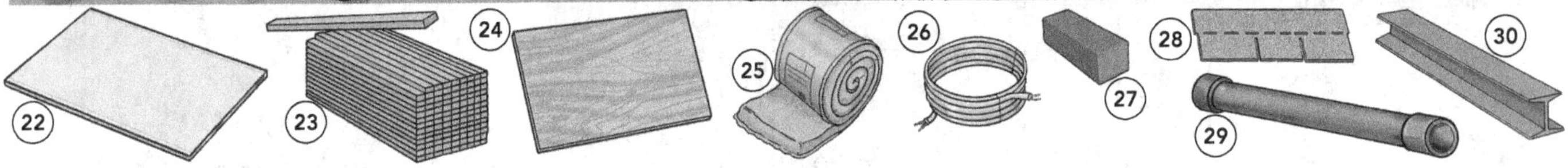

铁锤 **1** sledgehammer
镐 **2** pickax
铲子 **3** shovel
独轮手推车 **4** wheelbarrow
手提钻/风钻 **5** jackhammer/pneumatic drill
蓝图 **6** blueprints
梯子 **7** ladder
测量卷尺 **8** tape measure
工具皮带 **9** toolbelt
泥刀/小铲子 **10** trowel

水泥搅拌机 **11** cement mixer
水泥 **a** cement
脚手架 **12** scaffolding
倾卸车 **13** dump truck
前端装载机 **14** front-end loader
吊车 **15** crane
车载升降台 **16** cherry picker
推土机 **17** bulldozer
挖土机 **18** backhoe
混凝土搅拌车 **19** concrete mixer truck
混凝土 **a** concrete

敞篷载货小卡车 **20** pickup truck
汽车拖的流动屋 **21** trailer
石膏板 **22** drywall
木材 **23** wood/lumber
夹板/合板 **24** plywood
绝缘材料 **25** insulation
电线 **26** wire
砖块 **27** brick
瓦片 **28** shingle
水管 **29** pipe
梁 **30** girder/beam

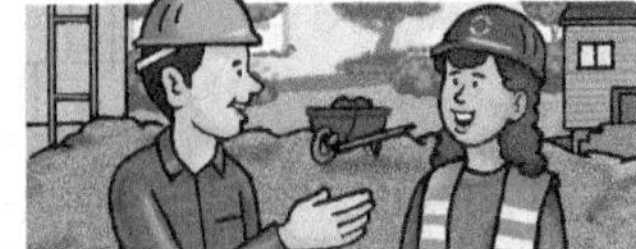

A. Could you get me that/those __[1–10]__?
B. Sure.

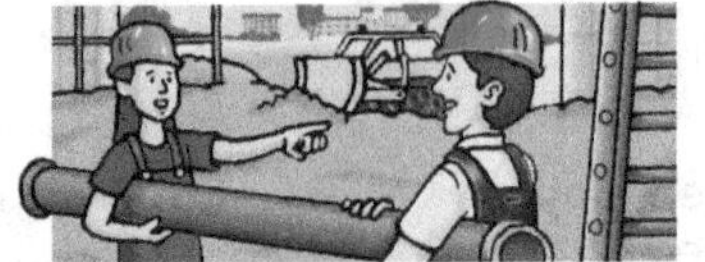

A. Watch out for that __[11–21]__!
B. Oh! Thanks for the warning!

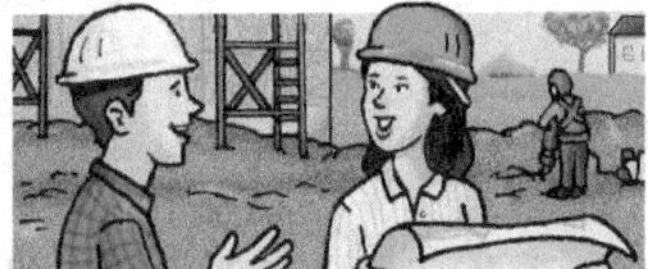

A. Do we have enough __[22–26]__ / __[27–30]__s?
B. I think so.

What building materials is your home made of?
When was it built?

Describe a construction site near your home or school.
Tell about the construction equipment and the materials.

工作安全

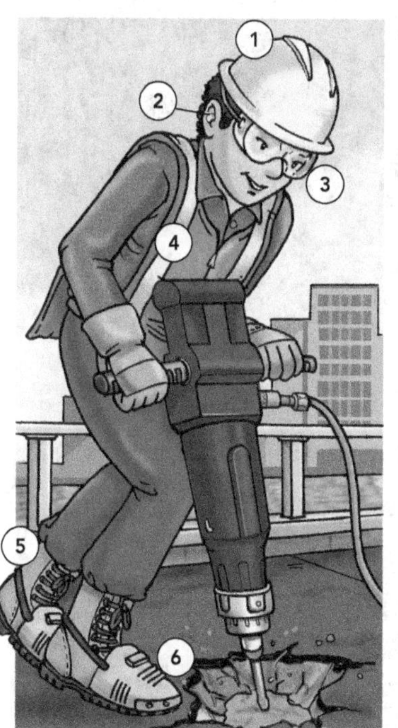

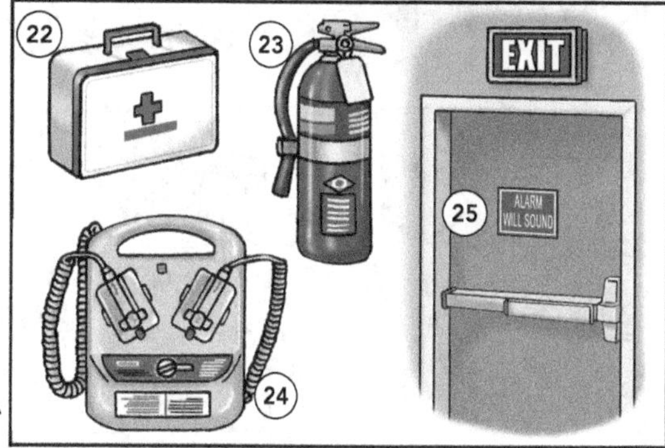

安全帽	**1**	hard hat/helmet	口罩	**10**	mask	危险的	**19**	hazardous
耳塞	**2**	earplugs	乳胶手套	**11**	latex gloves	生化危险	**20**	biohazard
护目镜	**3**	goggles	呼吸防护具	**12**	respirator	电力危险	**21**	electrical hazard
安全背心	**4**	safety vest	护目镜	**13**	safety glasses	急救箱	**22**	first-aid kit
安全靴	**5**	safety boots	易燃的	**14**	flammable	灭火器	**23**	fire extinguisher
护趾套	**6**	toe guard	有毒的	**15**	poisonous	电震发生器	**24**	defibrillator
腰背支撑	**7**	back support	具侵蚀性的	**16**	corrosive	紧急出口	**25**	emergency exit
安全耳罩	**8**	safety earmuffs	具放射性的	**17**	radioactive			
发网	**9**	hairnet	危险的	**18**	dangerous			

A. Don't forget to wear your ___[1–13]___!
B. Thanks for reminding me.

A. Be careful! { That material is ___[14–17]___! / That machine is ___[18]___! / That work area is ___[19]___! / That's a ___[20]___!/That's an ___[21]___! }
B. Thanks for the warning.

A. Where's the ___[22–25]___?
B. It's over there.

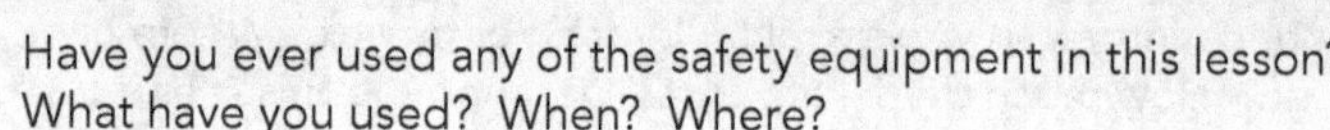

Have you ever used any of the safety equipment in this lesson? What have you used? When? Where?

Where do you see people using safety equipment in your community?

PUBLIC TRANSPORTATION

公共交通工具

公共汽车	**A**	**bus**
公车站	**1**	bus stop
公车路线	**2**	bus route
乘客	**3**	passenger/rider
公车费	**4**	(bus) fare
转车车票	**5**	transfer
公车司机	**6**	bus driver
长途巴士站	**7**	bus station
售票处	**8**	ticket counter
车票	**9**	ticket
行李箱	**10**	baggage compartment/ luggage compartment

火车	**B**	**train**
火车站	**11**	train station
售票窗口	**12**	ticket window
班机（车）抵达／离开时间看板	**13**	arrival and departure board
服务台/询问台	**14**	information booth
时刻表	**15**	schedule/ timetable
月台	**16**	platform
轨道	**17**	track
列车长	**18**	conductor

地铁	**C**	**subway**
地铁站	**19**	subway station
地铁票	**20**	(subway) token
旋转入口/十字转门	**21**	turnstile
储值卡	**22**	fare card
储值卡自售机	**23**	fare card machine
出租车	**D**	**taxi**
出租车招呼站	**24**	taxi stand
出租车	**25**	taxi/cab/taxicab
出租车计费表	**26**	meter
出租车司机	**27**	cab driver/taxi driver
渡轮	**E**	**ferry**

[A–E]
A. How are you going to get there?
B. {I'm going to take the [A–C, E].
{I'm going to take a [D].

[1, 7, 8, 10–19, 21, 23–25]
A. Excuse me. Where's the ________?
B. Over there.

How do you get to different places in your community? Describe public transportation where you live.

In your country, can you travel far by train or by bus? Where can you go? How much do tickets cost? Describe the buses and trains.

车辆种类

轿车	1	sedan
掀背车	2	hatchback
敞篷车	3	convertible
跑车	4	sports car
混合动力车	5	hybrid
旅行车	6	station wagon
休旅车/运动型多用途车	7	S.U.V. (sport utility vehicle)
吉普车	8	jeep
箱型车	9	van
小型箱型车	10	minivan
敞篷载货小卡车	11	pickup truck
加长豪华礼车	12	limousine
拖车	13	tow truck
露营车	14	R.V. (recreational vehicle)/camper
搬运用货车	15	moving van
厢式卡车	16	truck
牵引拖车/半拖货车	17	tractor trailer/ semi
自行车	18	bicycle/bike
小轮摩托车	19	motor scooter
机动脚踏两用车	20	moped
摩托车	21	motorcycle

A. What kind of vehicle are you looking for?
B. I'm looking for a **sedan**.

A. Do you drive a/an ________?
B. No. I drive a/an ________.

A. I just saw an accident between a/an ________ and a/an ________!
B. Was anybody hurt?
A. No. Fortunately, nobody was hurt.

What are the most common types of vehicles in your country?

What's your favorite type of vehicle? Why? In your opinion, which company makes the best one?

CAR PARTS AND MAINTENANCE

汽车零件及维修

保险杠	1	bumper
前灯	2	headlight
转弯指示灯	3	turn signal
停车灯	4	parking light
防护板/挡泥板	5	fender
轮胎	6	tire
轮毂罩	7	hubcap
引擎罩	8	hood
挡风玻璃	9	windshield
雨刷	10	windshield wipers
侧后视镜	11	side mirror
车顶行李架	12	roof rack
车顶天窗	13	sunroof
天线	14	antenna
后窗	15	rear window
后窗化霜器	16	rear defroster
行李箱	17	trunk
尾灯	18	taillight
煞车灯	19	brake light
倒车灯	20	backup light
汽车牌照	21	license plate
排气管	22	tailpipe/ exhaust pipe
消声器	23	muffler
变速箱	24	transmission
油箱	25	gas tank
千斤顶	26	jack
备胎	27	spare tire
十字扳手	28	lug wrench
照明灯	29	flare
汽车充电电缆	30	jumper cables
火花塞	31	spark plugs
空气过滤器	32	air filter
引擎/发动机	33	engine
燃料喷射系统	34	fuel injection system
水箱/散热器	35	radiator
散热器软管	36	radiator hose
风扇皮带	37	fan belt
交流发电机	38	alternator
量油尺	39	dipstick
电瓶	40	battery
气泵	41	air pump
加油机	42	gas pump
加油枪/加油嘴	43	nozzle
加油口	44	gas cap
汽油	45	gas
机油	46	oil
冷却剂	47	coolant
气	48	air

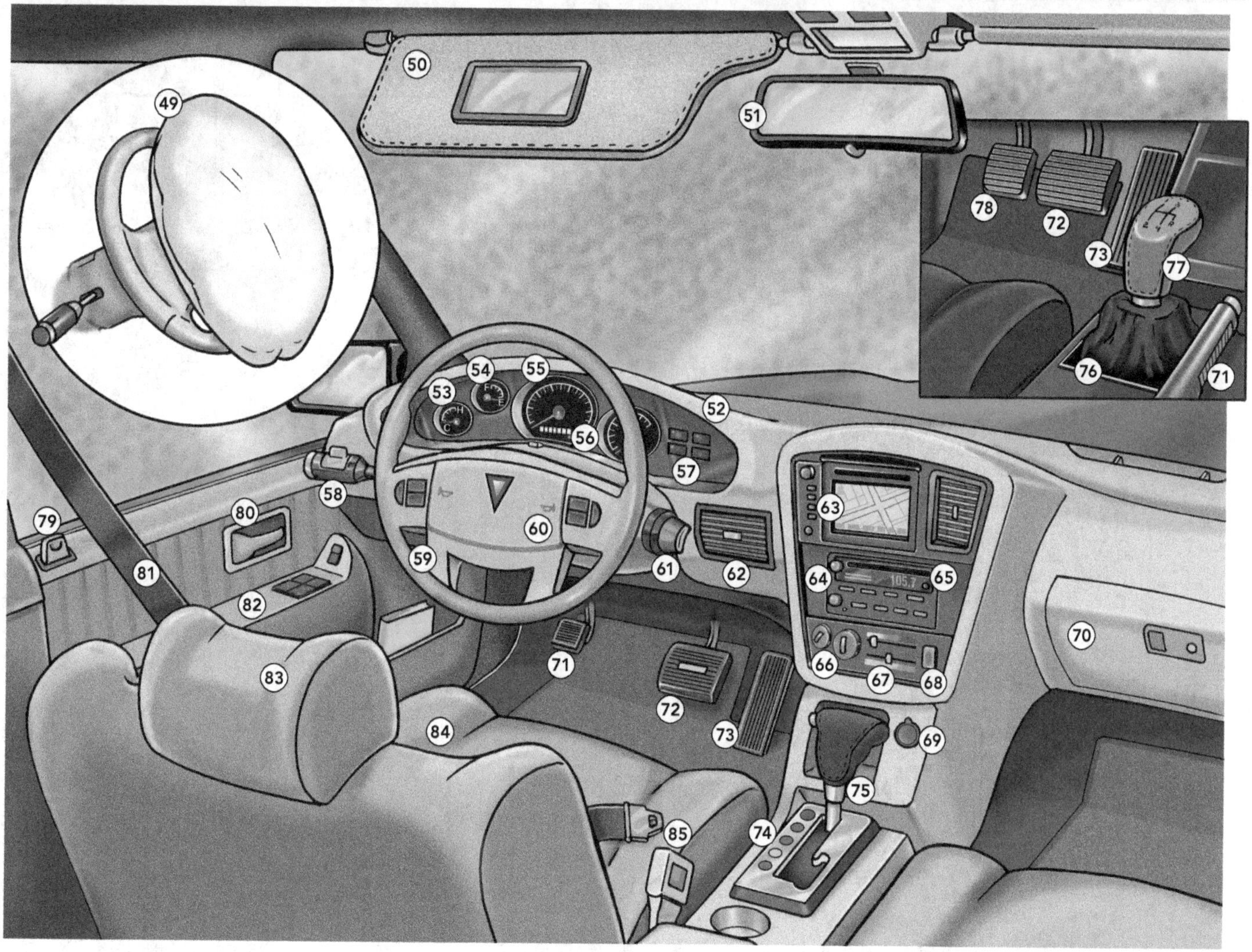

安全气囊 **49** air bag
遮阳板 **50** visor
后视镜 **51** rearview mirror
仪表盘 **52** dashboard/instrument panel
温度表 **53** temperature gauge
燃油表 **54** gas gauge/fuel gauge
时速表 **55** speedometer
里程表 **56** odometer
警告灯 **57** warning lights
转向灯控制杆 **58** turn signal
方向盘 **59** steering wheel

汽车喇叭 **60** horn
点火装置 **61** ignition
通风孔 **62** vent
导航系统 **63** navigation system
收音机 **64** radio
CD播放机 **65** CD player
暖气设备 **66** heater
空调 **67** air conditioning
除霜装置 **68** defroster
电源插座 **69** power outlet
储物小柜 **70** glove compartment
紧急煞车 **71** emergency brake
煞车踏板 **72** brake (pedal)
油门 **73** accelerator/gas pedal

自动排挡变速箱 **74** automatic transmission
变速杆/变速排挡 **75** gearshift
手动排挡变速箱 **76** manual transmission
手动变速杆 **77** stickshift
离合器 **78** clutch
车门锁 **79** door lock
车门把 **80** door handle
安全肩带 **81** shoulder harness
扶手 **82** armrest
头枕 **83** headrest
车座 **84** seat
安全带 **85** seat belt

[2, 3, 9–16, 24, 35–39, 49–85]
A. What's the matter with your car?
B. The ________(s) is/are broken.

[45–48]
A. Can I help you?
B. {Yes. My car needs ___[45–47]___.
   {Yes. My tires need ___[48]___.

[1, 2, 4–15, 17–23, 25]
A. I was just in a car accident!
B. Oh, no! Were you hurt?
A. No. But my ________(s) was/were damaged.

In your opinion, what are the most important features to look for when you buy a car?

Do you own a car? What kind? Tell about any repairs your car has needed.

HIGHWAYS AND STREETS

公路及街道

隧道 **1** tunnel
桥 **2** bridge
收费站 **3** tollbooth
路标 **4** route sign
公路 **5** highway
路面 **6** road
道路分隔栏/护栏 **7** divider/barrier
高架桥 **8** overpass
高架桥下车道 **9** underpass
入口坡道 **10** entrance ramp/ on ramp
州际公路 **11** interstate (highway)
路中安全岛 **12** median
左车道 **13** left lane
中央车道 **14** middle lane/ center lane
右车道 **15** right lane
路肩 **16** shoulder
虚线 **17** broken line
实线 **18** solid line
限速标志 **19** speed limit sign
出口坡道 **20** exit (ramp)
出口标志 **21** exit sign
街道 **22** street
单行道 **23** one-way street
双黄线 **24** double yellow line
行人穿越道/斑马线 **25** crosswalk
十字路口 **26** intersection
交通号志灯/红绿灯 **27** traffic light/ traffic signal
转角 **28** corner
街区 **29** block

[1–28]
A. Where's the accident?
B. It's on/in/at/near the ______.

Describe a highway you travel on.

Describe an intersection near where you live.

In your area, on which highways and streets do most accidents occur? Why are these places dangerous?

动态介词

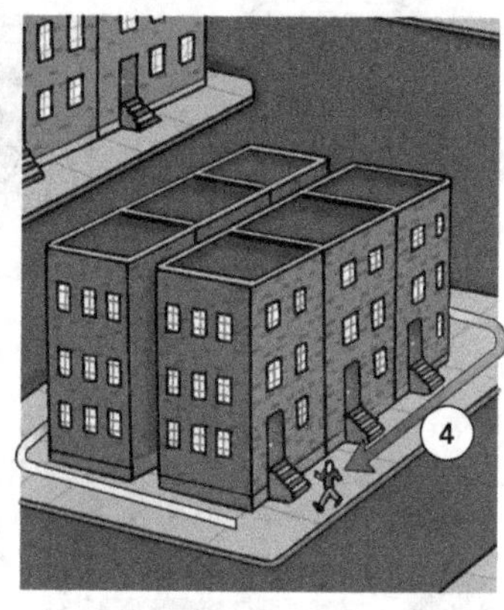

越过……的上面 **1** over
穿过……的下面 **2** under
穿过/通过 **3** through
环绕 **4** around

顺方向（行走）/上行 **5** up
逆方向（行走）/下行 **6** down
横越/穿过 **7** across
经过 **8** past

上 **9** on
下 **10** off
进 **11** into
出 **12** out of
进入 **13** onto

[1–8]
A. Go **over** *the bridge.*
B. **Over** *the bridge?*
A. Yes.

[9–13]
A. I can't talk right now. I'm getting **on** *a train.*
B. You're getting **on** *a train?*
A. Yes. I'll call you later.

What places do you go past on your way to school?

Tell how to get to different places from your home or your school.

交通标志及指示

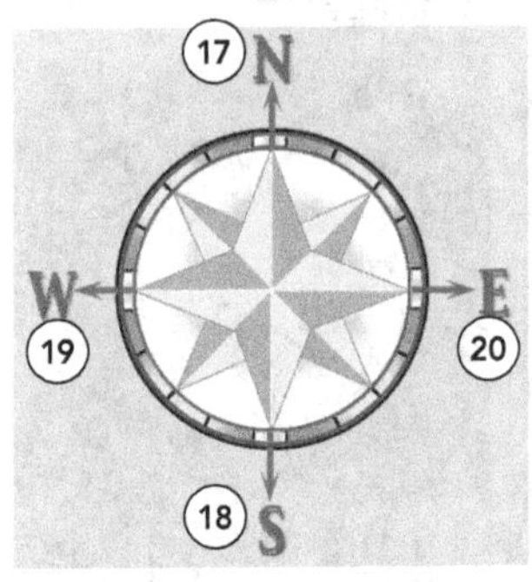

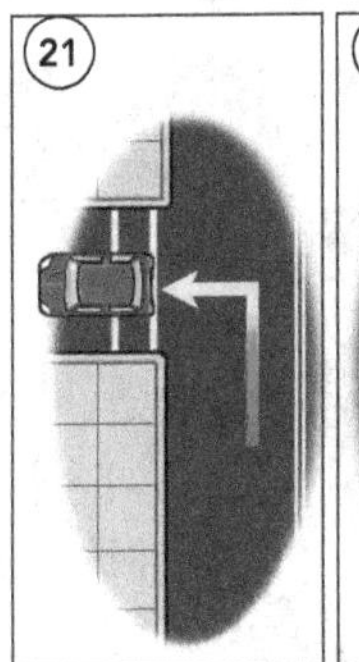
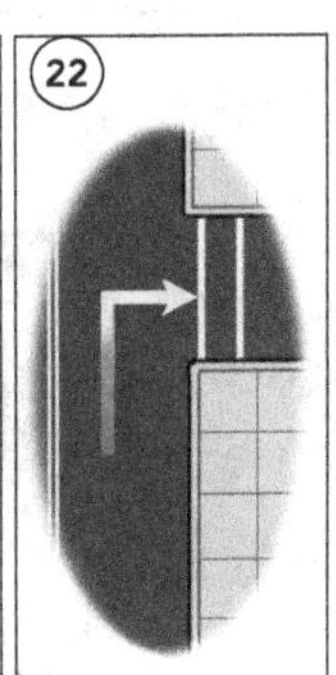
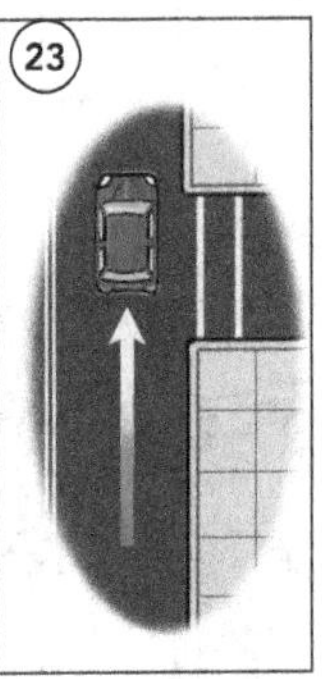
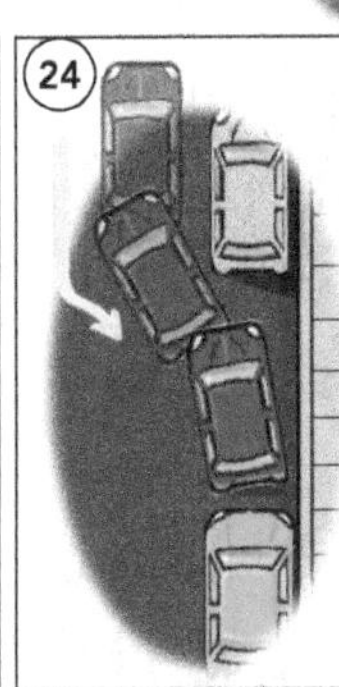
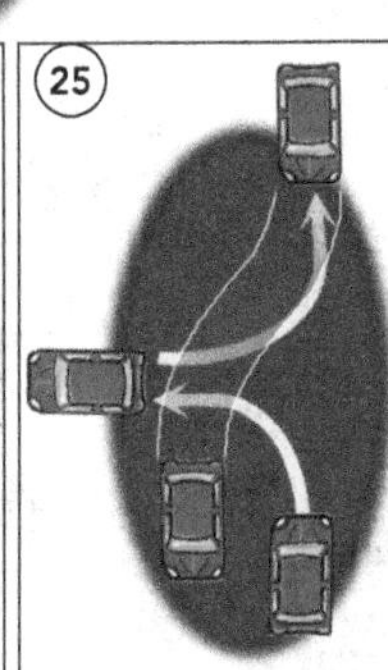

交通标志 Traffic Signs

- 停 **1** stop
- 禁止左转 **2** no left turn
- 禁止右转 **3** no right turn
- 禁止回转 **4** no U-turn
- 只准右转 **5** right turn only
- 禁止进入 **6** do not enter
- 单行道 **7** one way
- 此路不通 **8** dead end/no outlet
- 行人通道 **9** pedestrian crossing
- 铁路平交道 **10** railroad crossing
- 学童过路处 **11** school crossing
- 并道 **12** merging traffic
- 避让 **13** yield
- 绕道 **14** detour
- 路湿易滑 **15** slippery when wet
- 残障停车专位 **16** handicapped parking only

方向指示 Compass Directions

- 北 **17** north
- 南 **18** south
- 西 **19** west
- 东 **20** east

测路指示 Road Test Instructions

- 左转。 **21** Turn left.
- 右转。 **22** Turn right.
- 直走。 **23** Go straight.
- 平行停车。 **24** Parallel park.
- 做三点式转。 **25** Make a 3-point turn.
- 使用手势。 **26** Use hand signals.

[1–16]
A. Careful! That sign says "**stop**"!
B. Oh. Thanks.

[17–20]
A. Which way should I go?
B. Go **north**.

[21–26]
A. Turn **right**.
B. Turn **right**?
A. Yes.

Which of these traffic signs are in your neighborhood?
What other traffic signs do you usually see?

Describe any differences between traffic signs in different countries you know.

THE AIRPORT

飞机场

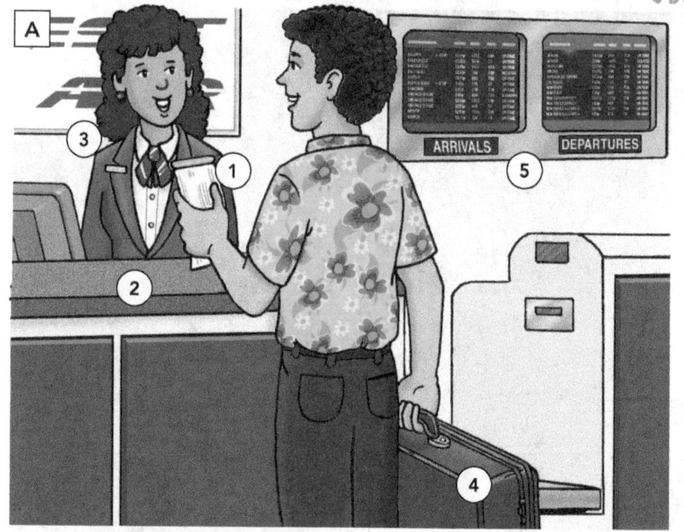

登机手续 **A Check-In**
机票 **1** ticket
票务柜台 **2** ticket counter
票务员 **3** ticket agent
旅行箱 **4** suitcase
班机抵达/出发时间显示屏幕 **5** arrival and departure monitor

安全检查 **B Security**
安全检查关口 **6** security checkpoint
金属物品探测器 **7** metal detector
保安员 **8** security officer
X光检测仪 **9** X-ray machine
随身行李 **10** carry-on bag

登机门 **C The Gate**
验票处 **11** check-in counter
登机证 **12** boarding pass
登机门 **13** gate
登机区 **14** boarding area

行李领取 **D Baggage Claim**
行李领取区 **15** baggage claim (area)
行李传送带/行李转盘 **16** baggage carousel
行李 **17** baggage
行李推车 **18** baggage cart/ luggage cart
行李小拖车 **19** luggage carrier
西装袋 **20** garment bag
行李牌 **21** baggage claim check

海关及出入境检查 **E Customs and Immigration**
海关 **22** customs
海关工作人员 **23** customs officer
海关申报表 **24** customs declaration form
出入境检查 **25** immigration
出入境检查官 **26** immigration officer
护照 **27** passport
签证 **28** visa

[2, 3, 5–9, 11, 13–16, 22, 23, 25, 26]
A. Excuse me. Where's the ________?*
B. Right over there.

* *With 22 and 25, use:* Excuse me. Where's ______?

[1, 4, 10, 12, 17–21, 24, 27, 28]
A. Oh, no! I think I've lost my ________!
B. I'll help you look for it.

Describe an airport you are familiar with. Tell about the check-in area, the security area, the gates, and the baggage claim area.

Have you ever gone through Customs and Immigration? Tell about your experience.

AIRPLANE TRAVEL

航空旅行

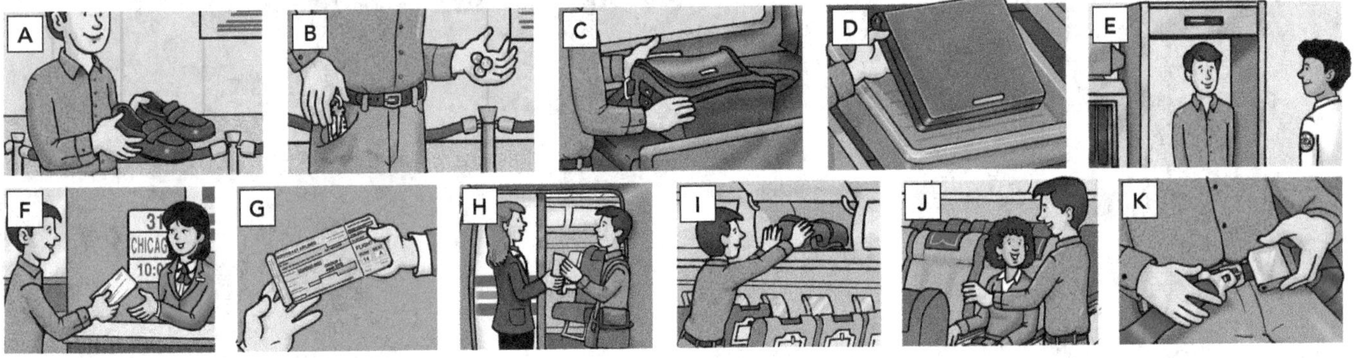

驾驶舱	1	cockpit
飞行员/机长	2	pilot/captain
副机长	3	co-pilot
洗手间	4	lavatory/bathroom
空服员	5	flight attendant
座位上方的行李箱	6	overhead compartment
走道	7	aisle
靠窗座位	8	window seat
中间座位	9	middle seat
靠走道座位	10	aisle seat
系上安全带指示灯	11	Fasten Seat Belt sign
禁止吸烟指示灯	12	No Smoking sign
呼叫钮	13	call button
氧气面罩	14	oxygen mask
紧急出口	15	emergency exit
(折叠式)小桌板	16	tray (table)
紧急措施说明	17	emergency instruction card
晕机袋/吐带	18	air sickness bag
救生衣	19	life vest/life jacket
飞机跑道	20	runway
航站大厦	21	terminal (building)
控制塔	22	control tower
飞机	23	airplane/plane/jet
脱鞋	A	take off your shoes
将口袋中的东西拿出来	B	empty your pockets
将手提袋放在传送带上	C	put your bag on the conveyor belt
将电脑放在托盘中	D	put your computer in a tray
通过金属物品探测器	E	walk through the metal detector
在登机门办登机手续	F	check in at the gate
拿登机证	G	get your boarding pass
登机	H	board the plane
存放随身行李	I	stow your carry-on bag
找座位	J	find your seat
系上安全带	K	fasten your seat belt

[1–23]
A. Where's the ________?
B. In/On/Next to/Behind/In front of/ Above/Below the ________.

[A–K]
A. Please ________.
B. All right. Certainly.

Have you ever flown in an airplane? Tell about a flight you took.

Be an airport security officer! Give passengers instructions as they go through the security area. Now, be a flight attendant! Give passengers instructions before take-off.

THE HOTEL

旅馆

看门人 **1** doorman
代客泊车 **2** valet parking
停车服务员 **3** parking attendant
行李员 **4** bellhop
行李推车 **5** luggage cart
行李员领班 **6** bell captain
一楼大厅 **7** lobby
饭店柜台 **8** front desk
柜台服务员 **9** desk clerk

客人 **10** guest
旅游服务台 **11** concierge desk
旅游服务台职员 **12** concierge
餐厅 **13** restaurant
会议室 **14** meeting room
礼品店 **15** gift shop
游泳池 **16** pool
健身房 **17** exercise room
电梯 **18** elevator

制冰机 **19** ice machine
走廊 **20** hall/hallway
房间钥匙 **21** room key
客房清洁推车 **22** housekeeping cart
饭店客房清洁员 **23** housekeeper
客房 **24** guest room
客房服务 **25** room service

A. Where do you work?
B. I work at the *Grand* Hotel.
A. What do you do there?
B. I'm a/an ___[1, 3, 4, 6, 9, 12, 23]___.

A. Excuse me. Where's the ___[1–19, 22, 23]___?
B. Right over there.
A. Thanks.

Tell about a hotel you are familiar with. Describe the place and the people.

In your opinion, which hotel employee has the most interesting job? the most difficult job? Why?

HOBBIES, CRAFTS, AND GAMES

嗜好，手工艺，游戏

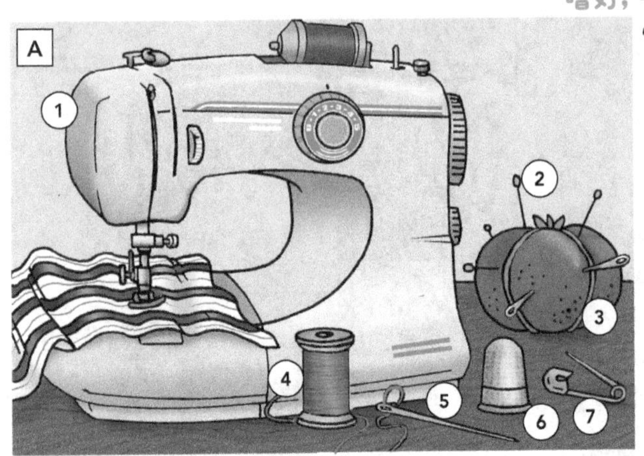

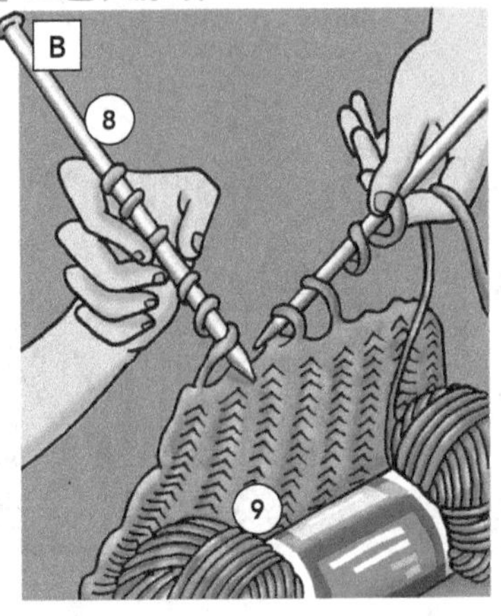

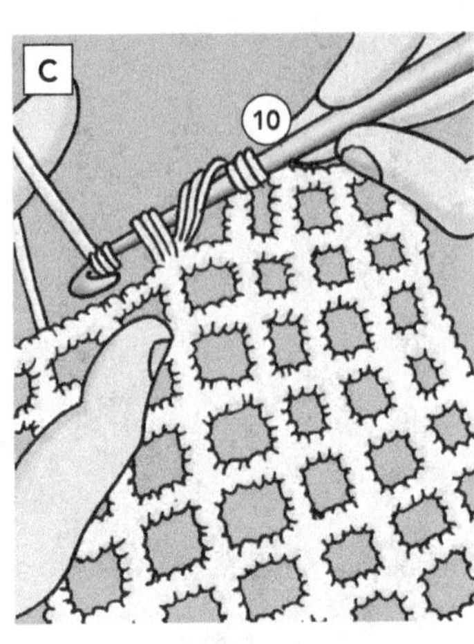

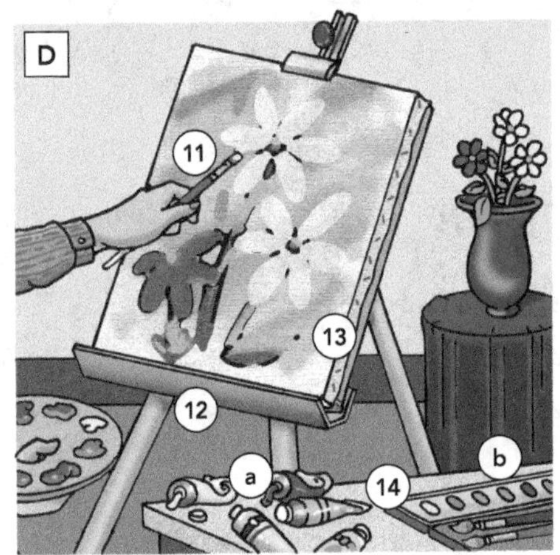

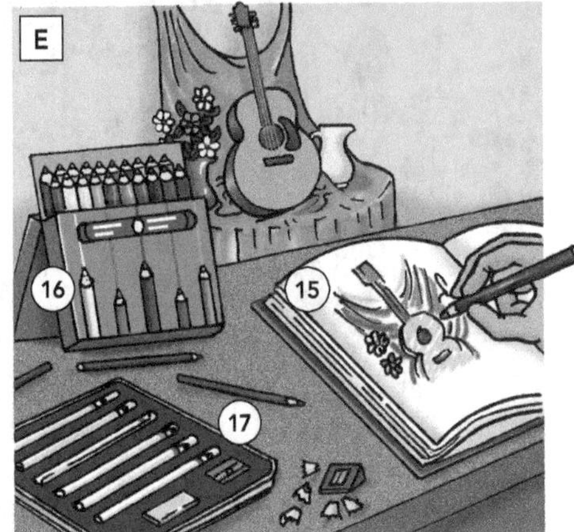

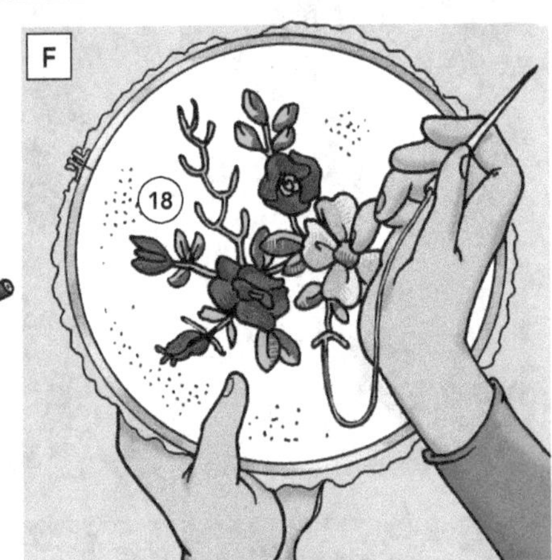

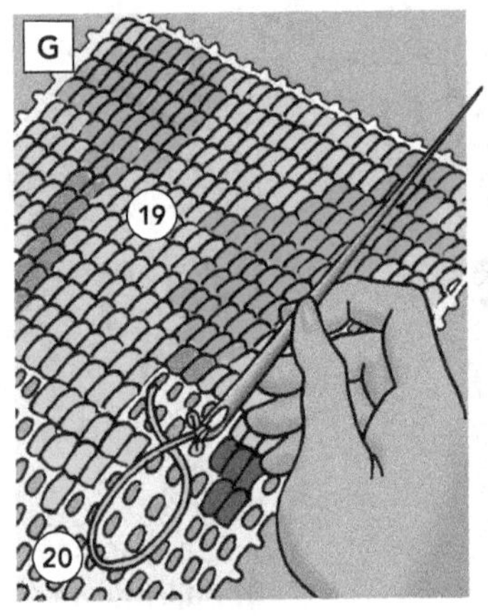

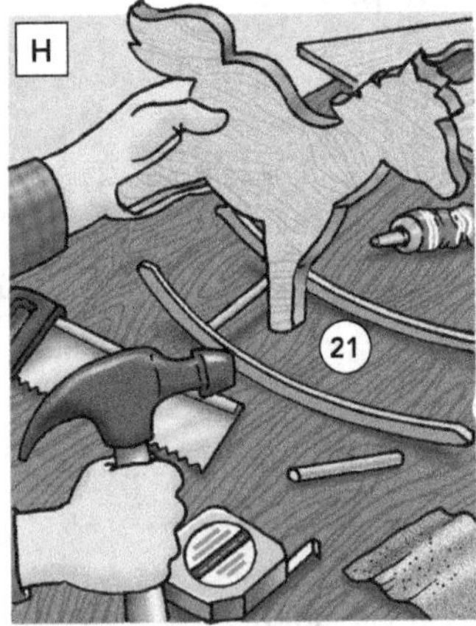

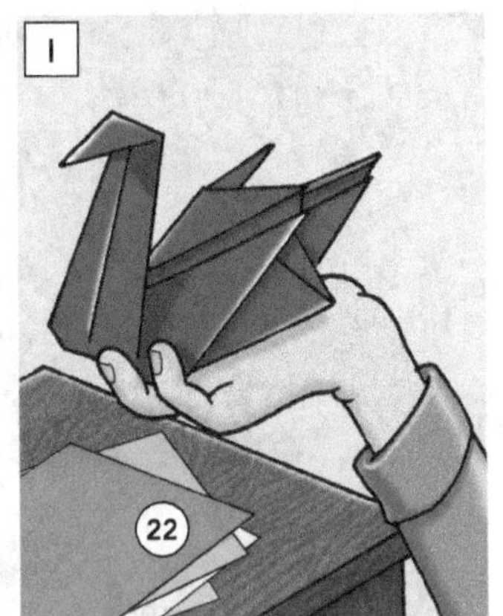

缝纫 **A sew**
缝纫机 **1** sewing machine
大头针 **2** pin
针插 **3** pin cushion
(一)卷线 **4** (spool of) thread
缝纫针 **5** (sewing) needle
顶针箍 **6** thimble
安全别针 **7** safety pin

毛衣编织 **B knit**
织针 **8** knitting needle
毛线 **9** yarn

钩针编织 **C crochet**
钩针 **10** crochet hook

(水彩/颜料)画 **D paint**
画笔 **11** paintbrush
画架 **12** easel
油画布 **13** canvas
颜料 **14** paint
油画颜料 **a** oil paint
水彩颜料 **b** watercolor

(硬笔)画 **E draw**
素描本 **15** sketch book
(一套)彩色铅笔 **16** (set of) colored pencils
绘图铅笔 **17** drawing pencil

做刺绣 **F do embroidery**
刺绣 **18** embroidery

做斜针十字绣 **G do needlepoint**
斜针十字绣 **19** needlepoint
图案 **20** pattern

做木工艺 **H do woodworking**
木工艺组合 **21** woodworking kit

折纸 **I do origami**
折纸用纸 **22** origami paper

制陶 **J make pottery**
陶土 **23** clay
陶轮/拉胚机 **24** potter's wheel

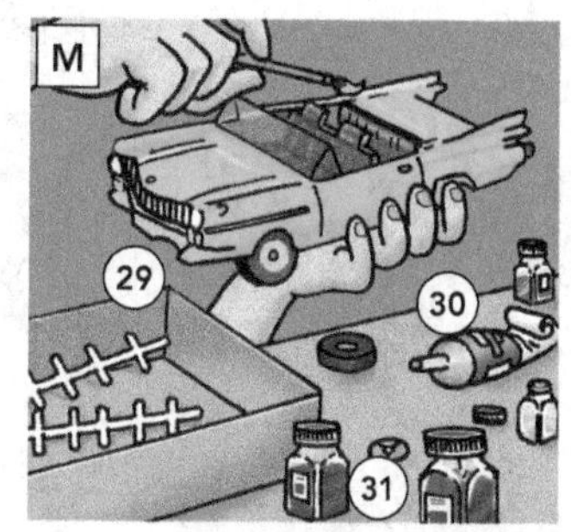

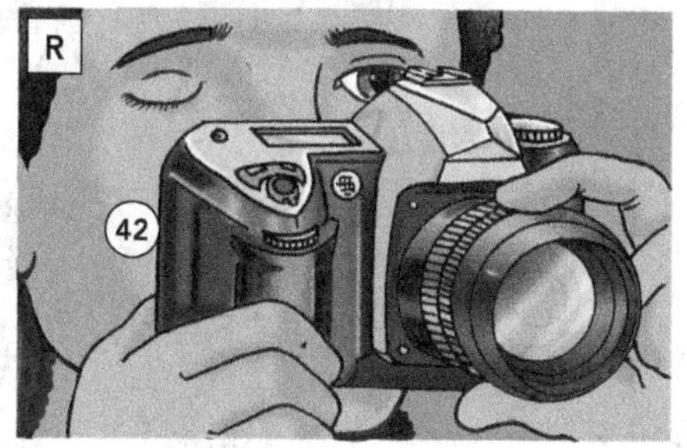

集邮 **K collect stamps**
集邮册 **25** stamp album
放大镜 **26** magnifying glass

集币 **L collect coins**
钱币目录 **27** coin catalog
集币册 **28** coin collection

制作模型 **M build models**
模型玩具组合 **29** model kit
胶水 **30** glue
压克力颜料 **31** acrylic paint

去观鸟 **N go bird-watching**
望远镜 **32** binoculars
图鉴 **33** field guide

玩纸牌 **O play cards**
(一)副纸牌 **34** (deck of) cards
梅花 **a** club
方块 **b** diamond
红心 **c** heart
黑桃 **d** spade

玩棋盘游戏 **P play board games**
国际象棋 **35** chess
西洋跳棋 **36** checkers
西洋双陆棋 **37** backgammon
大富翁游戏 **38** Monopoly
骰子 **a** dice
拼字游戏 **39** Scrabble

上网 **Q go online/ browse the Web/ "surf" the net**
网页浏览器 **40** web browser
网址 **41** web address/URL

摄影 **R photography**
照相机 **42** camera

天文学 **S astronomy**
(单筒)望远镜 **43** telescope

A. What do you like to do in your free time?
B. {I like to ___[A–Q]___.
{I enjoy ___[R, S]___.

A. May I help you?
B. Yes, please. I'd like to buy (a/an) ___[1–34, 42, 43]___.

A. What do you want to do?
B. Let's play ___[35–39]___.
A. Good idea!

Do you like to do any of these activities in your free time? Which ones?

What games are popular in your country? Describe how to play one.

PLACES TO GO

游玩去处

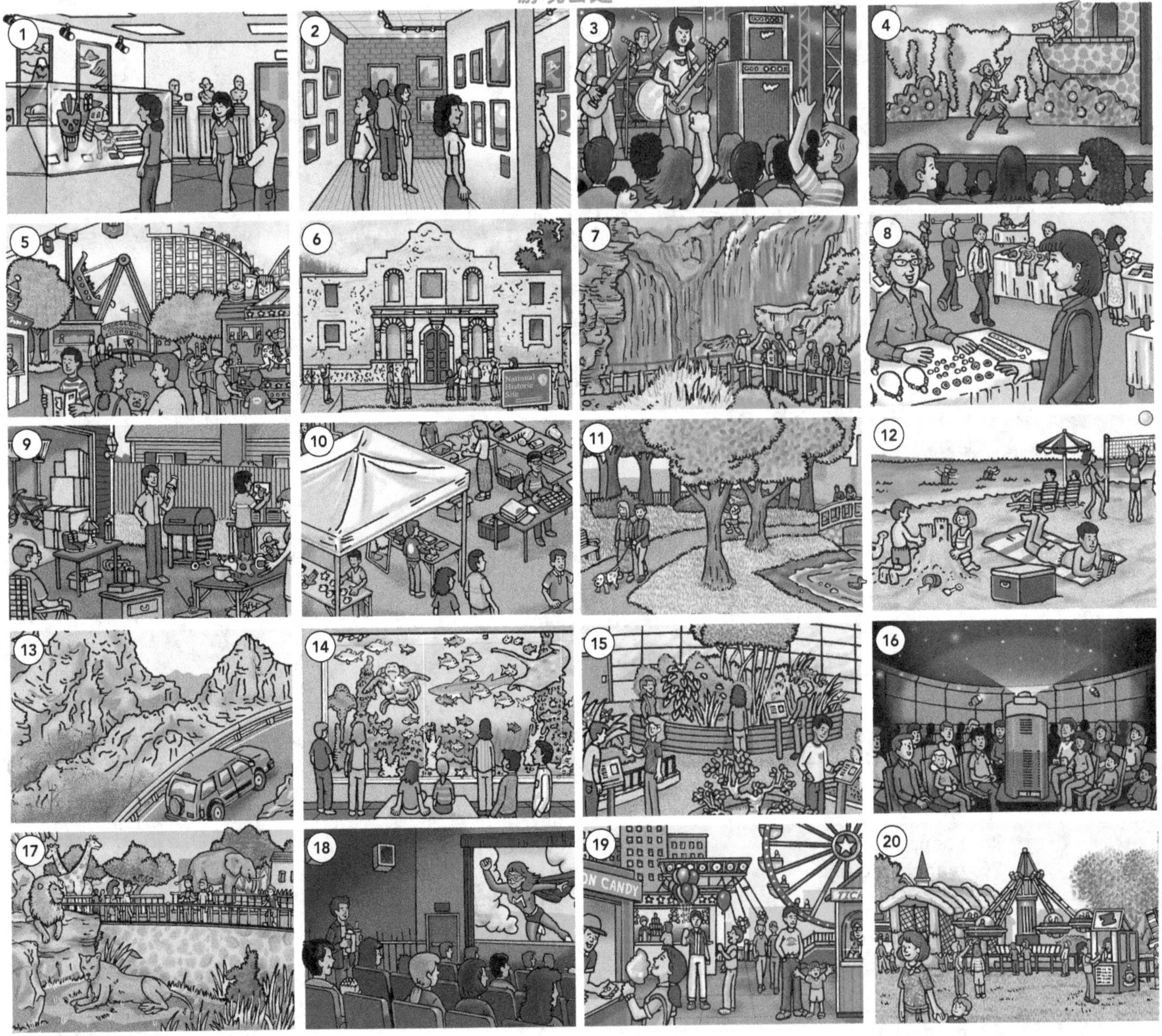

1
2
3
4
5
6
National Historic Site
7
8
9
10
11
12
13
14
15
16
17
18
19
ON CANDY
20

博物馆 **1** museum
美术馆 **2** art gallery
演唱会/音乐会 **3** concert
戏剧 **4** play
游乐园 **5** amusement park
古迹 **6** historic site
国家公园 **7** national park

手工艺展览 **8** craft fair
私人二手货出售 **9** yard sale
廉价市场/跳蚤市场 **10** swap meet/flea market
公园 **11** park
海边/海滩 **12** beach
山 **13** mountains

水族馆 **14** aquarium
植物园 **15** botanical gardens
天文馆 **16** planetarium
动物园 **17** zoo
电影院 **18** movies
嘉年华 **19** carnival
露天游乐场 **20** fair

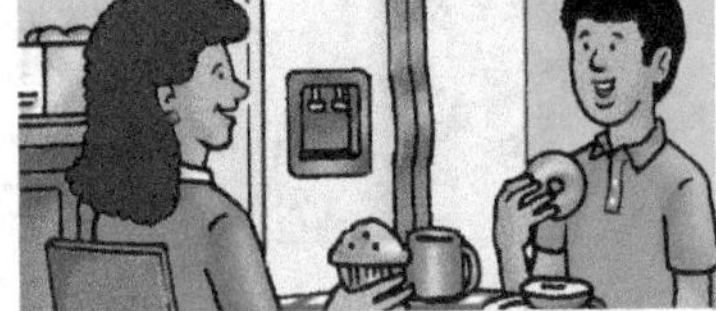

A. What do you want to do today?
B. Let's go to { a/an ___[1–9]___. / the ___[10–20]___.

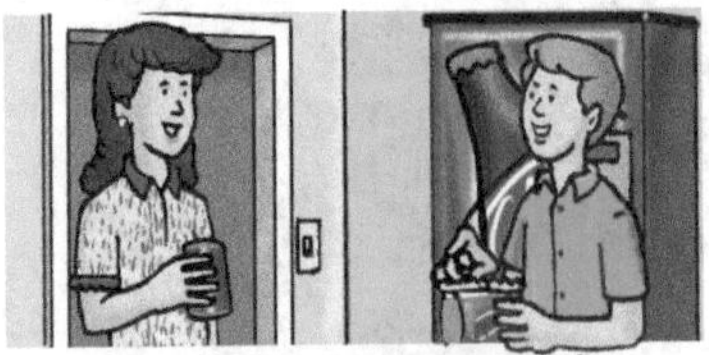

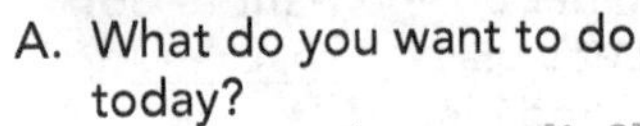

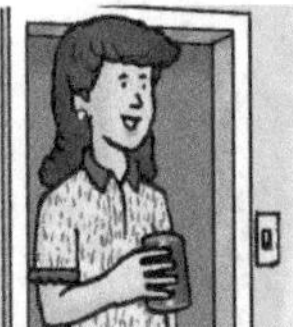

A. What did you do over the weekend?
B. I went to { a/an ___[1–9]___. / the ___[10–20]___.

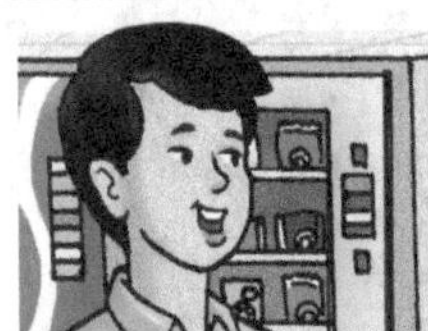

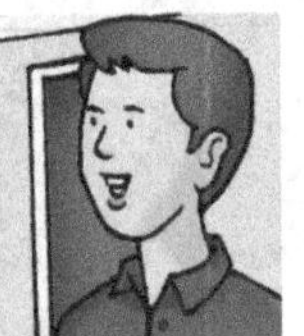

A. What are you going to do on your day off?
B. I'm going to go to { a/an ___[1–9]___. / the ___[10–20]___.

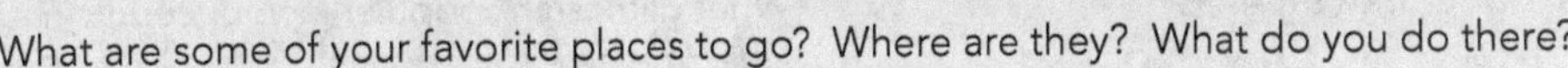

What are some of your favorite places to go? Where are they? What do you do there?

自行车道	1	bicycle path/ bike path/ bikeway
鸭池	2	duck pond
野餐区	3	picnic area
垃圾桶	4	trash can
烤肉架	5	grill
野餐桌	6	picnic table
饮水器	7	water fountain
慢跑道	8	jogging path
长凳	9	bench
网球场	10	tennis court
球场	11	ballfield
喷水池	12	fountain
脚踏车停放架	13	bike rack
旋转木马	14	merry-go-round/ carousel
滑板坡道	15	skateboard ramp
游乐场	16	playground
攀岩墙	17	climbing wall
秋千	18	swings
攀爬架	19	climber
滑梯	20	slide
翘翘板	21	seesaw
沙池	22	sandbox
沙	23	sand

[1–22]
A. Excuse me. Does this park have (a) ________?
B. Yes. Right over there.

[17–23]
A. { Be careful on the [17–21]! / Be careful in the [22, 23]!
B. I will, Dad/Mom.

Describe a park and playground you are familiar with.

THE BEACH

海边

救生员 **1** lifeguard
救生员看台 **2** lifeguard stand
救生圈 **3** life preserver
食品小卖部 **4** snack bar/ refreshment stand
小贩 **5** vendor
游泳者 **6** swimmer
海浪 **7** wave
冲浪者 **8** surfer
风筝 **9** kite

沙滩躺椅 **10** beach chair
沙滩太阳伞 **11** beach umbrella
沙堡 **12** sand castle
趴板 **13** boogie board
日光浴者 **14** sunbather
太阳镜 **15** sunglasses
沙滩巾 **16** (beach) towel
海滩球 **17** beach ball
冲浪板 **18** surfboard
贝壳 **19** seashell/shell

石头 **20** rock
小冷藏箱 **21** cooler
太阳帽 **22** sun hat
防晒油 **23** sunscreen/ sunblock/ suntan lotion
沙滩毯 **24** (beach) blanket
铲子 **25** shovel
桶子 **26** pail

[1–26]
A. What a nice beach!
B. It is. Look at all the ______s!

[9–11, 13, 15–18, 21–26]
A. Are you ready for the beach?
B. Almost. I just have to get my ______.

Do you like to go to the beach? Describe your favorite beach. What do you take when you go there?

户外休闲活动

露营 **A camping**
帐篷 **1** tent
睡袋 **2** sleeping bag
帐篷钉 **3** tent stakes
提灯 **4** lantern
短柄小斧 **5** hatchet
露营火炉 **6** camping stove
瑞士军刀 **7** Swiss army knife
驱虫剂 **8** insect repellent
火柴 **9** matches

徒步旅行 **B hiking**
背包 **10** backpack
(士兵等用)水壶 **11** canteen
指南针 **12** compass
山路图 **13** trail map
全球定位装置 **14** GPS device
登山靴 **15** hiking boots

攀岩 **C rock climbing/ technical climbing**
安全带 **16** harness
绳索 **17** rope

骑越野单车 **D mountain biking**
越野单车 **18** mountain bike
自行车安全帽 **19** (bike) helmet

野餐 **E picnic**
野餐毯 **20** (picnic) blanket
保温瓶 **21** thermos
野餐篮 **22** picnic basket

A. Let's go [A–E]* this weekend.
B. Good idea! We haven't gone [A–E]* in a long time.

**With E, say:* on a picnic.

A. Did you bring
{ the [1–9, 11–14, 16, 17, 20–22]?
{ your [10, 15, 18, 19]?
B. Yes, I did.
A. Oh, good.

Have you ever gone camping, hiking, rock climbing, or mountain biking? Tell about it: What did you do? Where? What equipment did you use?

Do you like to go on picnics? Where? What picnic supplies and food do you take with you?

个人运动与休闲活动

慢跑	A	**jogging**
慢跑衣裤	1	jogging suit
慢跑鞋	2	jogging shoes
跑步	B	**running**
跑步短裤	3	running shorts
跑步鞋	4	running shoes
步行	C	**walking**
步行鞋	5	walking shoes
(溜)直排轮滑	D	**inline skating/rollerblading**
直排轮滑鞋	6	inline skates/rollerblades
护膝	7	knee pads
(骑)自行车	E	**cycling/biking**
自行车/单车	8	bicycle/bike
自行车安全帽/单车安全帽	9	(bicycle/bike) helmet
(溜)滑板运动	F	**skateboarding**
滑板	10	skateboard
护肘	11	elbow pads
(打)保龄球	G	**bowling**
保龄球	12	bowling ball
保龄球鞋	13	bowling shoes
骑马	H	**horseback riding**
马鞍	14	saddle
缰绳	15	reins
马镫	16	stirrups
网球	I	**tennis**
网球拍	17	tennis racket
网球	18	tennis ball
网球短裤	19	tennis shorts
羽毛球	J	**badminton**
羽毛球拍	20	badminton racket
羽毛球	21	birdie/shuttlecock
短柄墙球	K	**racquetball**
护目镜	22	safety goggles
短柄墙球	23	racquetball
短柄墙球拍	24	racquet
乒乓球	L	**table tennis/ping pong**
乒乓球拍	25	paddle
乒乓球桌	26	ping pong table
乒乓球网	27	net
乒乓球	28	ping pong ball

高尔夫球 **M golf**
高尔夫球棍 **29** golf clubs
高尔夫球 **30** golf ball

飞盘 **N Frisbee**
飞盘 **31** Frisbee/
flying disc

台球 **O billiards/pool**
台球桌 **32** pool table
球杆 **33** pool stick
撞球 **34** billiard balls

武术 **P martial arts**
黑带 **35** black belt

体操 **Q gymnastics**
马 **36** horse
双杠 **37** parallel bars
垫子 **38** mat
平衡木 **39** balance beam
蹦床/弹床 **40** trampoline

举重 **R weightlifting**
杠铃 **41** barbell
哑铃 **42** weights

射箭 **S archery**
弓箭 **43** bow and arrow
靶 **44** target

拳击 **T box**
拳击手套 **45** boxing gloves
拳击短裤 **46** (boxing) trunks

摔跤 **U wrestle**
摔跤服 **47** wrestling uniform
摔角垫子 **48** (wrestling) mat

健身运动 **V work out/exercise**
跑步机 **49** treadmill
划艇机 **50** rowing machine
健身脚踏车 **51** exercise bike
多功能运动器材/运动器材 **52** universal/
exercise equipment

[A–V]
A. What do you like to do in your free time?
B. I like to go ____[A–H]____.
I like to play ____[I–O]____.
I like to do ____[P–S]____.
I like to ____[T–V]____.

[1–52]
A. I really like this/these new ________.
B. It's/They're very nice.

Do you do any of these activities? Which ones? Which are popular in your country?

TEAM SPORTS

团队运动

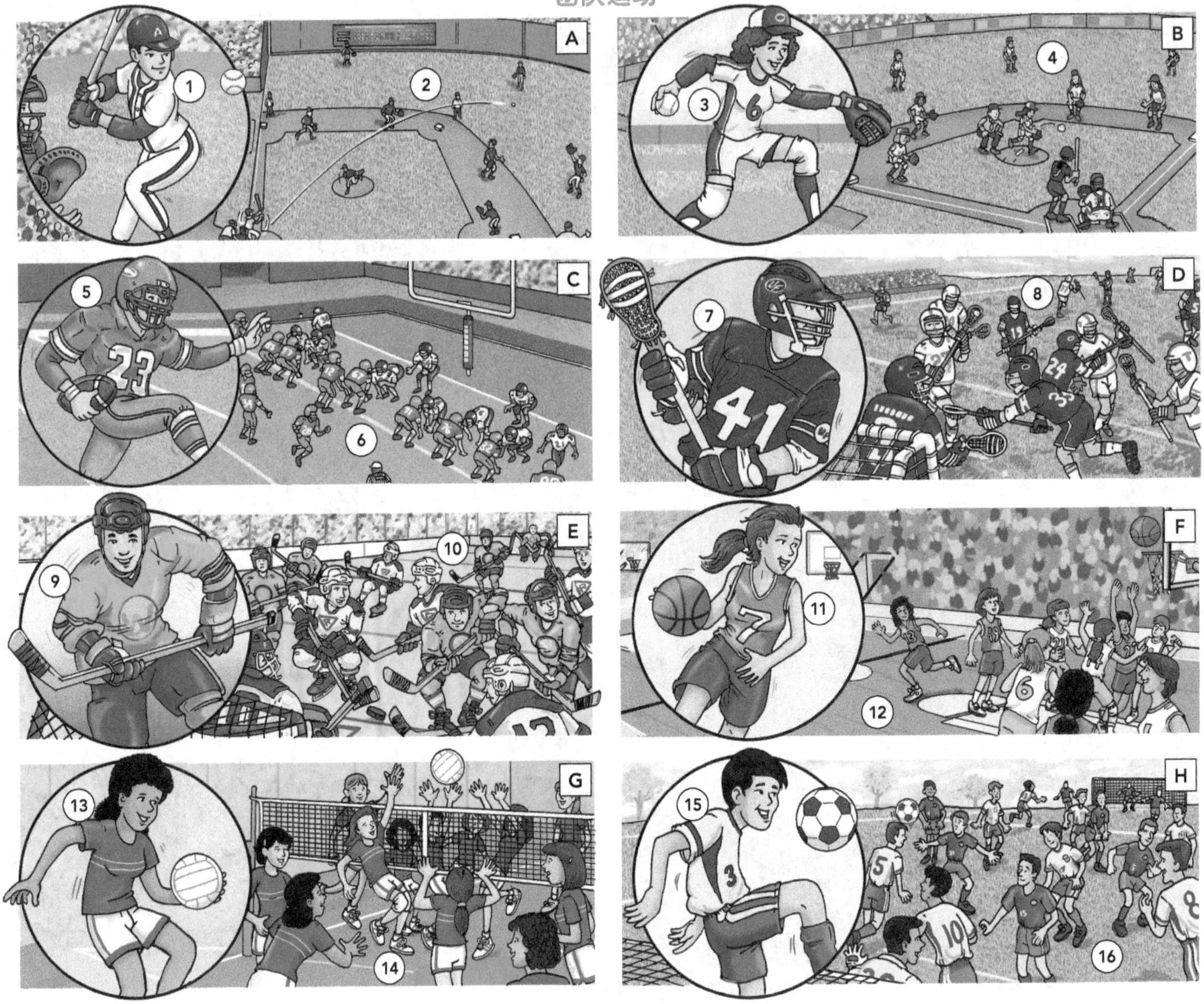

棒球	**A**	**baseball**
棒球队员	**1**	baseball player
棒球场	**2**	baseball field/ ballfield
垒球	**B**	**softball**
垒球队员	**3**	softball player
垒球场	**4**	ballfield
橄榄球	**C**	**football**
橄榄球队员	**5**	football player
橄榄球场	**6**	football field
长曲棍球	**D**	**lacrosse**
长曲棍球队员	**7**	lacrosse player
长曲棍球场	**8**	lacrosse field
冰球	**E**	**(ice) hockey**
曲棍球队员	**9**	hockey player
曲棍球场	**10**	hockey rink
篮球	**F**	**basketball**
篮球队员	**11**	basketball player
篮球场	**12**	basketball court
排球	**G**	**volleyball**
排球队员	**13**	volleyball player
排球场	**14**	volleyball court
足球	**H**	**soccer**
足球队员	**15**	soccer player
足球场	**16**	soccer field

[A–H]
A. Do you like to play **baseball**?
B. Yes. **Baseball** is one of my favorite sports.

A. .... plays [A–H] very well.
B. You're right. I think he's/she's one of the best ________s* on the team.

*Use 1, 3, 5, 7, 9, 11, 13, 15.

A. Now listen, team! I want all of you to go out on that ________† and play the best game of [A–H] you've ever played!
B. All right, Coach!

† Use 2, 4, 6, 8, 10, 12, 14, 16.

Which sports in this lesson do you like to play? Which do you like to watch?

What are your favorite teams?

Name some famous players of these sports.

团队运动设备

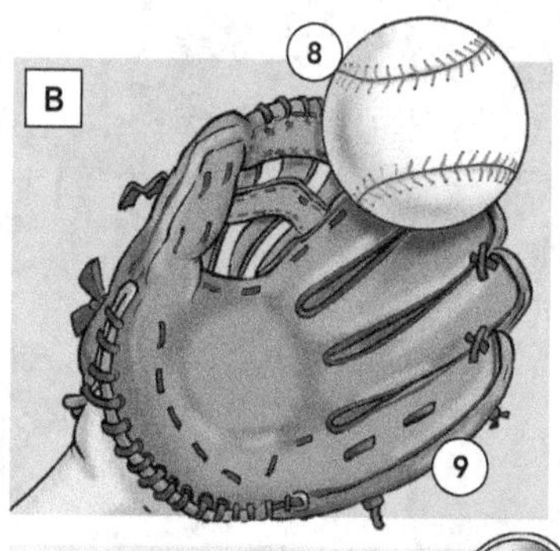

棒球 **A baseball**
棒球 1 baseball
棒球棍 2 bat
打击手头盔 3 batting helmet
棒球制服 4 (baseball) uniform
接球手面罩 5 catcher's mask
棒球手套 6 (baseball) glove
接球手套 7 catcher's mitt

垒球 **B softball**
垒球 8 softball
垒球手套 9 softball glove

橄榄球 **C football**
橄榄球 10 football
橄榄球头盔 11 football helmet
护肩 12 shoulder pads

长曲棍球 **D lacrosse**
长曲棍球 13 lacrosse ball
面具 14 face guard
长曲棍球杆 15 lacrosse stick

冰球 **E (ice) hockey**
曲棍球 16 hockey puck
曲棍球球杆 17 hockey stick
曲棍球面罩 18 hockey mask
曲棍球手套 19 hockey glove
曲棍球溜冰鞋 20 hockey skates

篮球 **F basketball**
篮球 21 basketball
篮板 22 backboard
篮圈 23 basketball hoop

排球 **G volleyball**
排球 24 volleyball
排球网 25 volleyball net

足球 **H soccer**
足球 26 soccer ball
护胫 27 shinguards

[1–27]
A. I can't find my **baseball**!
B. Look in the closet.*

*closet, basement, garage

[In a store]
A. Excuse me. I'm looking for (a) _[1–27]_.
B. All our _[A–H]_ equipment is over there.
A. Thanks.

[At home]
A. I'm going to play _[A–H]_ after school today.
B. Don't forget your _[1–21, 24, 26, 27]_!

Which sports in this lesson are popular in your country? Which sports do students play in high school?

冬季运动与休闲活动

下坡滑雪 **A (downhill) skiing**
滑雪板 **1** skis
滑雪靴 **2** ski boots
滑雪板皮靴固定器 **3** bindings
滑雪撑杆 **4** (ski) poles

越野滑雪 **B cross-country skiing**
越野滑雪板 **5** cross-country skis

溜冰 **C (ice) skating**
溜冰鞋 **6** (ice) skates
冰刀 **7** blade
冰刀套 **8** skate guard

花式溜冰 **D figure skating**
花式溜冰鞋 **9** figure skates

滑雪单板 **E snowboarding**
滑雪单板 **10** snowboard

滑雪橇 **F sledding**
雪撬 **11** sled
圆雪橇 **12** sledding dish/ saucer

滑大雪橇/滑连橇 **G bobsledding**
大雪橇/连雪橇 **13** bobsled

驾雪车 **H snowmobiling**
雪车 **14** snowmobile

[A–H]
A. What's your favorite winter sport?
B. **Skiing**.

[A–H]
[At work or at school on Friday]
A. What are you going to do this weekend?
B. I'm going to go ______.

[1–14]
[On the telephone]
A. Hello. *Sally's* Sporting Goods.
B. Hello. Do you sell ______(s)?
A. Yes, we do. / No, we don't.

Have you ever done any of these activities? Which ones?

Have you ever watched the Winter Olympics? Which event do you think is the most exciting? the most dangerous?

水上运动与休闲活动

驾帆船 **A sailing**
帆船 1 sailboat
救生衣 2 life jacket/life vest

划独木舟 **B canoeing**
独木舟 3 canoe
桨 4 paddles

划船 **C rowing**
划船 5 rowboat
橹 6 oars

划皮艇 **D kayaking**
皮艇 7 kayak
桨 8 paddles

激流泛舟 **E (white-water) rafting**
橡皮艇 9 raft
救生衣 10 life jacket/life vest

游泳 **F swimming**
游泳衣 11 swimsuit/bathing suit
蛙镜 12 goggles
泳帽 13 bathing cap

浮潜 **G snorkeling**
潜水镜 14 mask
潜水呼吸管 15 snorkel
蛙鞋 16 fins

潜水 **H scuba diving**
潜水衣 17 wet suit
压缩空气瓶 18 (air) tank
潜水镜 19 (diving) mask

冲浪 **I surfing**
冲浪板 20 surfboard

风帆冲浪 **J windsurfing**
风帆板 21 sailboard
风帆 22 sail

滑水 **K waterskiing**
滑水板/滑水橇 23 water skis
托缆/滑水绳 24 towrope

钓鱼 **L fishing**
钓鱼杆 25 (fishing) rod/pole
线轴 26 reel
鱼线 27 (fishing) line
鱼网 28 (fishing) net
鱼饵 29 bait

[A–L]
A. Would you like to go **sailing** tomorrow?
B. Sure. I'd love to.

A. Have you ever gone ___[A–L]___?
B. Yes, I have./No, I haven't.

A. Do you have everything you need to go ___[A–L]___?
B. Yes. I have my ___[1–29]___ (and my ___[1–29]___).
A. Have a good time!

Which sports in this lesson have you tried? Which sports would you like to try?

Are any of these sports popular in your country? Which ones?

SPORT AND EXERCISE ACTIONS

运动及练习动作

- 打球 **1** hit
- 投球 **2** pitch
- 掷球 **3** throw
- 接球 **4** catch
- 传球 **5** pass
- 踢球 **6** kick
- 发球 **7** serve
- 拍球 **8** bounce
- 运球 **9** dribble
- 投篮 **10** shoot
- 伸展 **11** stretch
- 弯腰 **12** bend
- 走 **13** walk
- 跑 **14** run
- 单脚跳 **15** hop
- 轻巧地跳 **16** skip
- 跳跃 **17** jump
- 伸臂 **18** reach
- 摆动 **19** swing
- 举起 **20** lift
- 游泳 **21** swim
- 潜水 **22** dive
- 射箭 **23** shoot
- 伏地挺身 **24** push-up
- 仰卧起坐 **25** sit-up
- 蹲 **26** deep knee bend
- 开合跳 **27** jumping jack
- 翻筋斗 **28** somersault
- 横翻筋斗 **29** cartwheel
- 倒立 **30** handstand

[1–10]
A. ________ the ball!
B. Okay, Coach!

[11–23]
A. Now ________!
B. Like this?
A. Yes.

[24–30]
A. Okay, everybody. I want you to do twenty ________s!
B. Twenty ________s?!
A. That's right.

Do you exercise regularly? Which exercises do you do?

Be an exercise instructor! Lead your friends in an exercise routine using the actions in this lesson.

娱乐

戏剧 **A play**
剧场 **1** theater
演员 **2** actor
女演员 **3** actress

演奏会/演唱会 **B concert**
音乐厅 **4** concert hall
管弦乐队 **5** orchestra
乐师 **6** musician
指挥 **7** conductor
乐团 **8** band

歌剧 **C opera**
歌剧演唱者 **9** opera singer

芭蕾舞 **D ballet**
芭蕾舞者 **10** ballet dancer
女芭蕾舞者 **11** ballerina

歌厅 **E music club**
演唱者/歌手 **12** singer

电影院 **F movies**
电影院 **13** (movie) theater
电影屏幕 **14** (movie) screen
女演员 **15** actress
演员 **16** actor

喜剧表演俱乐部 **G comedy club**
喜剧演员 **17** comedian

[A–G]
A. What are you doing this evening?
B. I'm going to { a ____[A, B, E, G]____. / the ____[C, D, F]____.

[1–17]
A. What a magnificent ________!
B. I agree.

What kinds of entertainment in this lesson do you like?
What kinds of entertainment are popular in your country?

Who are some of your favorite actors? actresses? musicians? singers? comedians?

TYPES OF ENTERTAINMENT

娱乐种类

A

B

音乐 **A music**
古典音乐 **1** classical music
流行音乐 **2** popular music
乡村音乐 **3** country music
摇滚音乐 **4** rock music
民俗音乐 **5** folk music

饶舌音乐 **6** rap music
福音音乐 **7** gospel music
爵士乐 **8** jazz
蓝调音乐 **9** blues
蓝草音乐(美国南方乡村音乐) **10** bluegrass
嘻哈音乐 **11** hip hop
雷鬼/雷盖音乐(源自牙买加) **12** reggae

戏剧 **B plays**
话剧/戏剧 **13** drama
喜剧 **14** comedy
悲剧 **15** tragedy
歌舞喜剧 **16** musical (comedy)

C

D

电影	**C**	**movies/films**
剧情片	**17**	drama
喜剧片	**18**	comedy
西部片	**19**	western
悬疑片	**20**	mystery
歌舞片	**21**	musical
卡通片/动画片	**22**	cartoon
记录片	**23**	documentary
动作片/探险片	**24**	action movie/ adventure movie
战争片	**25**	war movie
恐怖片	**26**	horror movie
科幻片	**27**	science fiction movie
外语片	**28**	foreign film
电视节目	**D**	**TV programs**
电视剧	**29**	drama
情境喜剧	**30**	(situation) comedy/ sitcom
脱口秀	**31**	talk show
游戏竞赛节目	**32**	game show/ quiz show
实境节目	**33**	reality show
肥皂剧/连续剧	**34**	soap opera
卡通影集/动画影集	**35**	cartoon
儿童节目	**36**	children's program
新闻节目	**37**	news program
体育节目	**38**	sports program
自然科学节目	**39**	nature program
购物节目	**40**	shopping program

A. What kind of ___[A–D]___ do you like?

B. { I like ___[1–12]___.
I like ___[13–40]___s.

What's your favorite type of music?
Who is your favorite singer? musician? musical group?

What kind of movies do you like?
Who are your favorite movie stars?
What are the titles of your favorite movies?

What kind of TV programs do you like?
What are your favorite shows?

MUSICAL INSTRUMENTS

乐器

弦乐器 **Strings**
- 小提琴 **1** violin
- 中提琴 **2** viola
- 大提琴 **3** cello
- 低音提琴 **4** bass
- 空心吉他 **5** (acoustic) guitar
- 电吉他 **6** electric guitar
- 班卓琴/五弦琴 **7** banjo
- 竖琴 **8** harp

木管乐器 **Woodwinds**
- 短笛 **9** piccolo
- 长笛 **10** flute
- 单簧管/黑管 **11** clarinet
- 双簧管 **12** oboe
- 直笛 **13** recorder
- 萨克斯管 **14** saxophone
- 巴松管 **15** bassoon

铜管乐器 **Brass**
- 小喇叭/小号 **16** trumpet
- 伸缩喇叭/长号 **17** trombone
- 法国号/圆号 **18** French horn
- 低音喇叭/大号 **19** tuba

打击乐器 **Percussion**
- 鼓 **20** drums
- 铙钹 **a** cymbals
- 铃鼓 **21** tambourine
- 木琴 **22** xylophone

键盘乐器 **Keyboard Instruments**
- 钢琴 **23** piano
- 电子琴 **24** electric keyboard
- 风琴 **25** organ

其它乐器 **Other Instruments**
- 手风琴 **26** accordion
- 口琴 **27** harmonica

A. Do you play a musical instrument?
B. Yes. I play the **violin**.

A. You play the **trumpet** very well.
B. Thank you.

A. What's that noise?!
B. That's my son/daughter practicing the **drums**.

Do you play a musical instrument? Which one?

Which instruments are usually in an orchestra? a marching band? a rock group?

Name and describe typical musical instruments in your country.

THE FARM AND FARM ANIMALS

农场及家畜

农舍	1	farmhouse
农夫	2	farmer
菜园	3	(vegetable) garden
稻草人	4	scarecrow
干草	5	hay
雇工	6	hired hand
牲口棚/谷仓	7	barn
马厩	8	stable
马	9	horse
谷仓旁院子	10	barnyard
火鸡	11	turkey
山羊	12	goat
小羔羊	13	lamb
公鸡	14	rooster
猪圈	15	pig pen
猪	16	pig
养鸡场	17	chicken coop
鸡	18	chicken
母鸡舍	19	hen house
母鸡	20	hen
农作物	21	crop
灌溉系统	22	irrigation system
拖拉机	23	tractor
田地	24	field
牧场	25	pasture
牛	26	cow
绵羊	27	sheep
果树园	28	orchard
果树	29	fruit tree
农场工人	30	farm worker
紫花苜蓿	31	alfalfa
玉米	32	corn
棉花	33	cotton
米	34	rice
黄豆	35	soybeans
小麦	36	wheat

[1–30]
A. Where's the ________?
B. In/Next to the ________.

A. The [9, 11–14, 16, 18, 20, 26] s/ [27] are loose again!
B. Oh, no! Where are they?
A. They're in the [1, 3, 7, 8, 10, 15, 17, 19, 24, 25, 28].

[31–36]
A. Do you grow ________ on your farm?
B. No. We grow ________.

Tell about farms in your country. What crops and animals are common on these farms?

动物及宠物

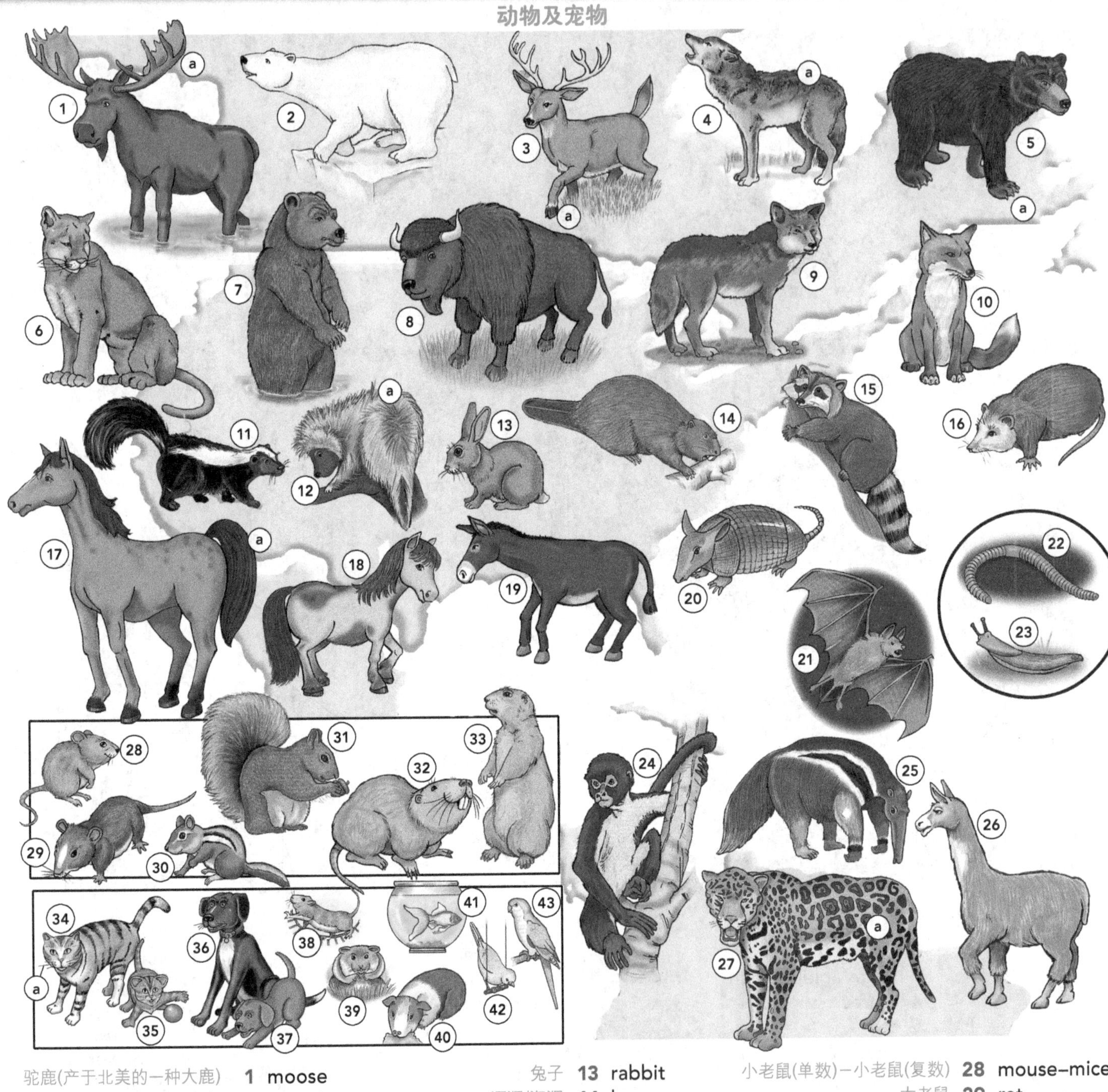

驼鹿(产于北美的一种大鹿) **1** moose
鹿角 **a** antler
北极熊 **2** polar bear
鹿 **3** deer
蹄(单数)－蹄(复数) **a** hoof–hooves
狼(单数)－狼(复数) **4** wolf–wolves
毛皮 **a** coat/fur
黑熊 **5** (black) bear
爪 **a** claw
美洲狮 **6** mountain lion
灰熊 **7** (grizzly) bear
北美野牛 **8** buffalo/bison
北美土狼 **9** coyote
狐狸 **10** fox
臭鼬 **11** skunk
豪猪 **12** porcupine
刺 **a** quill

兔子 **13** rabbit
河狸/海狸 **14** beaver
浣熊 **15** raccoon
负鼠 **16** possum/opossum
马 **17** horse
尾巴 **a** tail
小马 **18** pony
驴 **19** donkey
犰狳(中南美产) **20** armadillo
蝙蝠 **21** bat
蚯蚓 **22** worm
蛞蝓 **23** slug
猴子 **24** monkey
食蚁兽 **25** anteater
美洲驼 **26** llama
美洲虎 **27** jaguar
斑点 **a** spots

小老鼠(单数)－小老鼠(复数) **28** mouse–mice
大老鼠 **29** rat
花栗鼠 **30** chipmunk
松鼠 **31** squirrel
地鼠 **32** gopher
北美的草原土拨鼠 **33** prairie dog
猫 **34** cat
胡须 **a** whiskers
小猫 **35** kitten
狗 **36** dog
小狗 **37** puppy
仓鼠 **38** hamster
沙鼠 **39** gerbil
天竺鼠 **40** guinea pig
金鱼 **41** goldfish
金丝雀 **42** canary
鹦哥/小型鹦鹉 **43** parakeet

羚羊 **44** antelope
狒狒 **45** baboon
犀牛 **46** rhinoceros
角 a horn
熊猫 **47** panda
猩猩 **48** orangutan
黑豹 **49** panther
长臂猿 **50** gibbon

老虎 **51** tiger
掌 a paw
骆驼 **52** camel
驼峰 a hump
大象 **53** elephant
象牙 a tusk
象鼻 b trunk
土狼 **54** hyena

狮子 **55** lion
鬃 a mane
长颈鹿 **56** giraffe
斑马 **57** zebra
条纹 a stripes
黑猩猩 **58** chimpanzee
河马 **59** hippopotamus
豹 **60** leopard

大猩猩 **61** gorilla
袋鼠 **62** kangaroo
肚袋 a pouch
无尾熊/树袋熊 **63** koala (bear)
鸭嘴兽 **64** platypus

[1–33, 44–64]
A. Look at that _______!
B. Wow! That's the biggest _______ I've ever seen!

[34–43]
A. Do you have a pet?
B. Yes. I have a _______.
A. What's your _______'s name?
B. ....

What animals are there where you live?

Is there a zoo near where you live? What animals does it have?

What are some common pets in your country?

If you could be an animal, which animal would you like to be? Why?

Does your culture have any popular folk tales or children's stories about animals? Tell a story you know.

BIRDS AND INSECTS

鸟类及昆虫类

鸟类 Birds

知更鸟 **1** robin
鸟窝 **a** nest
鸟蛋 **b** egg
冠蓝鸦 **2** blue jay
翅膀 **a** wing
尾巴 **b** tail
羽毛 **c** feather
红衣凤头鸟/红衣主教鸟 **3** cardinal
乌鸦 **4** crow
海鸥 **5** seagull
啄木鸟 **6** woodpecker
鸟嘴 **a** beak
鸽子 **7** pigeon
猫头鹰 **8** owl
苍鹰 **9** hawk
老鹰 **10** eagle
爪 **a** claw
天鹅 **11** swan
蜂鸟 **12** hummingbird
鸭子 **13** duck
鸭嘴 **a** bill
麻雀 **14** sparrow
鹅(单数)–鹅(复数) **15** goose–geese
企鹅 **16** penguin
红鹤 **17** flamingo
鹤 **18** crane
鹳 **19** stork
鹈鹕 **20** pelican
孔雀 **21** peacock
鹦鹉 **22** parrot
驼鸟 **23** ostrich

昆虫类 Insects

苍蝇 **24** fly
瓢虫 **25** ladybug
萤火虫 **26** firefly/lightning bug
蛾 **27** moth
毛毛虫 **28** caterpillar
茧 **a** cocoon
蝴蝶 **29** butterfly
扁虱 **30** tick
蚊子 **31** mosquito
蜻蜓 **32** dragonfly
蜘蛛 **33** spider
蜘蛛网 **a** web
螳螂 **34** praying mantis
黄蜂 **35** wasp
蜜蜂 **36** bee
蜂窝 **a** beehive
蚱蜢 **37** grasshopper
甲虫 **38** beetle
蝎子 **39** scorpion
蜈蚣 **40** centipede
蟋蟀 **41** cricket

[1–41]
A. Is that a/an ________?
B. No. I think it's a/an ________.

[24–41]
A. Hold still! There's a ________ on your shirt!
B. Oh! Can you get it off me?
A. There! It's gone!

What birds and insects are there where you live?

Does your culture have any popular folk tales or children's stories about birds or insects? Tell a story you know.

FISH, SEA ANIMALS, AND REPTILES

鱼类，海洋动物，爬行动物

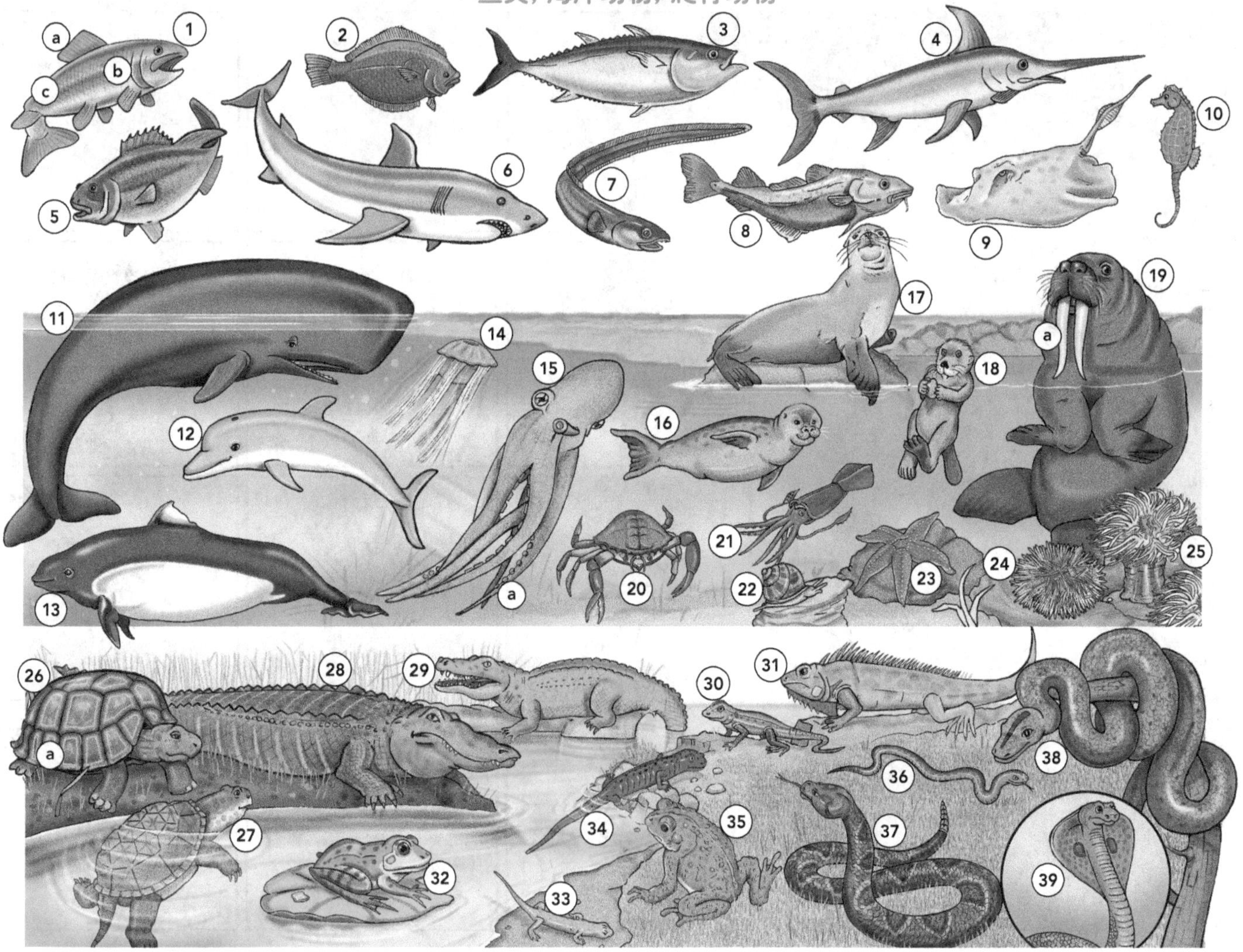

鱼 Fish

鳟鱼	1	trout
鳍		a fin
鳃		b gill
鳞		c scales
鲽鱼/比目鱼	2	flounder
金枪鱼	3	tuna
旗鱼	4	swordfish
鲈鱼	5	bass
鲨鱼	6	shark
鳗鱼	7	eel
鳕鱼	8	cod
刺魟	9	ray/stingray
海马	10	sea horse

海洋动物 Sea Animals

鲸鱼	11	whale
海豚	12	dolphin
鼠海豚	13	porpoise
水母	14	jellyfish
章鱼	15	octopus
触须		a tentacle
海豹	16	seal
海狮	17	sea lion
水獭	18	otter
海象	19	walrus
长牙		a tusk
螃蟹	20	crab
鱿鱼	21	squid
蜗牛	22	snail
海星	23	starfish
海胆	24	sea urchin
海葵	25	sea anemone

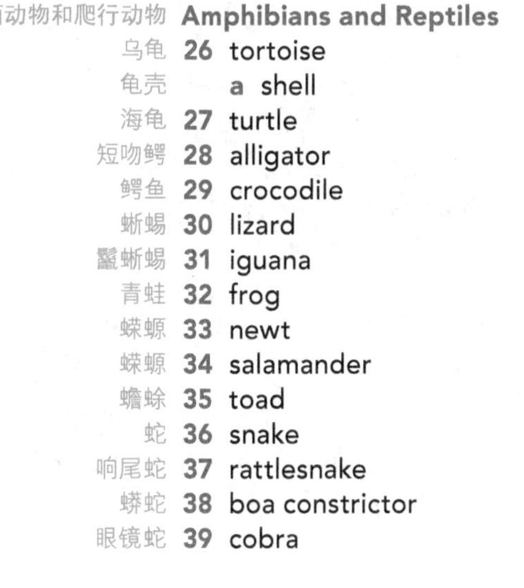

两栖动物和爬行动物 Amphibians and Reptiles

乌龟	26	tortoise
龟壳		a shell
海龟	27	turtle
短吻鳄	28	alligator
鳄鱼	29	crocodile
蜥蜴	30	lizard
鬣蜥蜴	31	iguana
青蛙	32	frog
蝾螈	33	newt
蝾螈	34	salamander
蟾蜍	35	toad
蛇	36	snake
响尾蛇	37	rattlesnake
蟒蛇	38	boa constrictor
眼镜蛇	39	cobra

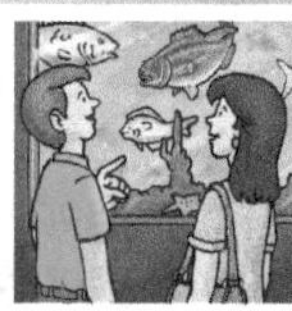

[1–39]
A. Is that a/an ________?
B. No. I think it's a/an ________.

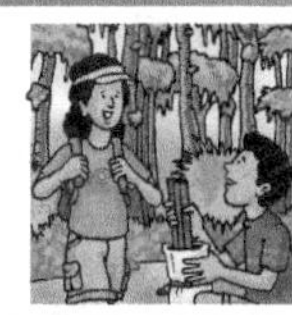

[26–39]
A. Are there any ________s around here?
B. No. But there are lots of ________!

What fish, sea animals, and reptiles can be found in your country? Which ones are endangered and need to be protected? Why?

In your opinion, which ones are the most interesting? the most beautiful? the most dangerous?

TREES, PLANTS, AND FLOWERS

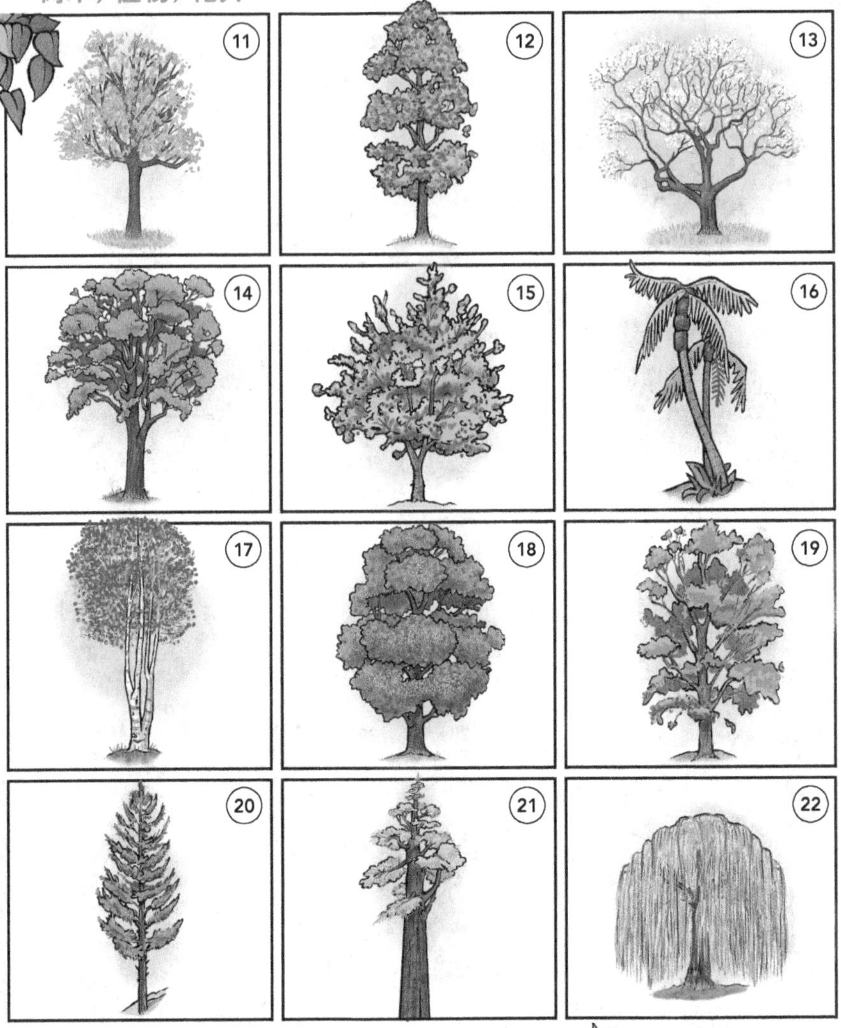

树	1	tree
叶子（单数）– 叶子（复数）	2	leaf–leaves
细枝	3	twig
树枝/树杈	4	branch
枝干	5	limb
树干/主干	6	trunk
树皮	7	bark
树根	8	root
针叶	9	needle
松果/松球	10	pine cone
山茱萸	11	dogwood
冬青树	12	holly
木兰	13	magnolia
榆树	14	elm
樱桃树	15	cherry
棕榈树	16	palm
白桦	17	birch
枫树	18	maple
橡树	19	oak
松树	20	pine
红杉	21	redwood
垂柳	22	(weeping) willow
灌木丛	23	bush
冬青树	24	holly
浆果	25	berries
灌木	26	shrub
蕨类植物	27	fern
植物	28	plant
仙人掌	29	cactus–cacti
藤蔓	30	vine
毒葛	31	poison ivy
(毒)盐肤木	32	poison sumac
毒栎	33	poison oak

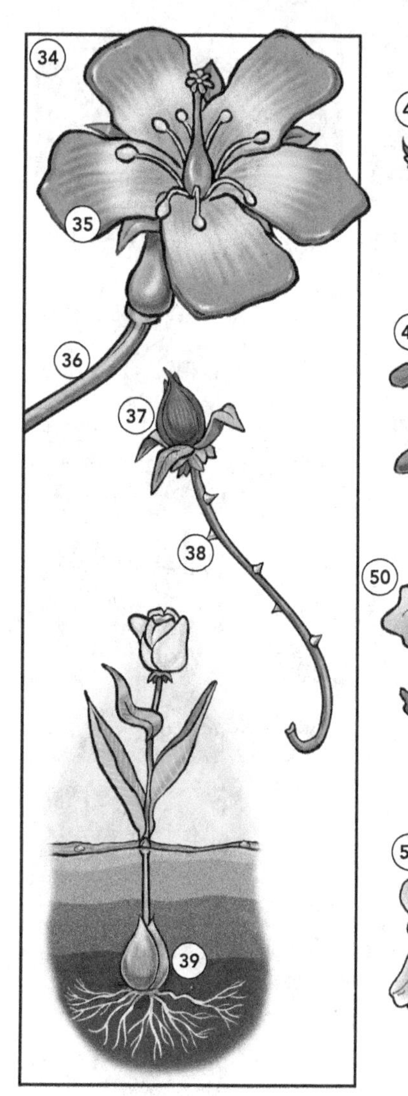

花 **34** flower
花瓣 **35** petal
茎 **36** stem
花蕾 **37** bud
刺 **38** thorn
球茎 **39** bulb
菊花 **40** chrysanthemum
水仙花 **41** daffodil
雏菊 **42** daisy

万寿菊/金盏花 **43** marigold
康乃馨 **44** carnation
栀子花 **45** gardenia
百合花 **46** lily
鸢尾花 **47** iris
三色堇/三色紫萝兰 **48** pansy
矮牵牛 **49** petunia
兰花 **50** orchid
玫瑰 **51** rose

向日葵 **52** sunflower
番红花 **53** crocus
郁金香 **54** tulip
天竺葵 **55** geranium
紫萝兰 **56** violet
猩猩木 **57** poinsettia
茉莉花 **58** jasmine
木槿 **59** hibiscus

[11–22]
A. What kind of tree is that?
B. I think it's a/an ______ tree.

[31–33]
A. Watch out for the ______ over there!
B. Oh. Thanks for the warning.

[40–57]
A. Look at all the ______s!*
B. They're beautiful!

**With 58 and 59, use:* Look at all the ___!

Describe your favorite tree and your favorite flower.

What kinds of trees and flowers grow where you live?

In your country, what flowers do you see at weddings? at funerals? during holidays? in hospital rooms? Tell which flowers people use for different occasions.

能源，环保，环境

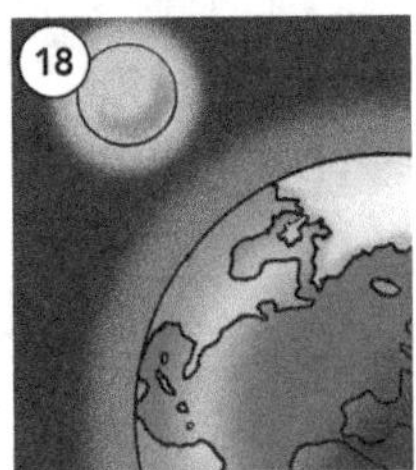

能源 **Sources of Energy**

石油 **1** oil/petroleum
天燃气 **2** (natural) gas
煤 **3** coal
核能 **4** nuclear energy
太阳能 **5** solar energy
水力发电 **6** hydroelectric power
风能 **7** wind
地热能 **8** geothermal energy

环保 **Conservation**

资源回收 **9** recycle
节约能源 **10** save energy/ conserve energy
节约用水 **11** save water/ conserve water
汽车共乘 **12** carpool

环境问题 **Environmental Problems**

空气污染 **13** air pollution
水污染 **14** water pollution
危险废物 **15** hazardous waste/ toxic waste
酸雨 **16** acid rain
放射物 **17** radiation
全球变暖 **18** global warming

[1–8]
A. In my opinion, _______ will be our best source of energy in the future.
B. I disagree. I think our best source of energy will be _______.

[9–12]
A. Do you _______?
B. Yes. I'm very concerned about the environment.

[13–18]
A. Do you worry about the environment?
B. Yes. I'm very concerned about _______.

What kind of energy do you use to heat your home? to cook? In your opinion, which will be the best source of energy in the future?

Do you practice conservation? What do you do to help the environment?

In your opinion, what is the most serious environmental problem in the world today? Why?

自然灾害

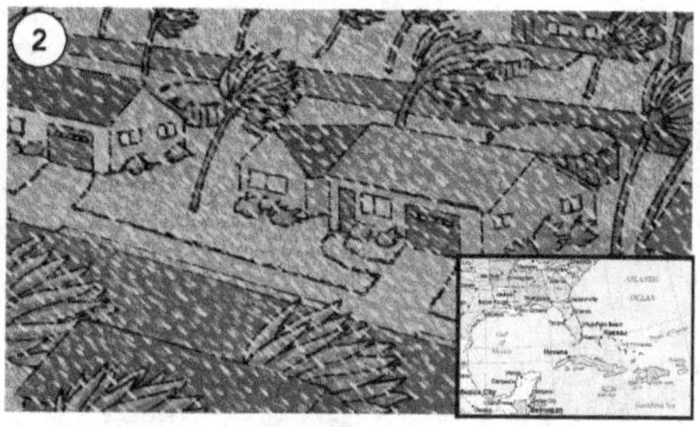

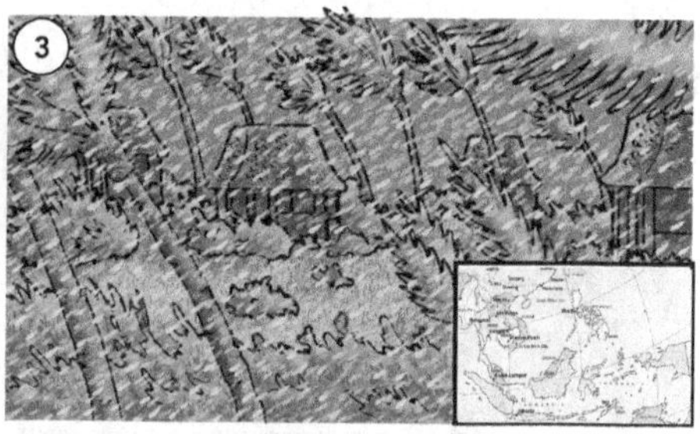

地震 **1** earthquake	洪水 **6** flood	山崩 **11** landslide
飓风 **2** hurricane	海啸 **7** tsunami	泥石流 **12** mudslide
台风 **3** typhoon	干旱 **8** drought	雪崩 **13** avalanche
暴风雪 **4** blizzard	森林大火 **9** forest fire	火山爆发 **14** volcanic eruption
龙卷风 **5** tornado	野火 **10** wildfire	

A. Did you hear about the ______ in ......(country)......?
B. Yes, I did. I saw it on the news.

Have you or someone you know ever experienced a natural disaster? Tell about it.

Which natural disasters sometimes happen where you live? How do people prepare for them?

FORMS OF IDENTIFICATION

身份证明种类

1

2

3

4

5

6 7
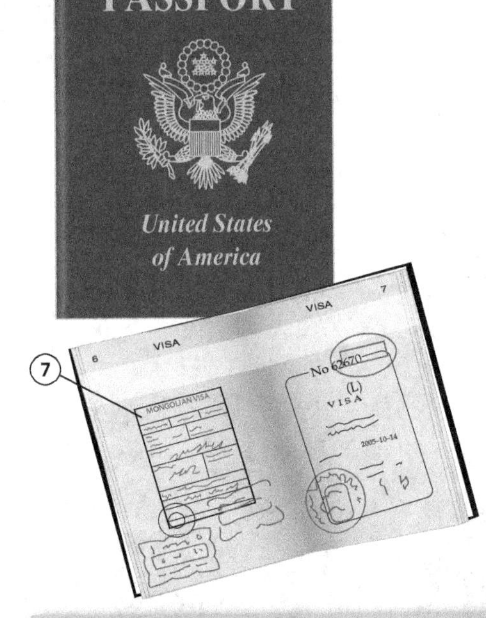

8
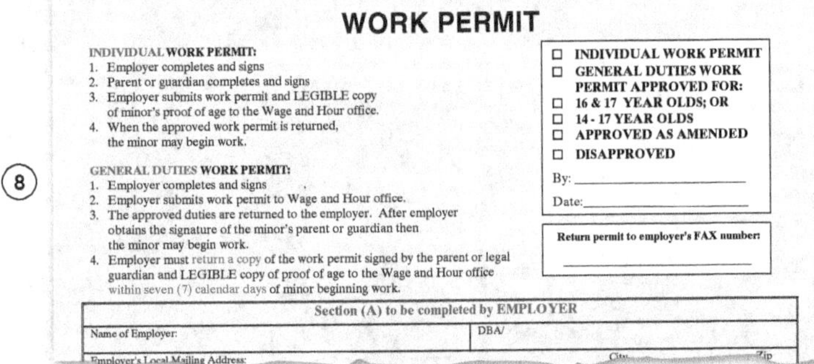

WORK PERMIT

INDIVIDUAL WORK PERMIT:
1. Employer completes and signs
2. Parent or guardian completes and signs
3. Employer submits work permit and LEGIBLE copy of minor's proof of age to the Wage and Hour office.
4. When the approved work permit is returned, the minor may begin work.

GENERAL DUTIES WORK PERMIT:
1. Employer completes and signs
2. Employer submits work permit to Wage and Hour office.
3. The approved duties are returned to the employer. After employer obtains the signature of the minor's parent or guardian then the minor may begin work.
4. Employer must return a copy of the work permit signed by the parent or legal guardian and LEGIBLE copy of proof of age to the Wage and Hour office within seven (7) calendar days of minor beginning work.

☐ INDIVIDUAL WORK PERMIT
☐ GENERAL DUTIES WORK PERMIT APPROVED FOR:
☐ 16 & 17 YEAR OLDS; OR
☐ 14 - 17 YEAR OLDS
☐ APPROVED AS AMENDED
☐ DISAPPROVED

By: ______
Date: ______

Return permit to employer's FAX number:

Section (A) to be completed by EMPLOYER

Name of Employer: DBA/

Employer's Local Mailing Address: City Zip

10
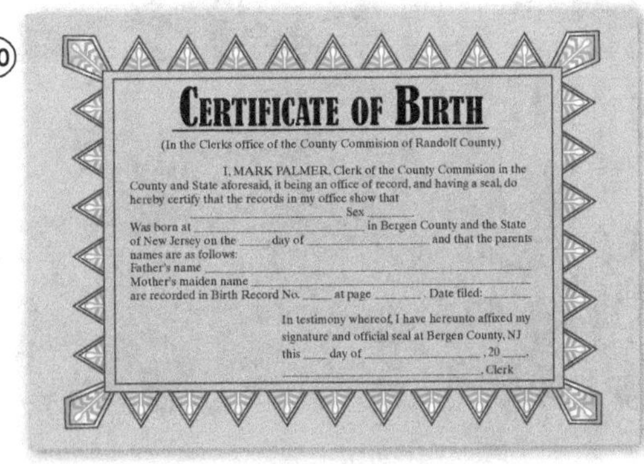

CERTIFICATE OF BIRTH

(In the Clerks office of the County Commission of Randolf County)

I, MARK PALMER, Clerk of the County Commission in the County and State aforesaid, it being an office of record, and having a seal, do hereby certify that the records in my office show that ______ Sex ______ Was born at ______ in Bergen County and the State of New Jersey on the ______ day of ______ and that the parents names are as follows: Father's name ______ Mother's maiden name ______ are recorded in Birth Record No. ____ at page ____. Date filed: ____

In testimony whereof, I have hereunto affixed my signature and official seal at Bergen County, NJ this ____ day of ______, 20__.
______ Clerk

9
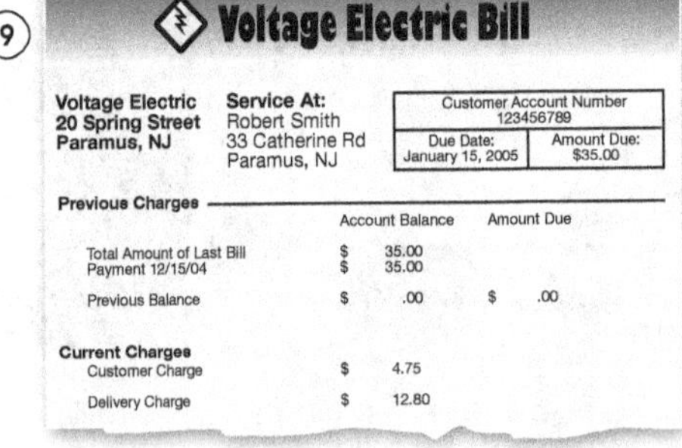

Voltage Electric Bill

Voltage Electric
20 Spring Street
Paramus, NJ

Service At:
Robert Smith
33 Catherine Rd
Paramus, NJ

Customer Account Number	
123456789	
Due Date: January 15, 2005	Amount Due: $35.00

Previous Charges

	Account Balance	Amount Due
Total Amount of Last Bill	$ 35.00	
Payment 12/15/04	$ 35.00	
Previous Balance	$ .00	$ .00

Current Charges

Customer Charge	$ 4.75	
Delivery Charge	$ 12.80	

驾驶执照 1 driver's license
社会安全卡 2 social security card
学生证 3 student I.D. card
员工识别证 4 employee I.D. badge
永久居留卡 5 permanent resident card
护照 6 passport
签证 7 visa
工作许可证 8 work permit
居住证明 9 proof of residence
出生证 10 birth certificate

A. May I see your ______?
B. Yes. Here you are.

A. Oh, no! I can't find my ______!
B. I'll help you look for it.
A. Thanks.

Which forms of identification do you have? When do you need to show them?

美国政府

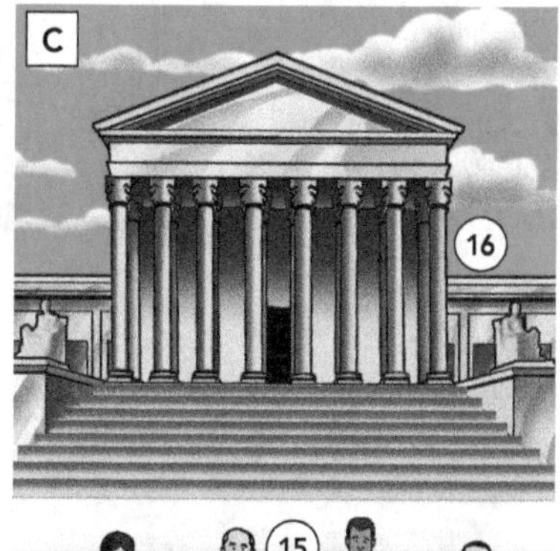

立法部门 **A legislative branch**
制定法律 **1** makes the laws
国会众议员/众议院议员/众议院女议员 **2** representatives/congressmen and congresswomen
众议院 **3** house of representatives
参议员 **4** senators
参议院 **5** senate
国会大厦 **6** Capitol Building

行政部门 **B executive branch**
执法 **7** enforces the laws
总统 **8** president
副总统 **9** vice-president
内阁 **10** cabinet
白宫 **11** White House

司法部门 **C judicial branch**
解释法律/司法审查 **12** explains the laws
最高法院法官 **13** Supreme Court justices
首席法官 **14** chief justice
最高法院 **15** Supreme Court
最高法院大楼 **16** Supreme Court Building

A. Which branch of government __[1, 7, 12]__?
B. The __[A, B, C]__.

A. Who works in the __[A, B, C]__ of the government?
B. The __[2, 4, 8–10, 13, 14]__.

A. Where do/does the __[2, 4, 8–10, 13, 14]__ work?
B. In the __[6, 11, 16]__.

A. In which branch of the government is the __[3, 5, 10, 15]__?
B. In the __[A, B, C]__.

Compare the governments of different countries you are familiar with. What are the branches of government? Who works there? What do they do?

宪法及人权法案

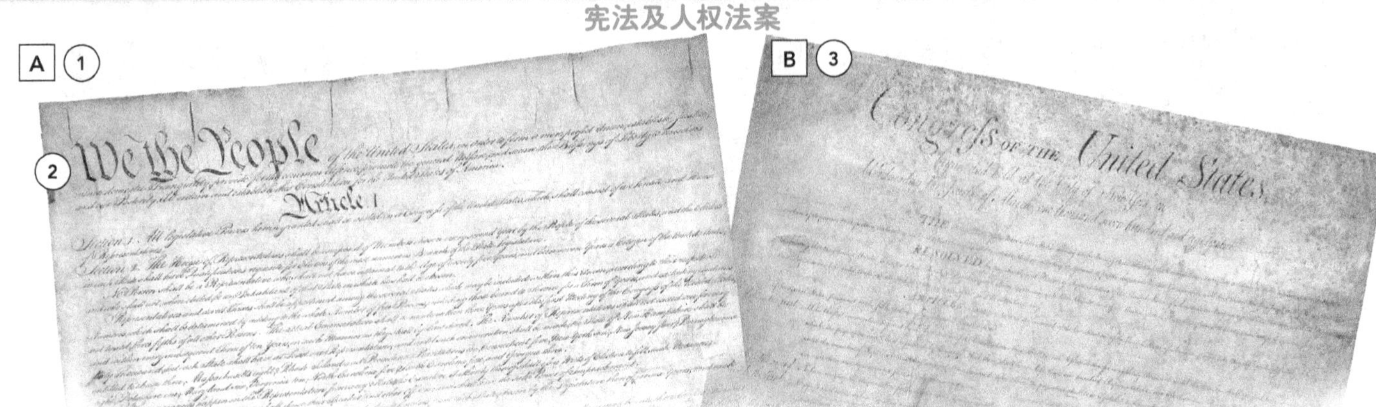

C

D

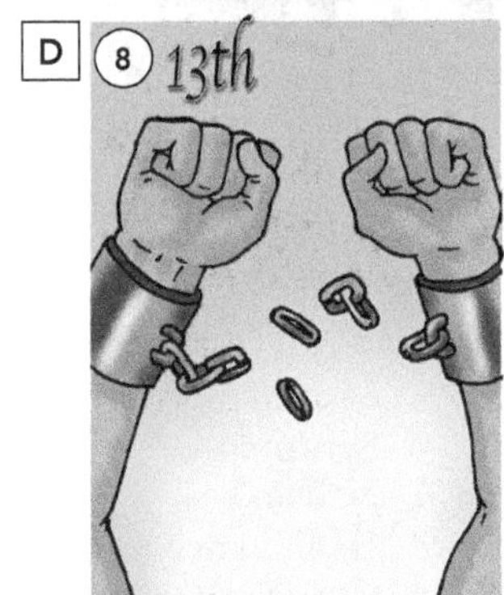

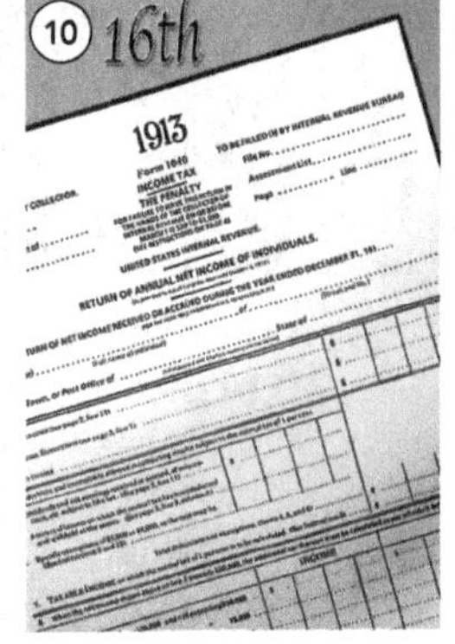

宪法 **A The Constitution**
“国家最高法律” **1** “the supreme law of the land”
宪法序言 **2** the Preamble

人权法案 **B The Bill of Rights**
宪法修正案第一至第十条 **3** the first 10 amendments to the Constitution

美国宪法第一修正案 **C The 1st Amendment**
言论自由 **4** freedom of speech
出版自由 **5** freedom of the press
宗教自由 **6** freedom of religion
集会自由 **7** freedom of assembly

其他修正案 **D Other Amendments**
终止奴隶制 **8** ended slavery
给非裔美国人投票权 **9** gave African-Americans the right to vote
建立所得税制度 **10** established income taxes
给与妇女得票权 **11** gave women the right to vote
给与满十八岁以上的公民投票权 **12** gave citizens eighteen years and older the right to vote

A. What is ___[A, B]___?
B. ___[1, 3]___.

A. Which amendment guarantees people ___[4–7]___?
B. The 1st Amendment.

A. Which amendment ___[8–12]___?
B. The ______ Amendment.

A. What did the ______ Amendment do?
B. It ___[8–12]___.

Describe how people in your community exercise their 1st Amendment rights. What are some examples of freedom of speech? the press? religion? assembly?

Do you have an idea for a new amendment? Tell about it and why you think it's important.

EVENTS IN UNITED STATES HISTORY

美国历史上的大事

TIMELINE

1607	Colonists come to Jamestown, Virginia. 殖民地开拓者来到维吉尼亚的詹姆士镇。
1620	Pilgrims come to the Plymouth Colony. 英国清教徒来到普利茅斯殖民地。
1775	The Revolutionary War begins. 美国独立战争爆发。
1776	The colonies declare their independence. 殖民地宣布独立。
1783	The Revolutionary War ends. 革命战争结束。
1787	Representatives write the United States Constitution. 国会众议员撰写美国宪法。
1789	George Washington becomes the first president. 乔治·华盛顿成为美国第一任总统。
1791	The Bill of Rights is added to the Constitution. 宪法中加入人权法案。
1861	The Civil War begins. 南北战争暴发。
1863	President Lincoln signs the Emancipation Proclamation. 林肯总统签颁解放宣言。
1865	The Civil War ends. 南北战争结束。
1876	Alexander Graham Bell invents the telephone. 亚历山大·格雷汉姆·贝尔发明电话。
1879	Thomas Edison invents the lightbulb. 托马斯·爱迪生发明电话。
1914	World War I (One) begins. 第一次世界大战开始。
1918	World War I (One) ends. 第一次世界大战结束。
1920	Women get the right to vote. 妇女获得投票权。
1929	The stock market crashes, and the Great Depression begins. 股市崩盘，经济大萧条开始。
1939	World War II (Two) begins. 第二次世界大战爆发。
1945	World War II (Two) ends. 第二次世界大战结束。
1950	The Korean War begins. 朝鲜战争爆发。
1953	The Korean War ends. 朝鲜战争结束。
1954	The civil rights movement begins. 民权运动开始。
1963	The March on Washington takes place. 举行向华盛顿进军大游行。
1964	The Vietnam War begins. 越南战争爆发。
1969	Astronaut Neil Armstrong lands on the moon. 太空人尼尔·阿姆斯特朗登陆月球。
1973	The Vietnam War ends. 越南战争结束。
1991	The Persian Gulf War occurs. 波斯湾战争爆发
2001	The United States is attacked by terrorists. 美国受到恐怖分子袭击。

A. What happened in ......(year)......?
B. ......(Event)......ed.

A. When did ......(event)......?
B. In ......(year)......

In your opinion, which event in this lesson is the most important? Why?

Tell about important events in the history of your country.

节日

新年 1 New Year's Day
马丁路德·金纪念日 2 Martin Luther King, Jr.* Day
情人节 3 Valentine's Day
阵亡将士纪念日 4 Memorial Day
(美国) 独立纪念日/ (美国) 国庆日 5 Independence Day/ the Fourth of July
万圣节 6 Halloween
退伍军人节 7 Veterans Day
感恩节 8 Thanksgiving
圣诞节 9 Christmas
回教斋月 10 Ramadan
宽扎节 11 Kwanzaa
(犹太教的) 光明节 12 Hanukkah

*Jr. = Junior

A. When is [1, 3, 5, 6, 7, 9]?
B. It's on (date).

A. When is [2, 4, 8]?
B. It's in (month).

A. When does [10–12] begin this year?
B. It begins on (date).

Which of these holidays do you celebrate? How?

What holidays do people celebrate in your country?

司法制度

被逮补 **A** be arrested
在警察局登记为案犯 **B** be booked at the police station
请律师 **C** hire a lawyer/ hire an attorney
出庭 **D** appear in court
受审 **E** stand* trial
被宣告无罪 **F** be acquitted
被宣告有罪 **G** be convicted
被宣告有罪 **H** be sentenced
被判决 **I** go to jail/prison
被释放 **J** be released
嫌疑犯 **1** suspect
警察 **2** police officer

*stand–stood

手铐 **3** handcuffs
米兰达权利（犯罪嫌疑人保持沉默的权利） **4** Miranda rights
指纹 **5** fingerprints
嫌犯面部照片 **6** mug shot/ police photo
律师 **7** lawyer/attorney
法官 **8** judge
被告 **9** defendant
保释金 **10** bail
法庭 **11** courtroom
检察官 **12** prosecuting attorney
证人 **13** witness

法庭记录员 **14** court reporter
辩护律师 **15** defense attorney
证据 **16** evidence
（在法庭上的）法警 **17** bailiff
陪审团 **18** jury
（陪审团的）裁决 **19** verdict
清白/无罪 **20** innocent/ not guilty
有罪 **21** guilty
判决 **22** sentence
罚金 **23** fine
监狱看守 **24** prison guard
囚犯 **25** convict/prisoner/ inmate

[A–J]
A. Did you hear about ....(name)........?
B. No, I didn't.
A. He/She ________ed.
B. Really? I didn't know that.

[A–J]
A. What happened in the last episode?
B. ....(name of character)........ ________ed.

[1, 2, 7–9, 12–15, 17, 24, 25]
A. Are you the ________?
B. No. I'm the ________.

Tell about the legal system in your country.
Describe what happens after a person is arrested.

Do you watch any crime shows on TV? Which ones?
Tell about an episode you remember.

CITIZENSHIP

公民身份/公民权

公民的权利与责任 Citizens' Rights and Responsibilities

投票 1 vote
遵守法律 2 obey laws
付税 3 pay taxes
陪审 4 serve on a jury
加入社区生活 5 be part of community life
关注新闻明了时事 6 follow the news to know about current events
向选征兵役体系登记* 7 register with the Selective Service System

*美国国内凡18到26岁的男子都必须向选征兵役体系登记。

成为公民的途径 The Path to Citizenship

申请公民身份/申请公民权 8 apply for citizenship
学习有关美国政府和历史 9 learn about U.S. government and history
参加公民入籍考试 10 take a citizenship test
接受归化面谈 11 have a naturalization interview
参加归化典礼 12 attend a naturalization ceremony
朗诵忠诚宣誓 13 recite the Oath of Allegiance

A. Can you name one responsibility of United States citizens?
B. Yes. Citizens should ___[1–7]___.

A. How is your citizenship application coming along?
B. Very well. I ___[8–11]___ed, and now I'm preparing to ___[9–13]___.
A. Good luck!

In your opinion, what are the most important rights and responsibilities of all people in their communities?

In your opinion, should non-citizens have all the same rights as citizens? Why or why not?

美国和加拿大

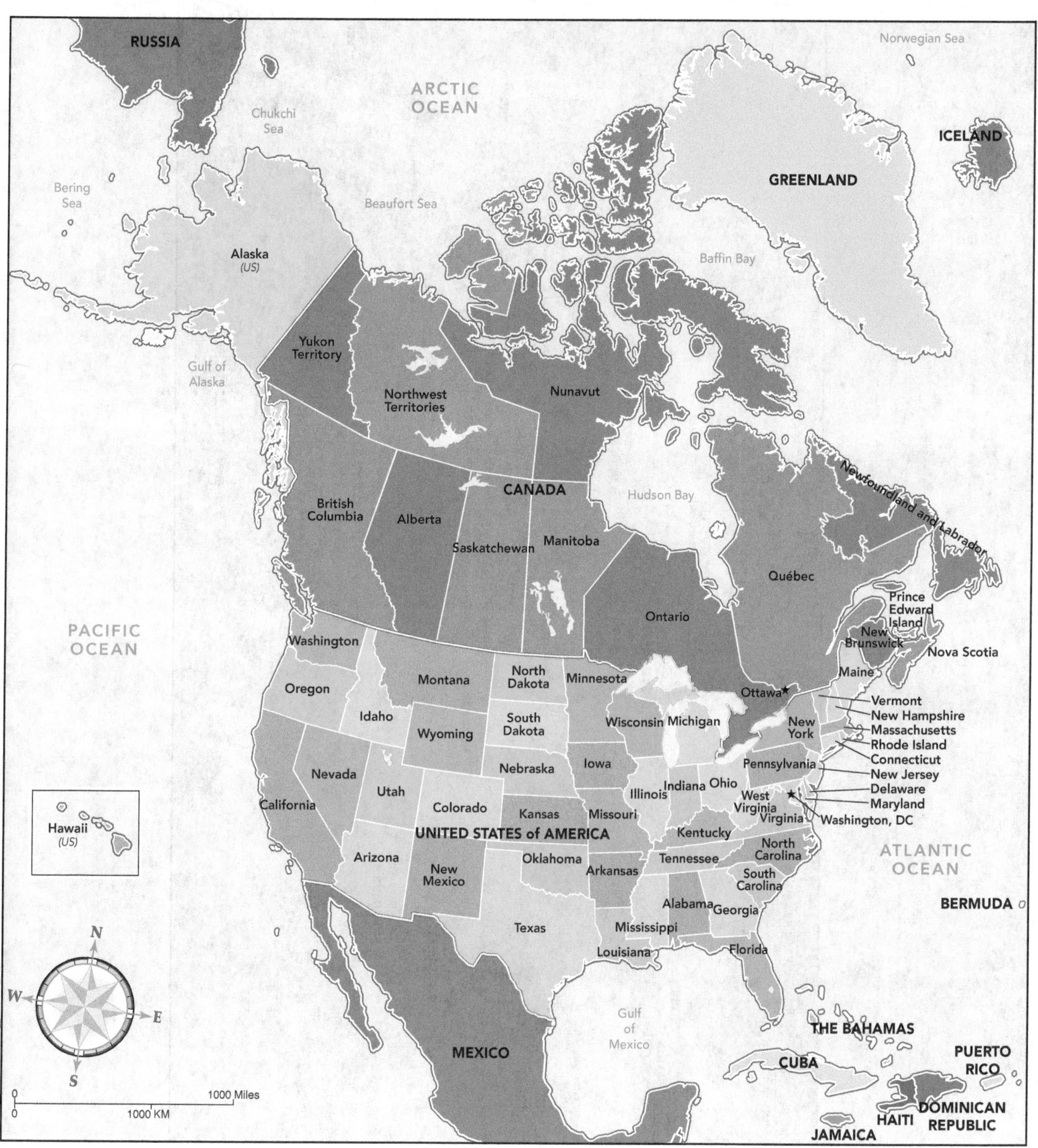
RUSSIA
ARCTIC OCEAN
Chukchi Sea
Norwegian Sea
ICELAND
GREENLAND
Bering Sea
Beaufort Sea
Alaska
(US)
Baffin Bay
Yukon Territory
Gulf of Alaska
Northwest Territories
Nunavut
CANADA
Hudson Bay
Newfoundland and Labrador
British Columbia
Alberta
Saskatchewan
Manitoba
Québec
Prince Edward Island
Ontario
New Brunswick
Nova Scotia
PACIFIC OCEAN
Washington
North Dakota
Minnesota
Maine
Montana
Oregon
Ottawa
Vermont
New Hampshire
Massachusetts
Rhode Island
Connecticut
New Jersey
Delaware
Maryland
Washington, DC
Idaho
South Dakota
Wisconsin
Michigan
New York
Wyoming
Nebraska
Iowa
Pennsylvania
Nevada
Illinois
Indiana
Ohio
Utah
West Virginia
Virginia
California
Colorado
Kansas
Missouri
Hawaii
(US)
UNITED STATES of AMERICA
Kentucky
North Carolina
Tennessee
ATLANTIC OCEAN
Arizona
Oklahoma
Arkansas
South Carolina
New Mexico
Alabama
Georgia
BERMUDA
Texas
Mississippi
Louisiana
Florida
N
W
E
S
Gulf of Mexico
THE BAHAMAS
MEXICO
CUBA
PUERTO RICO
0
1000 Miles
0
1000 KM
HAITI
DOMINICAN REPUBLIC
JAMAICA

墨西哥，中美洲，和加勒比海

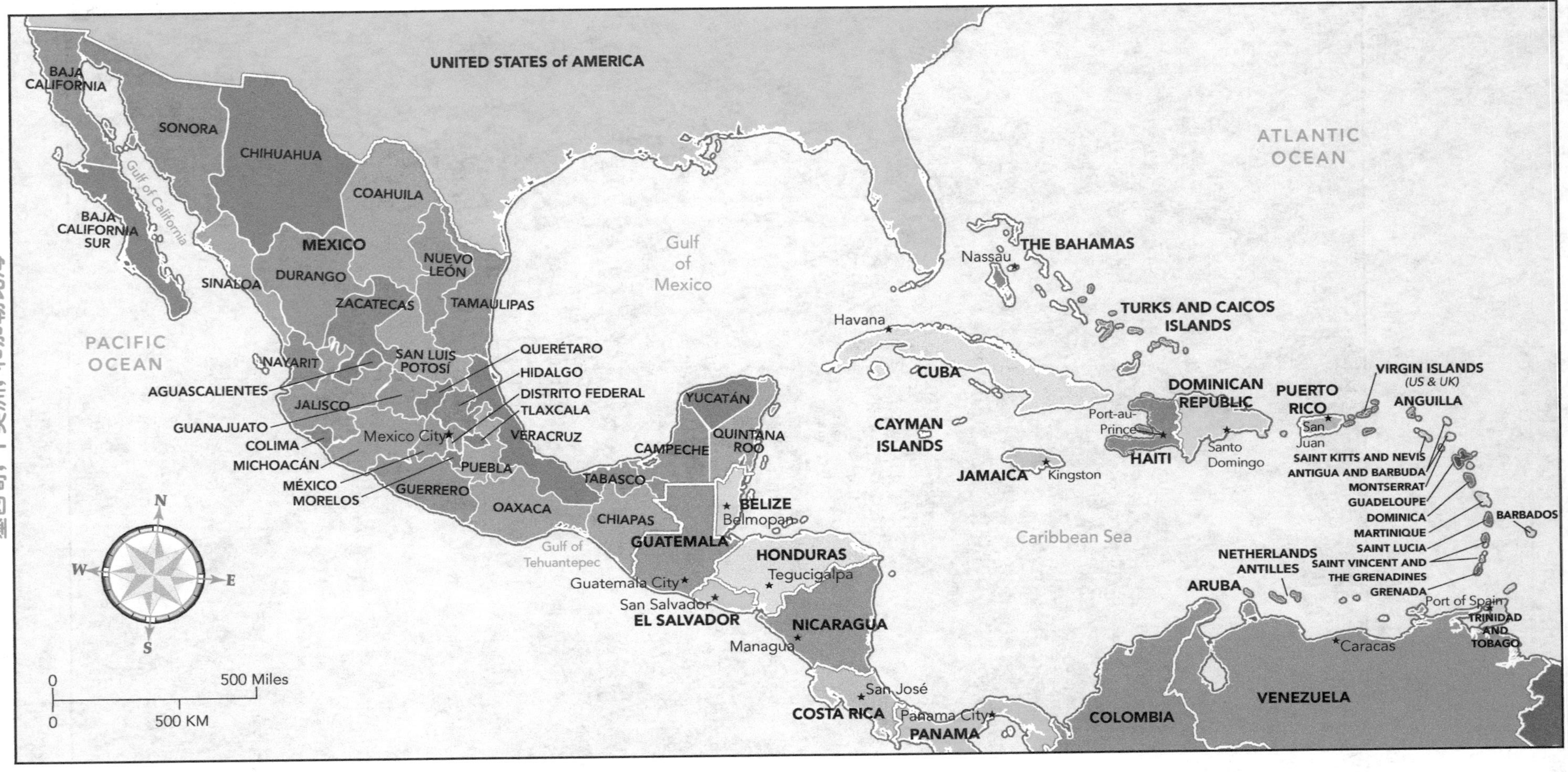

南美洲

Caribbean Sea
Barranquilla
Cartagena
Maracaibo
Valencia
Barquisimeto
Caracas
VENEZUELA
ATLANTIC OCEAN
Georgetown
Paramaribo
Cayenne
GUYANA
SURINAME
FRENCH GUIANA
Medellín
Bogotá
Cali
COLOMBIA
Equator
Quito
ECUADOR
Gulf of Guayaquil
Guayaquil
Belém
Manaus
Fortaleza
Teresina
Recife
PERU
BRAZIL
Lima
Salvador
Brasília
Goiânia
La Paz
BOLIVIA
Sucre
Belo Horizonte
Rio de Janeiro
Campinas
São Paulo
PARAGUAY
CHILE
Asuncion
Curitiba
PACIFIC OCEAN
ARGENTINA
Pôrto Alegre
Córdoba
Rosario
Santiago
URUGUAY
Buenos Aires
Montevideo
Gulf of San Matías
ATLANTIC OCEAN
Gulf of San Jorge
N
W
E
S
FALKLAND ISLANDS
Port Stanley
Strait of Magellan
SOUTH GEORGIA ISLAND
0
500 Miles
0
500 KM

世界

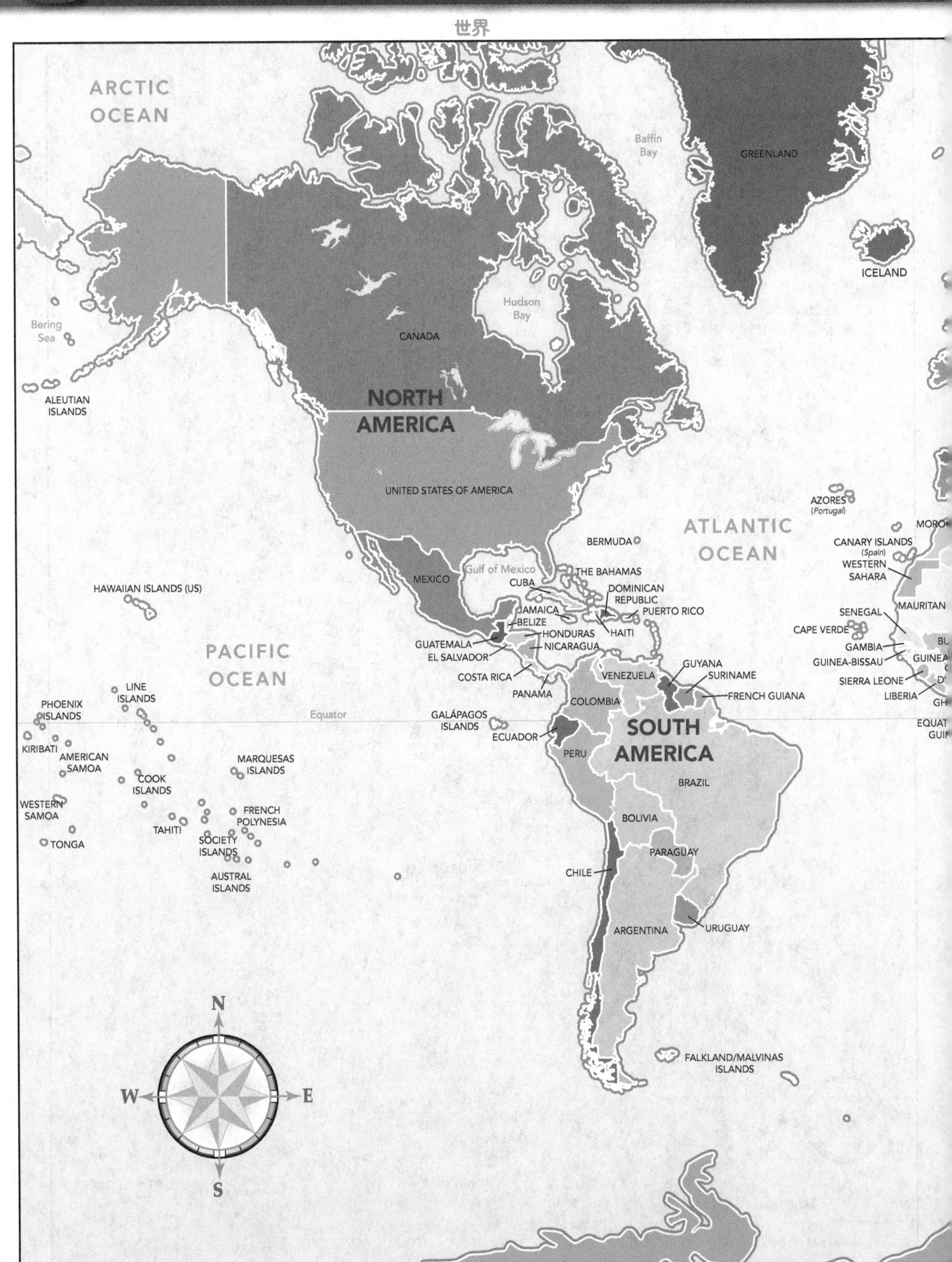
ARCTIC OCEAN
Baffin Bay
GREENLAND
ICELAND
Hudson Bay
Bering Sea
CANADA
ALEUTIAN ISLANDS
NORTH AMERICA
UNITED STATES OF AMERICA
AZORES (Portugal)
ATLANTIC OCEAN
BERMUDA
CANARY ISLANDS (Spain)
WESTERN SAHARA
Gulf of Mexico
THE BAHAMAS
MEXICO
CUBA
DOMINICAN REPUBLIC
HAWAIIAN ISLANDS (US)
JAMAICA
PUERTO RICO
BELIZE
HAITI
SENEGAL
CAPE VERDE
HONDURAS
GUATEMALA
NICARAGUA
GAMBIA
EL SALVADOR
GUYANA
GUINEA-BISSAU
PACIFIC OCEAN
COSTA RICA
VENEZUELA
SURINAME
SIERRA LEONE
LINE ISLANDS
PANAMA
FRENCH GUIANA
LIBERIA
PHOENIX ISLANDS
COLOMBIA
Equator
GALÁPAGOS ISLANDS
SOUTH AMERICA
ECUADOR
KIRIBATI
AMERICAN SAMOA
MARQUESAS ISLANDS
PERU
COOK ISLANDS
BRAZIL
WESTERN SAMOA
FRENCH POLYNESIA
BOLIVIA
TAHITI
TONGA
SOCIETY ISLANDS
PARAGUAY
AUSTRAL ISLANDS
CHILE
URUGUAY
ARGENTINA
N
W
E
S
FALKLAND/MALVINAS ISLANDS

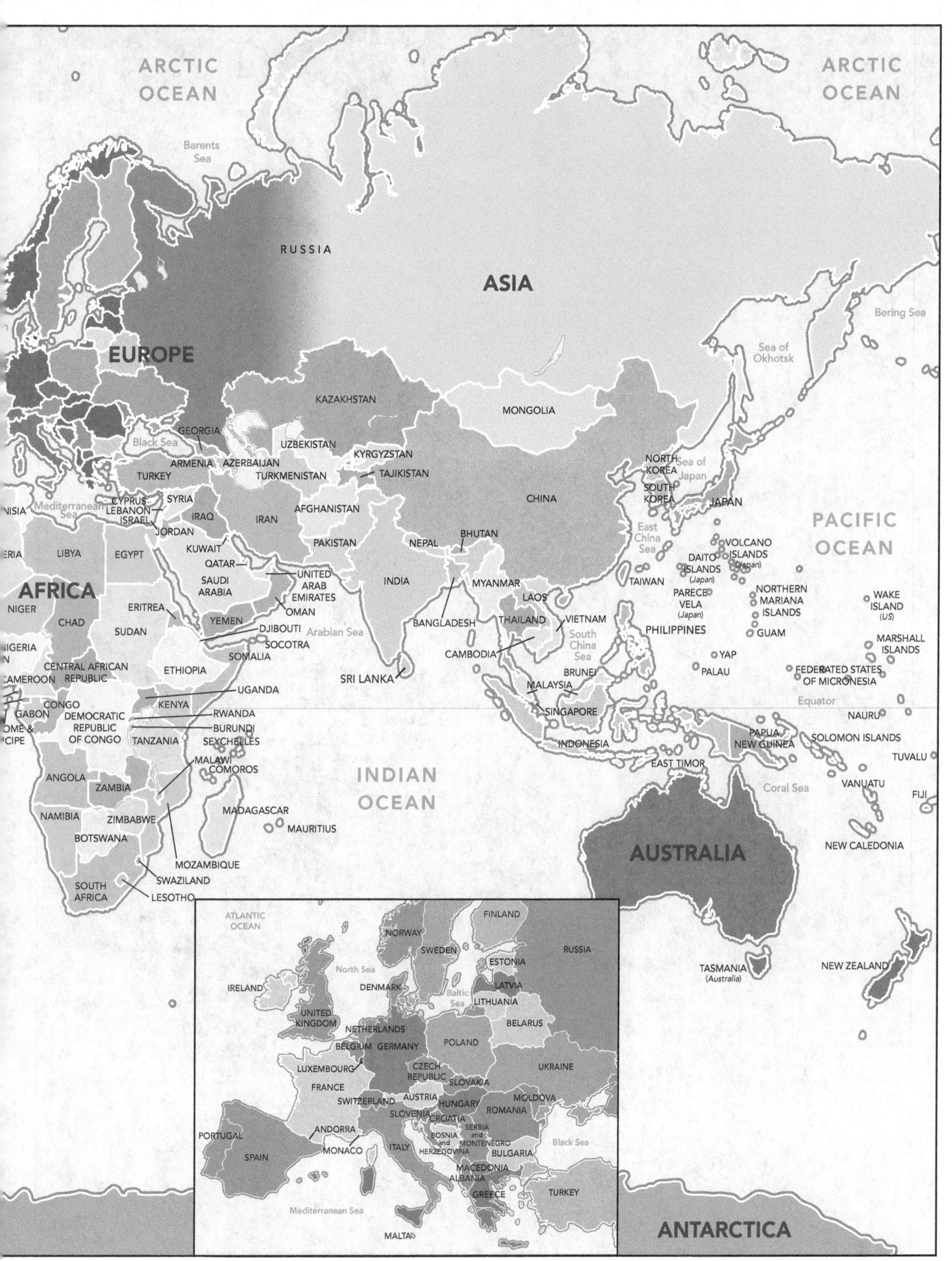
ARCTIC OCEAN
ARCTIC OCEAN
Barents Sea
RUSSIA
ASIA
EUROPE
Bering Sea
Sea of Okhotsk
KAZAKHSTAN
MONGOLIA
GEORGIA
Caspian Sea
Black Sea
UZBEKISTAN
KYRGYZSTAN
ARMENIA
AZERBAIJAN
TURKEY
TURKMENISTAN
TAJIKISTAN
NORTH KOREA
Sea of Japan
SOUTH KOREA
CHINA
JAPAN
CYPRUS
SYRIA
LEBANON
ISRAEL
IRAQ
IRAN
AFGHANISTAN
JORDAN
Mediterranean Sea
PACIFIC OCEAN
East China Sea
KUWAIT
PAKISTAN
NEPAL
BHUTAN
VOLCANO ISLANDS (Japan)
DAITO ISLANDS (Japan)
LIBYA
EGYPT
QATAR
UNITED ARAB EMIRATES
SAUDI ARABIA
INDIA
MYANMAR
TAIWAN
AFRICA
LAOS
PARECE VELA (Japan)
NORTHERN MARIANA ISLANDS
WAKE ISLAND (US)
NIGER
ERITREA
CHAD
OMAN
YEMEN
BANGLADESH
THAILAND
VIETNAM
SUDAN
DJIBOUTI
Arabian Sea
PHILIPPINES
GUAM
SOCOTRA
South China Sea
MARSHALL ISLANDS
CAMBODIA
SOMALIA
YAP
CENTRAL AFRICAN REPUBLIC
ETHIOPIA
PALAU
BRUNEI
FEDERATED STATES OF MICRONESIA
CAMEROON
SRI LANKA
MALAYSIA
UGANDA
KENYA
CONGO
Equator
GABON
RWANDA
SINGAPORE
NAURU
DEMOCRATIC REPUBLIC OF CONGO
BURUNDI
TANZANIA
SEYCHELLES
PAPUA NEW GUINEA
SOLOMON ISLANDS
INDONESIA
MALAWI
COMOROS
EAST TIMOR
TUVALU
ANGOLA
INDIAN OCEAN
ZAMBIA
Coral Sea
VANUATU
FIJI
MADAGASCAR
NAMIBIA
ZIMBABWE
MAURITIUS
BOTSWANA
NEW CALEDONIA
AUSTRALIA
MOZAMBIQUE
SWAZILAND
SOUTH AFRICA
LESOTHO
ATLANTIC OCEAN
FINLAND
NORWAY
SWEDEN
RUSSIA
ESTONIA
North Sea
TASMANIA (Australia)
NEW ZEALAND
IRELAND
DENMARK
LATVIA
Baltic Sea
LITHUANIA
UNITED KINGDOM
BELARUS
NETHERLANDS
BELGIUM
GERMANY
POLAND
LUXEMBOURG
CZECH REPUBLIC
UKRAINE
SLOVAKIA
FRANCE
MOLDOVA
AUSTRIA
SWITZERLAND
HUNGARY
ROMANIA
SLOVENIA
CROATIA
ANDORRA
SERBIA and MONTENEGRO
PORTUGAL
BOSNIA and HERZEGOVINA
Black Sea
MONACO
ITALY
BULGARIA
SPAIN
MACEDONIA
ALBANIA
GREECE
TURKEY
Mediterranean Sea
MALTA
ANTARCTICA

时区

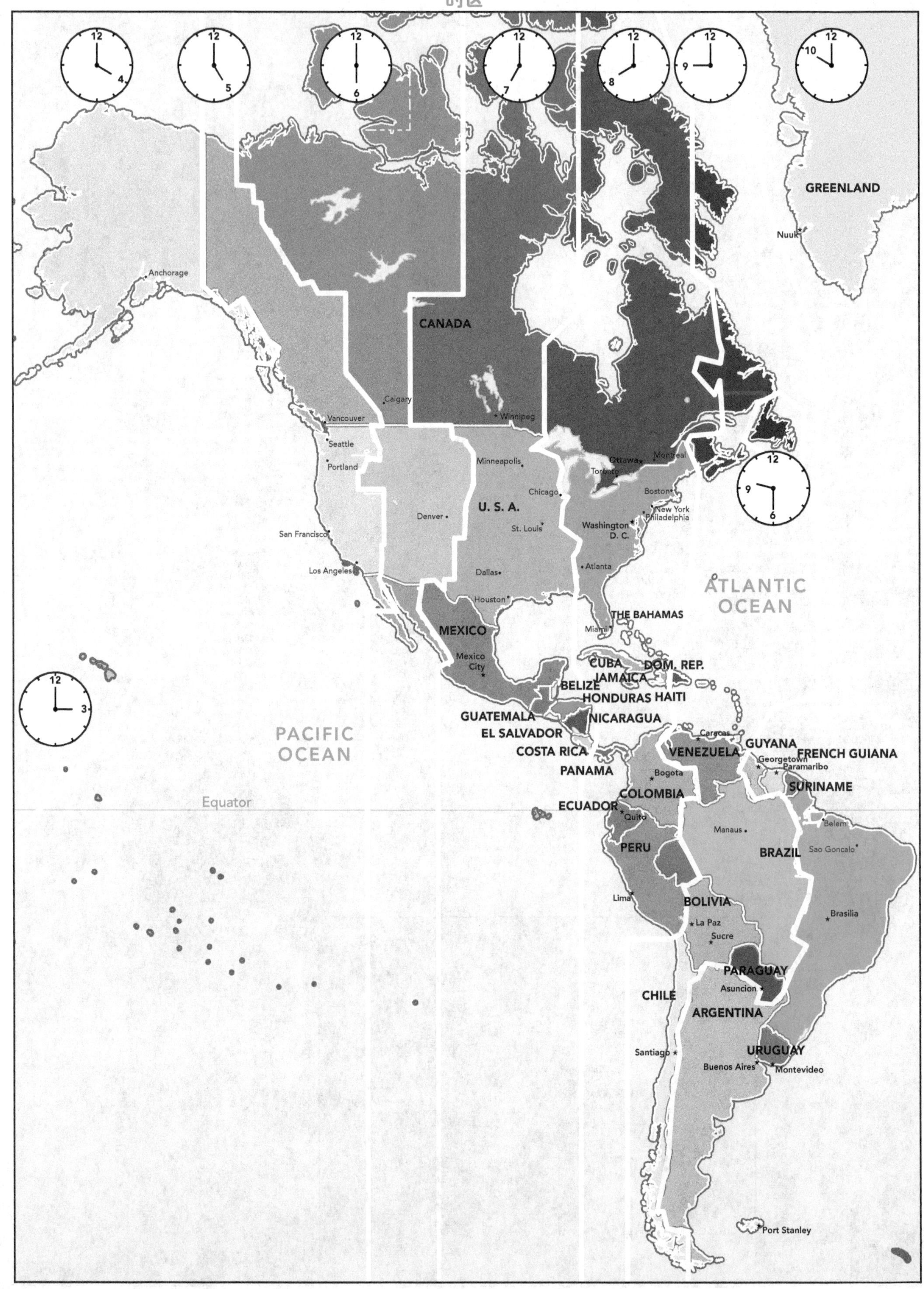

GREENLAND
Nuuk
Anchorage
CANADA
Calgary
Vancouver
Winnipeg
Seattle
Portland
Minneapolis
Ottawa
Montreal
Toronto
Chicago
Boston
New York
Philadelphia
Denver
U. S. A.
St. Louis
Washington D. C.
San Francisco
Los Angeles
Atlanta
Dallas
Houston
ATLANTIC OCEAN
THE BAHAMAS
Miami
MEXICO
Mexico City
CUBA
DOM. REP.
JAMAICA
BELIZE
HONDURAS
HAITI
GUATEMALA
NICARAGUA
EL SALVADOR
PACIFIC OCEAN
Caracas
COSTA RICA
VENEZUELA
GUYANA
FRENCH GUIANA
PANAMA
Georgetown
Paramaribo
Bogota
SURINAME
COLOMBIA
Equator
ECUADOR
Quito
Belem
Manaus
PERU
BRAZIL
Sao Goncalo
Lima
BOLIVIA
La Paz
Brasilia
Sucre
PARAGUAY
Asuncion
CHILE
ARGENTINA
URUGUAY
Santiago
Buenos Aires
Montevideo
Port Stanley

       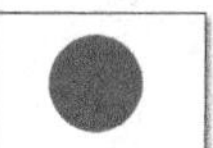 

Country	Nationality	Language
Afghanistan	Afghan	Afghan
Argentina	Argentine	Spanish
Australia	Australian	English
Bolivia	Bolivian	Spanish
Brazil	Brazilian	Portuguese
Bulgaria	Bulgarian	Bulgarian
Cambodia	Cambodian	Cambodian
Canada	Canadian	English/French
Chile	Chilean	Spanish
China	Chinese	Chinese
Colombia	Colombian	Spanish
Costa Rica	Costa Rican	Spanish
Cuba	Cuban	Spanish
(The) Czech Republic	Czech	Czech
Denmark	Danish	Danish
(The) Dominican Republic	Dominican	Spanish
Ecuador	Ecuadorian	Spanish
Egypt	Egyptian	Arabic
El Salvador	Salvadorean	Spanish
England	English	English
Estonia	Estonian	Estonian
Ethiopia	Ethiopian	Amharic
Finland	Finnish	Finnish
France	French	French
Germany	German	German
Greece	Greek	Greek
Guatemala	Guatemalan	Spanish
Haiti	Haitian	Haitian Kreyol
Honduras	Honduran	Spanish
Hungary	Hungarian	Hungarian
India	Indian	Hindi
Indonesia	Indonesian	Indonesian
Israel	Israeli	Hebrew

Country	Nationality	Language
Italy	Italian	Italian
Japan	Japanese	Japanese
Jordan	Jordanian	Arabic
Korea	Korean	Korean
Laos	Laotian	Laotian
Latvia	Latvian	Latvian
Lebanon	Lebanese	Arabic
Lithuania	Lithuanian	Lithuanian
Malaysia	Malaysian	Malay
Mexico	Mexican	Spanish
New Zealand	New Zealander	English
Nicaragua	Nicaraguan	Spanish
Norway	Norwegian	Norwegian
Pakistan	Pakistani	Urdu
Panama	Panamanian	Spanish
Peru	Peruvian	Spanish
(The) Philippines	Filipino	Tagalog
Poland	Polish	Polish
Portugal	Portuguese	Portuguese
Puerto Rico	Puerto Rican	Spanish
Romania	Romanian	Romanian
Russia	Russian	Russian
Saudi Arabia	Saudi	Arabic
Slovakia	Slovak	Slovak
Spain	Spanish	Spanish
Sweden	Swedish	Swedish
Switzerland	Swiss	German/French/ Italian
Taiwan	Taiwanese	Chinese
Thailand	Thai	Thai
Turkey	Turkish	Turkish
Ukraine	Ukrainian	Ukrainian
(The) United States	American	English
Venezuela	Venezuelan	Spanish
Vietnam	Vietnamese	Vietnamese

A. Where are you from?
B. I'm from **Mexico**.

A. What's your nationality?
B. I'm **Mexican**.

A. What language do you speak?
B. I speak **Spanish**.

Tell about yourself: Where are you from? What's your nationality? What languages do you speak?

Now interview and tell about a friend.

动词列表

规则动词

规则动词的过去式及过去分词有四种拼写形式。

1 在动词后加 **-ed**。例如:

act → act**ed**

act	cook	grill	pass	simmer
add	correct	guard	peel	sort
answer	cough	hand (in)	plant	spell
appear	cover	help	play	sprain
ask	crash	insert	polish	steam
assist	cross (out)	invent	pour	stow
attack	deliver	iron	print	stretch
attend	deposit	kick	reach	surf
bank	design	land	record	swallow
board	discuss	leak	register	talk
boil	dress	learn	relax	turn
box	drill	lengthen	repair	twist
brainstorm	dust	lift	repeat	unload
broil	edit	listen	request	vacuum
brush	end	load	respond	vomit
burn	enter	look	rest	walk
burp	establish	lower	return	wash
carpool	explain	mark	roast	watch
cash	faint	match	rock	wax
check	fasten	mix	saute	weed
clean	fix	mow	scratch	whiten
clear	floss	obey	seat	work
collect	fold	open	select	
comb	follow	paint	shorten	
construct	form	park	sign	

2 在动词最后的字母 **-e** 后加 **-d**。例如:

assemble → assemble**d**

assemble	declare	grate	pronounce	shave
bake	describe	hire	prune	slice
balance	dislocate	manage	raise	sneeze
barbecue	dive	measure	rake	state
bathe	dribble	microwave	recite	style
bounce	enforce	move	recycle	supervise
browse	erase	nurse	remove	translate
bruise	examine	operate	revise	type
bubble	exchange	organize	rinse	underline
change	exercise	overdose	save	unscramble
circle	experience	practice	scrape	use
close	file	prepare	serve	vote
combine	gargle	produce	share	wheeze

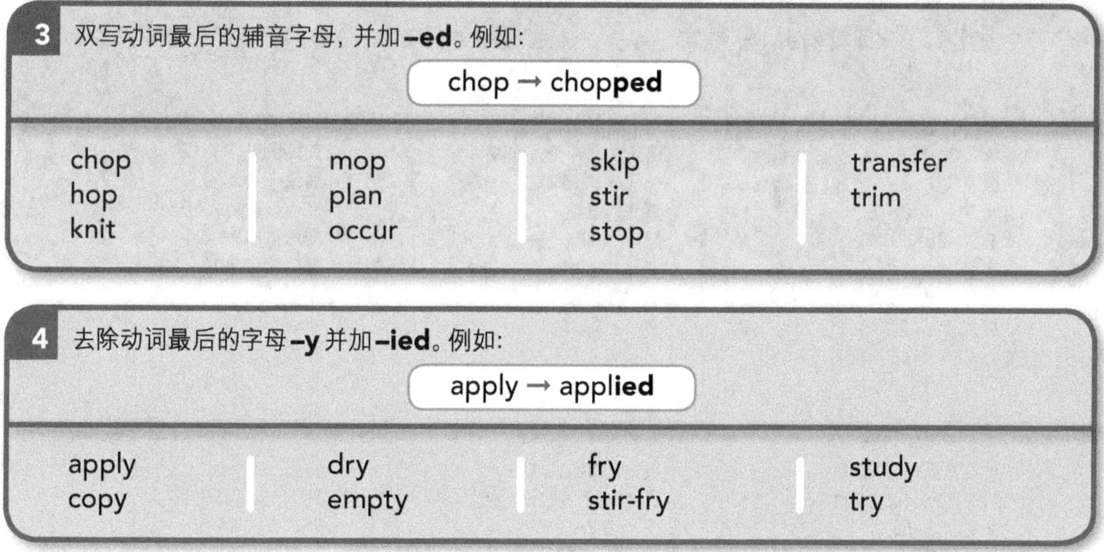

3 双写动词最后的辅音字母，并加**–ed**。例如：

chop → chop**ped**

chop	mop	skip	transfer
hop	plan	stir	trim
knit	occur	stop	

4 去除动词最后的字母**–y**并加**–ied**。例如：

apply → appl**ied**

apply	dry	fry	study
copy	empty	stir-fry	try

不规则动词

下列动词的过去式及过去分词是不规则的形式。

be	was/were	been
beat	beat	beaten
become	became	become
bend	bent	bent
begin	began	begun
bleed	bled	bled
break	broke	broken
bring	brought	brought
build	built	built
buy	bought	bought
catch	caught	caught
choose	chose	chosen
come	came	come
cut	cut	cut
do	did	done
draw	drew	drawn
drink	drank	drunk
drive	drove	driven
eat	ate	eaten
fall	fell	fallen
feed	fed	fed
fly	flew	flown
get	got	gotten
give	gave	given
go	went	gone
grow	grew	grown
hang	hung	hung
have	had	had
hit	hit	hit
hold	held	held
hurt	hurt	hurt
know	knew	known
leave	left	left
let	let	let
make	made	made
meet	met	met
pay	paid	paid
put	put	put
read	read	read
rewrite	rewrote	rewritten
run	ran	run
ring	rang	rung
say	said	said
see	saw	seen
sell	sold	sold
set	set	set
shoot	shot	shot
sing	sang	sung
sit	sat	sat
sleep	slept	slept
speak	spoke	spoken
stand	stood	stood
sweep	swept	swept
swim	swam	swum
swing	swung	swung
take	took	taken
teach	taught	taught
throw	threw	thrown
understand	understood	understood
withdraw	withdrew	withdrawn
write	wrote	written

词汇表（中文）

以黑体呈现的数字表示该单词所在的页数。该黑体数字后的数字表示该单词在该页图解及单词表中的位置。例如：「地址 **1**-5」表示「地址」在第 1 页单词表的第 5 项。

D

K

V

W

X

词汇表（英文）

The bold number indicates the page(s) on which the word appears. The number that follows indicates the word's location in the illustration and in the word list on the page. For example, "address 1-5" indicates that the word *address* is on page 1 and is item number 5.

Expressions

主题索引